Multitudes

Multitudes

How Crowds Made the Modern World

Dan Hancox

VERSO
London • New York

First published by Verso 2024
© Dan Hancox 2024

1 3 5 7 9 10 8 6 4 2

Verso
UK: 6 Meard Street, London W1F 0EG
US: 388 Atlantic Avenue, Brooklyn, NY 11217
versobooks.com

Verso is the imprint of New Left Books

ISBN-13: 978-1-80429-448-2
ISBN-13: 978-1-80429-450-5 (UK EBK)
ISBN-13: 978-1-80429-451-2 (US EBK)

British Library Cataloguing in Publication Data
A catalogue record for this book is available from the British Library

Library of Congress Cataloging-in-Publication Data

Names: Hancox, Dan, author.
Title: Multitudes : how crowds made the modern world / Dan Hancox.
Description: London ; New York : Verso, 2024. | Includes bibliographical
   references and index.
Identifiers: LCCN 2024017547 (print) | LCCN 2024017548 (ebook) | ISBN
   9781804294482 (hardback) | ISBN 9781804294512 (ebook)
Subjects: LCSH: Collective behavior—History. | Crowds—History. | Social
   change—History.
Classification: LCC HM871 .H36 2024 (print) | LCC HM871 (ebook) | DDC
   302.33—dc23/eng/20240515
LC record available at https://lccn.loc.gov/2024017547
LC ebook record available at https://lccn.loc.gov/2024017548

Typeset in Sabon by Biblichor Ltd, Edinburgh
Printed and bound by CPI Group (UK) Ltd, Croydon CR0 4YY

Contents

Preface: El Carnaval de Cádiz

Cádiz is an anomaly in modern Spain in all sorts of ways. It is a spectacular ancient city, the oldest in the Western world, once an island, now squeezed onto the fingertip of a thin, sandy spit of land, jutting out into the Atlantic Ocean on Spain's south-western coast, a maze of cobblestones gently polished into gold by centuries of ocean spray and bone-dry sherry. Gusts batter the city's sixteenth-century walls, while the February sky is so bright as to feel blinding, a vast and gleaming pool of azure. Things melt into each other that elsewhere would have hard borders: the salty sea into the air, the pavement into the road, the outdoors into the indoors.

There are crenellations, forts, cannons and watchtowers scattered across the rake-like promontory – bringing to mind the many armies, armadas, vanguards and garrisons that once fought over the city, from Carthaginians to Moors, Byzantines to Visigoths. Today, the descendants of these sword-wielding crowds look and behave a little differently. A group of middle-aged men heave into view. They are dressed in cheap blue-and-yellow Minions costumes, howling with laughter and swigging from oversized bottles of Cruzcampo lager.

Public space here means slow-moving streets and squares, under slender Juliet balconies, unaccommodating to the grim hierarchy of the modern city, which prioritises private cars above all else. At one point, in the four days I spent at the city's famous pre-Lenten

Carnival, I witnessed a perfect collision of twenty-first-century life and Cádiz's venerable *casco antiguo*: a Monster Energy Drink promotional van having to do a thirty-point turn just to get around a corner, with a crowd of tipsy *carnavaleros* laughing and cheering when it finally made it.

The streets are perilously narrow, like goat paths, and for eleven days every February are decorated with a festive array of confetti, feathers, streamers and spilled beer. Some are so narrow that, should the desire suddenly possess me, I could lie down across them, my face griddled by cobbles, and span the whole width of the road. It takes just fifteen minutes to walk across the old town, from one palm-tree-lined Atlantic coast to the other. And yet it hosts one of the biggest carnivals in Europe, drawing hundreds of thousands of visitors. Obviously, this dichotomy presents certain challenges: squeezing revellers down the streets like a ball of plasticine through a child's toy spaghetti maker, extruding into little channels of gaiety before reconvening in the next available leafy square.

The 2023 Carnival is the first in three years, the first since the pandemic, the resumption of an event so essential to Cádiz's anti-establishment culture that even General Franco did not manage to crush it. In Plaza de San Juan de Dios, the grand square that serves as the gateway to the old town, people are getting ready to head into the throng, finding their friends, eating *bocadillos de jamón* out of tinfoil, inspecting each other's costumes and carrier bags of booze. It's like a broad open-air foyer, lined with palm trees, bustling and mobile. Nonetheless the thirty or so young people who are dancing to a portable reggaeton sound system have consciously hemmed themselves in, like they've been circled by an invisible sheepdog, to make a kind of virtual dancefloor.

Elsewhere in the city a few live bands and DJs are scheduled to play, but there is little in the way of spectacle: people are here to see each other. Heading north into the maze, *carnavaleros* of all ages are slow-shuffling, doing pigeon steps down the crammed side streets towards Plaza de las Flores, and all in good humour, patiently, sometimes holding their rucksacks and children above their heads so they can squeeze by more easily. Everyone is trying to make do and accommodate everyone else, squishing themselves into doorways to let buggies and wheelchairs past, and doing so without stewarding or signposting – the crowd has arranged itself into two distinct streams, one going north, one going south.

Part of what makes Cádiz Carnival such a physical, multi-sensory experience is that, like any festival, there is just a hell of a lot of walking involved – so, while I'm feeling the spirit of Carnival deep in my soul, I'm also feeling it in my calves, my quads and the soles of my feet, which are positively humming with warm blood. My Google Maps 'timeline' function, the one which creepily traces your movements, looks like one of those experiments where they give a spider LSD.

In the city's most impressive square, Plaza de la Catedral, beneath the domes of the broad, baroque Cádiz Cathedral, the giant palms are flailing melodramatically in the wind like harpies, and the assembled crowd of drinkers (2,000? 3,000?) vibrates with colour and buzzes with whistles and laughter. Standing on the cathedral steps, I can see, scattered across the packed square, twinkling LED tiaras, rainbow mohicans, fireman's helmets, and people dressed as velociraptors, Vikings, shrimp, jailbirds, referees, pirates, centurions, Barbies, Mario Men, Minnie Mice, Batmen, a Volkswagen, a Casio watch, and a swarm of bees.

On the first weekend, and indeed the last weekend, as well as much of the week in between, the singing, dancing and drinking goes on all day and all night. To my astonishment, the first ten hours passes without sight of a single police officer, and even then, the presence is sparse.

At 1 a.m. on the first Friday night of Carnival, the older folks are still out in their flat caps and wax jackets, strolling by the Atlantic, eating ice creams and smiling fondly at the children and young people in their daft costumes. A group of lads in pink nuns' habits salute a passing group of Power Rangers, as if they were different platoons from the same army, while a geisha waits for her partner, Zorro, to finish at the pissoir. Around one corner, two groups of young women heading in different directions break their stride to sing along to Shakira's new single, which is playing from an upstairs window. They wail mock-theatrically, arms aloft to the cold February sky.

With a carefree lack of urgency, the Carnival crowd seems to follow itself: driven by FOMO and drifting by instinct to find which square has the buzziest atmosphere at any one time, across the long week of festivities – there are quiet side streets if you want a breather, but why would you spend any time there? You came to be part of the crowd. It's also cosier in the heart of things, huddled together under clouds of warm, boozy breath, the human density and the mottled city walls offering much-needed shelter from the fierce winds howling off the Atlantic.

More than once, I see a gang of friends arrive at a fork in the road and pause to discuss the best route. The path to the left is densely packed, while the path to the right is largely empty – an option that would allow them to quickly and efficiently circle round and arrive at their destination. But they will almost always plough on into the melee, rather than steal a march on their fellow *carnavaleros*. Carnival crowds are not just unhurried, but unafraid of greater density. In fact, they seem to be actively attracted to the pinch points and bottlenecks they can see ahead, as if these prove they are going the right way. A quiet, almost-empty street suggests a mistake – a path away from all this fun, all this clamour; back to normality.

One function of the layout of the old town is that you can't get lost, but you also can't *not* get lost – maintaining your sense of orientation is almost impossible on such winding streets. But if you walk for long enough you'll either emerge into a familiar square, or start to hear waves crashing against the coastal rock armour, and hit the ocean, and then you're set right again. I keep heading off in search of food; then I hear laughter and singing emanating from around a corner or behind an old church and have to change route again, ducking down a side street to see what's happening.

Cádiz Carnival is, like all carnivals, a hybrid. It has elements of some ancient pagan celebrations, but also roots in medieval Christianity – it is an exercise in pre-Lenten profanity – and displays influences from Old and New Worlds alike. Cádiz juts out into the wider world, towards the great Carnival cities of Havana, Genoa, Nice and Venice, and has pulled in celebratory rituals and motifs from them all. Its overall atmosphere feels quaintly antiquated. The saturnalian rites of Carnival can seem at odds with the modern world, and they are certainly at odds with late capitalism and its determination to manage, fence in and monetise any expressions of public, popular festivity and culture.

In Cádiz the primary and most distinctive Carnival practice is the singing of spiky and irreverent satirical songs, with a limited accompaniment of mandolins, lutes and kazoos, by amateur groups ranging in size from four to forty-five performers. It's a highly gestural, theatrical genre, lots of arched eyebrows and shocked expressions to go with the singers' elaborate costumes – all very much in cabaret style. For local aficionados, it is a high art that deserves to be considered, discussed and critiqued like any other. It is also formally judged, in an official competition broadcast and debated across Andalusia and culminating in an all-night final in the city's Teatro Falla on the first Friday.

But it is the street itself, as the official website reminds us, which is 'the protagonist of Carnival', and so the groups featured in the official contest also perform at random across the city, like wandering minstrels, along with street-only singing groups known as *ilegales*. One of the most alluring aspects of Carnival is that the groups singing in the streets are on the same plane as their audience. They come from the same local neighbourhoods, the same communities; they are not performing on a stage or for money, but only for applause, on the pavement – and they roam the streets at whim, singing to each other, to no one, to whomever is passing by. In the lush, sun-dappled Plaza de la Candelaria on Saturday afternoon, I watched the forty members of the 'Al-Ándalus' choir perform their rousing finale, a rallying cry in defiance of the increasingly popular far-right political party Vox: 'For the blood, the rage and the joy / For the fiesta and the melancholia / For the Moor, the Christian and the Jew / For the flowers of the rebellion / We were, we are and we will be: Andalusia!'

Carnival songs cover everything from local gossip to social mores and issues of class and politics, targeting corrupt politicians, the clergy, the press, the hated Guardia Civil military police, and US/NATO 'invaders' ensconced in their military base across the bay in Rota. Two centuries ago, during the Peninsular War with France, when the Spanish government had to retreat to fortified Cádiz, the citizens wrote Carnival songs mocking Napoleon. Carnival is, the revered local songwriter Paco Rosado once said, 'the only chance a people have for denouncing what doesn't work and for pointing out those responsible for it'. It is a time when political hierarchies and social rules dissolve, and the crowd takes over. The world is turned upside down and then dressed as a penguin.

As a consequence, Cádiz Carnival has long been under threat of laws and prohibitions of one kind or another – push-back from a Spanish elite ostensibly concerned by obscene dancing, sexually provocative performances, cross-dressing, and parodic lyrics aimed at their religious, military and political brethren. In bygone centuries, outrages emanating from the Carnival crowd included firecrackers and lewd gestures, the throwing of flour bombs from balconies, and kids knocking off men's hats as they walked in the street. These individual acts of outré behaviour no doubt offended the sententious Spanish upper classes. But their objection was much more elemental: a revulsion against working-class people gathering, en masse, in public. A self-assembled crowd is always a problem for the establishment.

When they weren't trying to ban Carnival, the Spanish aristocracy tried to co-opt it and enclose it for themselves, holding private pre-Lenten balls in expensive restaurants, drawing attention and energy, and bribing some of the singing groups away from the streets. In February 2023, as joy abounded throughout Cádiz, a few critics griped online that the Carnival crowd had become too big, too dense, too drunk, too uncultured, too Covid-risky, too full of 'tourists' from Seville (less than ninety minutes away), or that the young had forgotten the true spirit of Carnival. As long as there is a crowd enjoying itself, there will always be someone sitting comfortably in a well-appointed office, projecting their worst fears and most reactionary instincts onto it, and demanding that it disperse.

As I left Cádiz, shattered, hungover, legs full of lactic acid, synapses firing with all that collective joy, humming my favourite Carnival tunes, I spotted an official Carnival poster in the form of a cartoon, where someone dressed as Superman asks a group of fellow revellers: 'What have you come as?' The three strangers reply: 'As people who understand that Carnival is the cry of the masses, and not just any old party!'

They are in fact dressed as a frog, a banana, and a clown; but people take levity very seriously here. When you consider the potency of hundreds of thousands of instinctively anarchist Andalusians, gathered together in the public squares of Cádiz to sing scathing songs about the Spanish establishment, it is no wonder General Franco tried so hard to abolish Carnival: at various points censoring lyrics, banning masks, and forbidding all festivities in the streets. Nor is it any wonder that the people of Cádiz worked so hard, and risked so much, to resist this suppression – nor that they won, forcing their military dictator to give in to a scrappy, impoverished little port city in south-western Spain. The slogan on the official 2023 Cádiz Carnival t-shirts translated as 'I believe in the eternal life of Carnival.' You would be a fool to believe otherwise.

Introduction: The Age of the Crowd

The dogmas whose birth we are witnessing will soon have the force of the old dogmas; that is to say, the tyrannical and sovereign force of being above discussion. The divine right of the masses is about to replace the divine right of kings.
– Gustave Le Bon, 'The Crowd: A Study of the Popular Mind'

It had all been so different, so recently. As the first Covid-19 lockdown began in Britain in March 2020, a grey cloak of uncertainty and fear descended with alarming speed. In the uneasy days that followed, it dawned on me that the pandemic was not just heartbreaking because it locked us away from our loved ones, but because it locked us away from strangers too. In a moment, this unprecedented experience had flipped what it meant to be human – what it meant to be a social animal – inside out. Festivals, congregations, assemblies, raves, processions, rallies, gigs, demonstrations; audiences in stadiums, concert venues, lecture halls, clubs, theatres, cinemas: gatherings of any kind became not only unethical, not only illegal, but potentially fatal. At a stroke, the UK's 40,000 choirs fell silent, its 47,000 pubs closed their doors, and the 2 million fans who go to matches every weekend learned that for the first time since the Second World War, *football was cancelled.*

Isolated in our homes, we scowled and shook our heads at rumours of illicit parties, and shared photographs of the last pre-lockdown 'super-spreader' sporting events and rock concerts like they were clips from horror films. As the weeks passed, I had an unexpected opportunity to think about what crowds meant to me – about what was suddenly glaringly absent from my life. I missed being among thousands of total strangers with whom I shared something profound, people who, despite our never having exchanged a word in conversation, made me feel like a different person. Late capitalism has already atomised us, severed us from many of the nurturing bonds of community – all those youth clubs, pubs, libraries and community centres shut down under austerity since 2010, the local park fenced off for half the summer for expensive festivals, and the unionised workplace replaced with piecework, 'rise and grind' ideology, and the solitary confinement of 'WFH'. All of a sudden we'd been plunged into a hyperbolised, disaster-movie caricature of our increasingly solitary lives.

Iconic tourist sites around Britain were suddenly transformed into surreal 3D models of themselves. I cycled from my south London flat into the West End, riding through what would normally be the most overwhelming and chaotic parts of town: the House of Commons and Parliament Square, and then onto Trafalgar Square, to Piccadilly Circus, to St Paul's Cathedral. The traffic lights changed for nobody's benefit, just the occasional passer-by in a mask; sirens wailed in the distance. It was thrilling, and at the same time it was ghastly. In that absence, and emptiness, there was a glaring reminder of just how wrong things had gone.

And such was our yearning for this missing human warmth that we attempted to reconstruct the crowd digitally, through our screens. We opened cans of beer and the Zoom app to chat in a 'virtual pub', we attended virtual quizzes and comedy gigs (bizarre experiences, when the comedian is, like you, alone in their living room, their punchlines hollow without the punctuation of laughter), while one of my friends coordinated watch-alongs of old World Cup matches on YouTube, which we discussed in real time via WhatsApp, as if it were live. These ersatz crowd experiences, born of our innate longing to be with others, were, alas, just deeply discombobulating and unsocial. The glitches in the transmission of our loved ones' faces and voices via video chat became unbearable. It wasn't that it 'wasn't quite the same'. It wasn't even *close*.

I found myself craving songs that reminded me of being among a vast number of strangers. I watched videos of stirring terrace football chants on a loop, hundreds of thousands of strained, untrained voices bellowing with unguarded emotion the words to 'Bella Ciao', 'Sunshine on Leith', 'Grace', or 'You'll Never Walk Alone'. From there I progressed to audience sing-alongs of Rihanna's 'Umbrella' and Koffee's 'Toast', which took me back to swaying in the boozy crush of Notting Hill Carnival, and conjured the smell of mingled sweat and sunblock on my temples and spilt rum and ginger beer on my shoes; the sensation of being giddily overwhelmed, as the juddering sub-bass moved in waves through 1 million rib cages.

I missed the intimate vibrations and disinhibition of dancing, elbows pumping in time to thrumming bass lines alongside total strangers, in a dark, low-ceilinged club. I missed the transgression of screaming swear words into the icy winter air of the AFC Wimbledon terraces following an outrageous refereeing decision. I missed the vast spectacle and delirious, arms-aloft singalongs of massive music festivals. I missed the righteous solidarity of being on a political demo, chanting and feeling my own reedy voice being fattened and made whole by others joining it in unison. I missed the tingling mixture of anxiety and vertigo the moment you first step out into a carnival or football or protest crowd, the feeling of bug-eyed overstimulation, the undulating ripples of noise and colour leaping and competing for your attention. I missed the psychic alchemy of congregation, the energy-transfer where your brain pulses with the validation of strangers, and the joy of mass physical proximity to those who have chosen the same path. *How could I be wrong? Look, all these people are here too.*

~

Why do we join crowds? There is much to deter us from doing so, even outside of a viral pandemic. The level of anxiety they induce varies enormously from one person to the next, but it's a feeling which will be familiar to us all – even to those of us who love being in crowds: the fear there is no escape, the possibility of violence, of panic, groping, crushes and clashes, arrest, pick-pocketing, unfair judgement from those outside the crowd, the loss of control, of freedom, of peace and quiet, the suffocating of our individual agency, the muffling of our own voice. So why do we join them? I know the answer, because I felt the visceral pull of the phantom crowd throughout the mind-numbing isolation of the pandemic.

We join crowds because located there, in the midst of all that commotion and movement, is something fundamental about what it is to be human. We are swept along on an emotional tide, fired up and inspired by our fellow travellers. Our individual failings are submerged: we become greater than the sum of our meagre parts. We join crowds with tentative enthusiasm and leave them beaming with joy, or roaring about the need for change – yelling for one more tune, or one more push for revolution. Crowds are empowering – indeed, they are life-changing. Social psychologists have found that crowd membership doesn't just engender feelings of joy and belonging, but actually forms in us new social identities. It transforms our psychology, our sense of who we are and what we are capable of. In some cases, when we choose to join the right crowds, we become new people entirely.

Confined to the seventy square metres of my south London flat with my flatmate and two cats in the spring of 2020, I realised that many of the most formative and memorable experiences of my life (and of my work, in twenty years' reporting as a journal-ist) had been in crowds. There was the 2012 general strike in Madrid, where I joined 900,000 protesters against mass redun-dancies and austerity, and ended a feverish and overwhelming twenty-four hours dodging rubber bullets fired by the heavily armed Spanish riot police. There was the historic, 1.5-million-strong march against the Iraq War in London in February 2003, a day still burned into my memory more than two decades later. There was the loudest and most spine-tingling football crowd I'd ever been part of, among the deafening volume of the 30,000-strong, anarchist ultras of Beşiktaş in Istanbul in 2010.

Then there was the much darker experience of seeing an iconic London red double-decker bus go up in flames as I was reporting on the biggest riots in English history, in 2011 – where the seismic anger of the crowd seemed to send tremors down Tottenham High Street, as police horses weighing up to a tonne charged at us, and fireworks were let off in the other direction. Likewise, the most affecting moments of my music writing career unfolded in explosive, subterranean grime raves, in vast moshpits at Reading Festival or on asphalt dance floors at Notting Hill Carnival. Fiestas, festivals, football matches, political marches, rallies, riots, and raves – all were about my fellow travellers in the crowd, as much as they were about the thing that had drawn us all there in the first place.

Lately I have acquired a growing fear for the crowd's present and its future. In my work I have charted the emerging threats to it: the often innovative ways those with a monopoly on power disperse, repress and monetise it. These include the draconian, paramilitary policing and media demonisation of numerous political protests; the mass sell-off of public buildings under austerity and the creeping privatisation of once-open public spaces; the sad atomisation of our lives under late capitalism and the resulting crisis of loneliness; the way London's vibrant youth subcultures are attacked by the media, politicians and the police, and marginalised by gentrification. All of these are attacks on forms of collectivity, on the self-assembling crowd. For every transcendentally brilliant grime rave I attended in the 2000s, there were two more shut down by racist policing.[1] For every transformative political protest, there has been another knocked back by baton charges and libelled by media distortions.

Realising how vital crowd experiences have been to me has also meant realising how much they are now in jeopardy, and how crucial it is that they be defended. The crowd will only become more important as our cities become more densely populated. The history of the crowd is the history of civilisation, and that is not about to change: no one is returning to small hunter-gatherer communities. Human density and how we manage it will be the key to the twenty-first century.

Moments of epiphany are easier to come by when your senses are heightened by being among fellow travellers, and you're carried along by a flowing tide of collective energy. In fact, the most formative and radicalising political experience of my life took place because I had entered the heart of a crowd. It was 9 December 2010, a freezing cold winter day in Westminster in central London, the feverish climax of a month of rowdy, grassroots student protests that seemed to have erupted from nowhere – in protest at the Conservative–Liberal Democrat coalition government's swingeing cuts to public services, and their controversial decision to allow university tuition fees to triple to £9,000 a year. I was one of around 40,000 people to join this last-ditch effort to get the measures stopped, marching from the University of London Union in Bloomsbury to the House of Commons.

This was the historic peak of the Metropolitan Police's use of 'kettling', which had never been applied on such a scale before. Kettling is a brutal and dangerous public order policing tactic, whereby peaceful protesters are illegally detained for hours, without charge, without access to food, toilets, warm clothing, or medical assistance, by solid lines of baton-wielding riot cops. That long day and night was certainly an ending – the tuition fees vote was passed, while those it would impoverish were detained, dragged and beaten, right outside, in Parliament Square – but it also felt like the beginning of something new, for a generation of students and young people who would not willingly acquiesce to the deliberately inflicted misery of Conservative Britain.

But it was the intensely physical experience of *being right there* in the throng that changed me. As darkness fell in Parliament Square at 4 p.m., and the temperature dropped from four degrees centigrade to zero, you could see teenagers, eyes bulging with adrenaline, testing the limits of the police 'kettle' and feeling its barbed-wire edges. An hour before that, they had been happily passing around hip flasks, dancing to grime and rap on an impromptu sound system, swapping political leaflets and chanting about fees, cuts and austerity – and then, as the police closed ranks, conviviality turned to intense anger: that same full-body blood-rush of fear and energy you get if you've been in any kind of physical confrontation. It affects you physiologically, your nerves fizz and jangle, your heart races, and you simply cannot settle back down to where you were before.

There were terrifying horse charges into the crowd. A Porta-kabin was set on fire, spewing choking black fumes into the frigid evening air. At around 7 p.m., protesters stopped battling to escape the police lines on Whitehall and turned their attention to the Treasury, where riot police desperately tried to keep the double doors shut from the inside, as teenagers used metal fences as battering rams. By 10 p.m. we had been forced back by lines of riot cops, and crushed – thousands of us – onto the low-walled Westminster Bridge, packed in as tight as a moshpit, for hours, without explanation.

It was an enraging epiphany for me, as it was for so many people who would become close friends and comrades in the months and years that followed. It was an intense education in how the solidarity of the crowd works, and how power responds to that solidarity, and it would sharpen and radicalise my politics forever. Crammed together and bullied by the riot police, screaming desperately for freedom and justice under the silent, watchful eye of Big Ben, we wondered with each crowd surge if we were going to be plunged into the icy Thames below. Being in the crowd that day made flesh what were once abstract thoughts, feelings and things I'd read about state power and democracy: a truly collective experience that fired me up in ways that have not dimmed one bit, in the more than a decade that has passed since.

What *is* a crowd? One way to tackle this question is to list some things that I would argue are *not* crowds: eight family members gathered in a private house for Sunday lunch are not a crowd. Nor are the 47,790 inhabitants of Inverness. Nor are 700 people on the concourse of Victoria train station, streaming in different directions, with different agendas and destinations. Nor are the three billion users of Facebook. Nor are 100 shoppers in the aisles of a Tesco Extra on a Saturday afternoon. Nor are 350 rush-hour commuters, headphones plugged in, walking silently over London Bridge towards the City. Crowd psychologists make the distinction between 'psychological crowds' and 'physical crowds', which sometimes overlap, and sometimes do not. Some of the above might be physical crowds, but they have no psychological component binding them together. There's no technical lower limit on how many people constitute a crowd, and there's certainly no upper limit. More important than numbers is the powerful, sometimes ineffable sense of a shared group identity and purpose.

There are many types of crowd, of course. Some are more organic than others, some are more open to new members than others, and some are more polite and well-behaved than others. Some crowds have been specifically invited to form by the authorities or event organisers, and will arrive on time, show their tickets, speak or clap only when it is the accepted social norm to do so, sit quietly, leave on time, and comport themselves throughout with the unflinching discipline of an army regiment. Other crowds come together almost spontaneously, apparently on a whim, without warning, and seem to behave erratically, unpredictably, and to ebb and flow indefinitely. Some appear anarchic and disconnected up close, and then move swiftly and with purpose, aligning, dipping and swooping with the elegance of a murmuration of starlings. While their behaviour varies, these are all crowds because they are bound together by some shared social identity or goal, and that shared identity, that kinship and strength, will intensify and deepen precisely because they have gathered together.

Crowds matter because of what they do to the world around them: they escalate commonly held individual grievances into collective demands for change, they overthrow governments, they start wars, and can help end them too. They are the most direct and physical expression of democracy that we have – indeed, for centuries of human history, riots caused by hunger, exploitation or unfair and unequal treatment were the primary available expression of popular will – and yet they have been enlisted to legitimise and deify the most brutal dictators. They frequently have a profound cultural impact, beyond the moment when everyone drifts off home: the era-defining, 400,000-strong crowd at Woodstock in 1969 was the 'main character' of that festival, rather than Janis Joplin or Jimi Hendrix. And how political leaders and police forces respond to crowds – from horrific historical massacres, like Amritsar or Peterloo, to recent draconian laws clamping down on free assembly, to violent or racist public-order policing, from Hillsborough to the Notting Hill Carnival – tells us a great deal about the societies we live in.

Crowds also matter because of what they do to us when we join them. While most of us may have experienced varying degrees of anxiety or claustrophobia in a crowd, the simple fact is that crowd membership is overwhelmingly good for us, and makes us happy. There is a reason for this: because we have evolved to become social animals, there is an evolutionary imperative for us to come together with strangers, to forge bonds with people outside our family groups. In spite of what tabloid headlines, scolding politicians or popular wisdom would have you believe, crowds are complex and dynamic, and far more rational in their general character than they are given credit for. In any context, whether they are screaming blue murder or singing along to Blu Cantrell, every multitude contains multitudes. Crowd membership empowers and thrills us; it boosts our sense of self-worth and affirms our identity. In 2012, a substantial peer-reviewed study of hundreds of participants in the Mela – the vast Hindu pilgrimage event in northern India, attracting millions – became the latest in a growing body of evidence proving at last what many of us have instinctively known all along: that participating in mass gatherings actively improves our well-being.[2]

If the miserable solitude of the pandemic brought anything home, it's that we need other people around us. In the summers of 2020 and 2021, the joyous rush of the return to sports stadiums, festivals, illegal raves and block parties, along with the political imperatives of protests against racist violence or the climate crisis, overrode our concerns about a deadly virus. Even if we did so with face masks on, even if many of us did so nervously at first, most of us leaped back into the crowd before we had been vaccinated against Covid-19, because we needed it – as a vehicle for justice, or a vehicle for joy and debauchery, but either way, because an elemental, libidinal drive for the social was pulling us out of our homes.

This book makes the argument that the crowd is both the agent and the protagonist of history; the harbinger of change, the forcer of arguments. Crowds bring things to a head, they catalyse and accelerate. Crowds are 'the bearer of the new', as the political historian J. S. McClelland wrote. They hold this thrillingly progressive position, at the same time as they hark back millennia to something vital and innate to our development as social animals – marking our transformation from isolated, cave-dwelling family units to groups of humans working together towards bigger goals, to build communities and civilisations. Perhaps there's an unconscious awareness of these ancient roots in the denigration of crowds as animalistic, as 'stampeding hordes', an awareness that this was our elemental social state when we hunted and gathered and lived communally off the land, before we became *homo economicus* – before we became atomised, self-interested individuals with Netflix accounts and no mates.

Crowds have held great historical power since people first gathered in large groups in the Palaeolithic era, long before the ancient Greeks got together in the agora for political assemblies, performances, socialising and trade, or Stormzy headlined Glastonbury. This book focuses on the last 150 years, as the period in which the crowd, via the global surge towards representative democracy, grassroots revolutions, mass-party dictatorships, mass popular culture and urbanisation, has been the primary motor of history. This, I will argue, is the age of the crowd.

It might seem odd, given that primacy, but the history of the modern world is also the history of the defamation of the crowd as a poisonous influence on society. A crowd, we have forever been told, and are still told today, is always just a riot in waiting or a mob in disguise. From up on their pedestal, society's gatekeepers denounce the mindless thuggery of the crowd, its criminality and savagery, the ravings of its ringleaders, the base instinct for violence among the masses, the loss of all sense and propriety, the wilful derangement of the senses, the brainwashed, craven, gullible fools who would give up their agency and their individual wits to become a depraved and brainless horde. As you will discover in the chapters ahead, these are not just blatant falsehoods, but ones deliberately constructed and repeated to serve those in power.

After the student protests in 2010 I was horrified, if not surprised, to see how we had been described in the press. The *Sun*'s front page ran with 'BRAINLESS . . . that's the yobs who hijacked uni demo AND Met chief who let them.' The *Times* front page led with 'Thuggish and disgraceful', the *Daily Express* with 'Disgrace of the student hooligans', and the *Daily Mail* with 'Hijacking of a very middle-class protest'. It's not that the responses are pejorative – these are all right-wing newspapers, opposed to street protests in general and left-wing protests in particular – it's the language that is significant. The protesters are thugs, they are brainless, they have been 'hijacked' by sinister agitators; even if you are pro-Conservative and pro-austerity, on a purely factual basis you'll have to take my word for it that not one of those things was true (the 'very middle-class protest' jibe from the *Mail* is amusing, and partly although by no means entirely correct).

The 'brainless' or 'mindless' tag is particularly important, and worth unpacking: it is used so freely about rioters, protesters, ravers and football fans that our eyes might slide over it as a cliché, but it's fundamentally untrue, even when describing the most reprehensible crowd violence. Unless you are drunk or drugged to the point of near-unconsciousness, you know exactly what you're doing, even if that thing is illegal or highly morally dubious. And in the case of the 2010 student protests, I'm not sure I've ever encountered a political movement more dedicated to self-education, to sharing knowledge and making it freely accessible to all, and to thoughtful, strategic, creative activism – to mindful or *brainful* collective activity. You are welcome to disapprove of the crowd's actions, or the politics underpinning them, but it's fundamentally false, and very telling, to call them 'brainless'.

Yet the image of the crowd as a mindless mob prevails across different cultural forms throughout the modern age – in politics, the media, literature, art, cinema and TV. It is such a familiar scene in our culture that it has reached the point of knowing pastiche. Accusations of witch hunts and mob mentality never seem to leave our newspapers. The Angry Mob in *The Simpsons*, complete with flaming torches, placards and pitchforks, appears in the series so often – in no fewer than fifty different episodes – that it has its own dedicated page on the programme's Wiki site, as if it were a single character. The crowds in Dickens's *A Tale of Two Cities* conform to the same caricature – braying for violence, they are moved 'capriciously' to tears and calls for retribution. Our pop culture is stacked from front to back with mindless mobs, where in reality a sentient crowd should be.

How did this come to be the case? To my astonishment, as I delved deeper into the history of crowd psychology, I discovered that the popularly accepted wisdom about crowd behaviour – accepted by everyone from presidents to civilians – is overwhelmingly based on the work of one highly partisan and eccentric French conservative. That man, usually identified as 'the founder of crowd theory', author of the best-selling, endlessly reprinted and translated 1895 book *Psychologie des foules* (*The Crowd: A Study of the Popular Mind*), was Gustave Le Bon.

As I read about his idiosyncratic life and works, I concluded that Le Bon almost certainly formulated his theory of the crowd as a young soldier in 1871, watching with horror as the half-starved revolutionaries of the Paris Commune burned down the royal Tuileries Palace. Traumatised by that experience and haunted by the threat of mass democracy, he persuaded a world that was approaching the exhilarating, mind-altering crest of modernity that the violence and madness of crowds was innate, inevitable, and had to be crushed at all costs. He believed that the looming age of the crowd was to be an age of barbarism: that even the most civilised of men become animals upon joining with others. Le Bon was certainly a misanthrope, and it would be no exaggeration to label him a proto-fascist.

Few people outside of a handful of university social science departments seem to have noticed, but it is precisely this wildly distorted perspective that has prevailed ever since: *The Crowd* may be the most influential work of popular psychology ever written. Even the most socially minded of twenty-first-century humanists are apt to echo Le Bon's fictions about mob mentality and madding crowds, seemingly without realising.

Crowd psychology came into existence in the nineteenth century as a tool to explain the insurgent energy of the masses of angry, impoverished people crammed into the rapidly overflowing great cities of Europe – the newly formed slums of industrial workers who were demanding revolution. It also overlapped with the period's intense focus on decoding the 'criminal mind' and the 'criminal class', along with the racist and classist pseudoscience of physiognomy. Le Bon's deeply felt, *fin-de-siècle* bourgeois angst was extremely typical of its time. When faced with the wild-eyed, amoral tyranny of the crowd, Le Bon argued, the only option was to disperse it by force, or channel its chaotic energy towards the maintenance of hierarchical order – towards, as it would turn out, the terrifying spectacle of the Nazis' Nuremberg rallies.

The pipeline of nineteenth-century crowd theory to twentieth-century fascism was direct, and personal: *The Crowd* was read and Le Bon's ideas adopted by Mussolini, Hitler and Goebbels, and further implemented by the dictatorships of Stalin and the DPRK's Kim dynasty. The totalitarian performance of vast mass games, political rallies and military parades, with orderly, worshipful crowds prostrate before a dictator's personality cult, sought to absorb what were seen as the contagious passions of the masses, and put them to use for the benefit of those already at the top. The crowd, when properly marshalled, can still be a useful idiot for would-be despots today, as Donald Trump's barely concealed respect for the Capitol Hill rioters of 6 January 2021 demonstrates.

Despite these grim ideological bedfellows and legacies, Le Bon's ideas about crowds are all around us. His work is still regularly and approvingly cited as supposedly intellectual ballast for criticism of everyone from Black Lives Matter protesters to sports fans. 'The madness of crowds' is an idiom in itself in modern English, taken as an implicitly correct description, a perfectly natural and obvious pairing of the two nouns. This is an individualistic society's default position regarding mass participation in pretty much anything at all. That we all lose our heads in crowds is taken as read: foolishness and mob mentality are contagious, and we are all gullible enough to succumb to them. Almost all of the language we have to describe crowds draws on this same embedded prejudice: police engage in 'crowd control' to prevent 'crowd trouble' descending into 'crowd violence' – we never speak of 'crowd joy', 'crowd care' or 'crowd comfort'. There is no 'gentle mob' in the English language. No friendly pack. No thoughtful herd.

In fact, the spectre of 'mob rule' has become a way of damning democratic impulses and political participation in general, and crops up whenever there are protests – even in advance of them. A British newspaper op-ed before one of the 2023 Palestine solidarity demos warned that a march planned for 11 November, a march doing something so controversial as to call for a ceasefire on Remembrance Day, 'might be blighted by baying mobs of lefties, anarchists, and other assorted troublemakers . . . mob rule must not be allowed to prevail.'[3] That same week, the prominent author and columnist Adrian Wooldridge, who worked at the *Economist* for three decades, cited Gustave Le Bon to argue that politics belongs in parliament, not on the streets. Sometimes, a phantom mob is attacked when there are no physical gatherings of human beings at all: merely an appeal for political change, conducted politely and calmly. The 'woke mob' and the 'online mob' have become targets for right-wing ire in the absence of a substantive organised left. A single anonymous Twitter user calling a politician or pundit 'a muppet' is immediately liable to gin up histrionic cries to this effect from their fellow power-mongers. The way power speaks about the crowd is always a calculated attempt to diminish the humanity, and the complex, multilayered varieties of intent, behaviour and personality of people who have been denied the freedom to express these things.

Le Bon's theories have persisted as the default position on crowd behaviour and psychology because they serve a purpose as old as the crowd itself. That purpose is very simple: to shore up the powerful, and delegitimise the public. To hold back democracy, and maintain elite dominance. In the chapters that follow I'm going to show you – from inside and outside the throng – not just how completely all-pervasive Le Bon's antiquated version of the crowd is, but also that his theories are provably nonsense.

While this book addresses the war on the crowd in the modern age, Gustave Le Bon's theories did not fall fully formed from the sky in 1871, as he watched Paris burning. Plato's *Republic* gave us the idea that democracy's noble intentions could be corrupted and corroded to become mob rule, descending into tyranny. The foundational story of Christianity itself echoes this account of the irrational, violent and homogeneous crowd: according to the Gospel of Matthew, it is just this kind of sinister mob that condemns Jesus Christ. 'Crucify him!' they shout. When Pontius Pilate asks 'Why? What crime has he committed?' they do not respond to these reasonable questions with reasoned answers, but simply shout 'all the louder, "Crucify him!"'

Across the entire history of civilisation, the establishment has loathed and feared the crowd. Emperors, generals, nobles, church elders, and magistrates, and modern-day politicians, newspaper barons and police commanders, have all understood the threat and acted accordingly. Whether that threat takes the form of a direct political challenge to power, such as a protest or a riot or some other collective demand for change, or is more obliquely contained in a raucous grassroots celebration, or a cultural ritual, any crowd that has political agency or is making its own fun can arouse panic in our leaders.

Recent work by anthropologists of early human life has shown that coming together for singing, dancing and other revels is fundamental to our evolution as a species – it bonded us together and motored us into the first villages and societies. In 2003, a cave was unearthed in Nottinghamshire with 13,000-year-old paintings of what seem to be 'conga lines' of dancers. According to the archaeologist Paul Pettitt, the paintings matched others across Europe, and demonstrated a continent-wide Palaeolithic culture of collective singing and dancing. Evolutionary psychologists like Robin Dunbar have argued that singing and dancing together played a role in the evolutionary success of modern humans over other proto–*Homo sapiens*.[4] When a football crowd spontaneously begins a chant, they are following an evolutionary imperative tens of thousands of years old.

And those in power have never approved. The medieval and early modern Christian Church fought an epic battle to eradicate unruly and ecstatic dancing from its congregations – to reassert control over mass worship. As first the Reformation and then the Industrial Revolution swept through Europe, festivals, feast days, fairs, sports, revels and ecstatic rituals of countless kinds were outlawed for their tendency to result in drunken, pagan or otherwise ungodly behaviour. The crowd needed to be dispersed and disciplined, because there was work to be done in the mills and the factories, and church to go to on Sunday. 'The civilising process' described by Norbert Elias in his 1939 book of the same name was positioned against the freedom of the crowd. Elias charts the long transformation of public behaviour since the feudal era, a gradual process of inhibition: the social mandating of shame and decorum that was required to support the power structures of the modern, civilised world. The magistrate, the priest, the boss and the nobleman lined up to discipline and disperse subaltern masses that had become entirely too comfortable with public carousing.

Between the seventeenth and twentieth centuries, there were 'literally thousands of acts of legislation introduced which attempted to eliminate carnival and popular festivity from European life,' wrote Peter Stallybrass and Allon White in *The Politics and Poetics of Transgression* (1986). This was, in Max Weber's famous phrase, the period in which 'asceticism descended like a frost on the life of "Merrie old England".' Just as the evolution of industrial capitalism required acts of enclosure to capture our common lands and squirrel them away for a tiny, wealthy elite, a similar process was occurring which sought to abolish or recuperate our festive rituals and acts of collective joy.

From medieval dance manias to the pandemic's illegal plague raves, priests and politicians have panicked because they know that participation in crowds makes us stronger versions of ourselves – that crowds empower their individual members to do what they had always wanted, but didn't have the confidence to do alone: to declare their political beliefs or proclaim their sexual orientation in public, to belt out their heartfelt feelings for Mo Salah, to occupy a bank, to throw a brick, to fight with strangers, to dance to ABBA on the concourse of a major intercity railway station.

The point is not to decide which of these are right and which are wrong, and this book will not ignore fascist coups and witch hunts, acts of violence and intimidation, sinister attempts at mass manipulation and indoctrination, Nazi rallies, and other unpalatable stories from the history of crowds. I have joined countless crowds in pursuit of delirious hedonism and collective joy, or because they accord with my political beliefs – but in the name of journalism I have also borne witness to such sinister crowds as the fascist paramilitary group the Magyar Gárda in Budapest, or a proto-Trump Tea Party rally in White Plains, New York; I have even been to watch Chelsea at Stamford Bridge. Instead of acting as some kind of adjudicator between Good Crowds and Bad Crowds, I hope to lay out an accurate account of how crowds function, how susceptible we really are to being swept along by those around us, and why we have been sold so many lies about crowds, for so long.

This book will, I hope, make you think differently about this riotous history. I aim to show how Le Bon's deeply distorted but generally accepted 'story of the crowd' came to be – how governments, police chiefs and other elites have sought to disperse, defame, or otherwise exert control over gatherings of the public, and how the peculiar character of Gustave Le Bon came to loom over the modern age. I also set out to provide a more accurate account of the power of crowds by reporting from inside them in all their variety, plunging deep into the sights, sounds and visceral emotions of crowd membership, and tracing the revolution in crowd theory that is now finally taking place, thanks to the radical breakthroughs of a new generation of crowd psychologists who have dared to engage with the crowd empirically, rather than lob stones at it from on high. Finally, my third aim is to consider the pernicious threats to free assembly we face in an age of mass urbanisation, militarised policing, surveillance, social isolation and the chokehold of the corporate events industry over our play – over our cultural, social and sporting lives.

This is not an attempt to tell the history of every crowd that ever existed, or every modern crowd that ever existed, or even to outline every major type of crowd – worshipful, ecstatic religious crowds are absent, for example (please don't smite me, I'm an atheist and I wanted this book to be relatively short). It presents an argument about how corrupting, reactionary and devoid of evidence traditional crowd theory is, and how it has shaped the Western understanding of the crowd in the modern age, with dreadful consequences for anyone who appreciates democracy, socialism, and a decent party. The modern age is the age of the crowd, as far as this book is concerned: the age of mass culture, mass media, densely populated cities and universal suffrage. In selecting a few key categories of crowds which have been particularly pathologised as stupid or violent, and crowds which have been particularly brutally policed and wilfully misrepresented, I hope to show that the ideological needs of society's elites – rather than any sincere attempt to describe group psychology and behaviour – have determined how we view the crowd for far too long.

This is a book built around one central argument, but that argument is not 'you must all love all crowds all the time'. If you are personally hesitant about joining crowds, I would urge you to read on. 'I have something to confess,' the Turner Prize–nominated artist Rory Pilgrim said at an event I attended recently on the power of collective speech and song. He seemed nervous about his admission. 'I actually . . . *hate* crowds.' A striking number of people have said this to me during my research. For some people fear of crowds is a psychological issue, of course, rather than an aesthetic preference. Crowded spaces are a potential trigger for a panic attack for some, and a potential nightmare for anyone with claustrophobia or agoraphobia; while the sensory overload, the noise and the tumult, can be horribly unpleasant, frightening or alienating for non-neurotypical people. I have seen this firsthand,

and have had to escort my companion out of the throng and into A&E – I wouldn't wish it on anyone.

For those who do not have specific health reasons for avoiding crowds, there's something bigger and more nebulous going on: crowds have become a scapegoat for the pressures and anxieties of modern urban life. To be told that the place you are heading to is 'crowded' is never a pleasing discovery – it is effectively a pejorative, and implies that the space is not in its ideal state. My strong suspicion is that many people who say they hate crowds actually love being in the *right* crowd – one they have chosen to enter for pleasure, rather than encountered by accident. They might hate what they think of as the 'typical' crowd (say, 60,000 screaming football fans, if they hate football and lad culture; Glastonbury, if it all sounds like far too much effort; thousands of people darting through King's Cross Station at rush hour), but put the same person in an audience of 200 people for their favourite singer, and they're filled with warmth and joy. If dirt is simply 'matter out of place', then for many people 'the crowd' is social matter that has been corrupted, misaligned, badly arranged (i.e. it contains the *wrong* people) or that has accumulated to an undesirable excess.

While the twenty-first-century crowd has faced police riot squads and relentless demonisation by the media and political classes, it has also encountered an altogether new kind of threat: total domestication. Under mass surveillance, on streets that were once public space, now privatised, opportunities for free assembly in the modern city – to dance, celebrate, talk or protest – have been whittled away with alarming speed. In the place of such 'open crowds', we have the centrepiece of the modern, tourism-focused city dominated by the events industry, where the tamed, carefully marshalled crowd becomes a vital source of profit extraction. *Pay for your ticket, submit your personal data, empty your pockets in this tray, step this way for a bag check, look into the camera, verify your photo ID, stay in your seat, do as the steward says, leave in an orderly fashion, do not pass GO.*

This is the crowd's moment. Repressed around the world by the Covid-19 pandemic, because our lives depended on it, it was not long before crowds rushed back to the public square, in celebration and in anger. The history of the modern world is the history of the violent controversies and brutal crackdowns, joyful festivities and vigorous energies unleashed when humans gather together: for crowds change not just who we are, but also the course of history.

1

Paris Is Burning: Revolutionary Crowds

In 1871, the arrival of spring in Paris was even more welcome than usual, for it had been an almost unimaginable winter. France had suffered a resounding defeat in the Franco–Prussian War in September 1870, and Napoleon III had been captured. This humiliation was followed by a Prussian siege of Paris that dragged agonisingly across the long winter. It was a desperate, dreadful five months which left as many as 50,000 Parisians dead, many from malnutrition. Food supply lines were shut down. Sanitation and refuse disposal became ever harder. The Prussian army shelled the city relentlessly, and those that didn't die were driven half-mad from sleep deprivation. Communications with the outside world were cut off – Parisian officials had to resort to using hot-air balloons and pigeons.

Conditions became increasingly macabre. The menus of Paris's restaurants began advertising dishes made with the meat of cats, dogs and rats. Horse meat became an expensive luxury, and so too did wood, when it was needed to keep the deathly winter cold away. The pride of the city's Jardin des Plantes zoo, the famous elephants Castor and Pollux, were eaten. And these grim delicacies were a treat for the Parisian bourgeoisie. The city's poorest – the vast majority, in fact – were not able to afford such delights as fricassée of mouse, or ragout of cat. Instead there was only hunger, cold and desperation and, rising from it, a burgeoning collective desire for change: not just an end to the siege, but something more. Things could not simply go back to the way they were.

Along with the government of the Second French Empire, all of French civilisation seemed to be collapsing. The Prussian siege finally concluded at the end of January 1871, and six weeks later, into the power vacuum left by the French establishment, lurched the Paris Commune. This was a democratic, self-governing socialist-anarchist city republic, opposed to the national government in Versailles. It was powered by mass popular discontent, not least from the working-class National Guard soldiers stationed in the capital. While the Commune produced historically notable revolutionary thinkers and leaders like Louis Blanqui, Pierre-Joseph Proudhon and Louise Michel, it was not a Bolshevik-style vanguardist uprising of a few key figures, but one forged out of the revolutionary exhaustion of the Parisian citizenry at large. It was an insurrection that came from the crowd.

Half-starved by the siege, the Communards ripped down what was left of the existing hierarchy of French society. They separated Church and state, appropriated all Church property, cancelled rent owed to landlords during the siege, abolished child labour and night work, instituted maximum salaries for public employees, and empowered workers to take over their businesses. The Parisians, wrote Karl Marx in a letter to Dr Louis Kugelmann in April 1871, were 'heroic' and 'glorious', doing nothing less than 'storming heaven' and tearing down the 'old order'.

Crowds give a physical expression to the ideas of the society around them, and the Communards gave flesh to their revolutionary instincts not just with these radical new policies, but with public acts of collective ritual and festivity. Many of the public events organised by the Communards were celebratory: there were free concerts in the gardens of the royal Tuileries Palace, attended by people of all ages and social classes. The palace doors were thrown open to the crowd for all to enjoy. The *ancien régime* – the French elites and military based outside the city at Versailles – began bombarding Paris, but even as the shells rained down, over 10,000 people attended a Sunday concert in the palace gardens. Far from cowering in fear, the crowd were 'in raptures' according to one eyewitness.

For a population under siege – this time from their own masters – the Parisians did not act like it. Throughout the Commune's seventy-two days, there was a 'festival-like atmosphere' across the city, wrote the journalist Prosper-Olivier Lissagaray. People sang revolutionary songs in the streets, and thronged to concerts and theatres. 'The boulevards', he reported, were 'sparkling with life and gaiety, the bright cafés swarming with visitors'. The Commune's sense of in-group identity was also cemented via public rituals such as the staged burning of a guillotine, to the joy of a public who had lived in fear of its tyranny.

These mass actions were deeply symbolic, but symbolic acts do not exist only in the abstract – these public events had very real-world consequences: they bonded the Communard crowd more tightly together against the external enemies who were attacking them from beyond the city's walls. A crowd that is surrounded and assailed from outside only becomes more united, more incensed, and more sure of its righteousness.

On 16 May 1871, two months into the Commune, the most significant of all the Communards' great acts of public icono-clasm took place: the destruction of the Vendôme Column. Pulling it down was, wrote historian John Merriman, 'a spectac-ular attempt at exorcism through demolition'. It was neither impulsive nor perfunctory, but a well-planned, theatrical cere-mony designed to thrill, and to galvanise the suffering people of Paris. It was a glorious spring day, and underneath a cloudless blue sky, in the centre of the cobbles of the grand Place Vendôme, stood the forty-four-metre-high monument to Napoleon, his army and the old order. To the Communards, it was a monument to despotism, hierarchy, feudal inequality and imperialism: everything that was wrong with nineteenth-century France. As the preparations began around noon, a military band enlisted for the occasion, their brass sparkling in the sunshine, played the French revolutionary anthems 'La Marseillaise' and 'Chant du Départ'. Members of the Commune's political council stood around in red belts and scarves, enjoying the mounting excitement.

A scaffold had been erected around the monument, with ropes attached to the statue of Napoleon at the top and a red flag fixed to the balustrade, waving softly in the spring breeze, as 'an immense crowd thronged all the neighbouring streets', growing first to thousands, then tens of thousands of people.[1] Many were dirt-poor strangers to the *beaux quartiers*, lifelong Parisians who in normal times would have been accosted by police officers merely for setting foot in the posh part of town. It's a common thread to urban protests throughout history: a crowd whose political point is partly made by *where* they assemble – by the transgression of what is often an invisible boundary between slum and bourgeois square. It sends a clear message: 'Our very presence here shows how things can be different.' It is a principle which manifests itself in a common modern-day call-and-response protest chant I have heard countless times: 'Whose streets?' 'Our streets!'

Around Place Vendôme, the crowd enjoyed their collective act of transgression and the prospect of the event to come. The excitable chatter grew as the afternoon wore on. People leaned out of balconies and windows, even on adjoining streets, craning their necks to see this moment of spectacular iconoclasm. The shop fronts were all closed for the occasion, and a bed of sand and dung had been spread out beneath the column, to lessen the impact. At 5:30 p.m., after several hours of sawing, chiselling and pulling, the monument finally came crashing down, breaking in two on the cobbles below. The globe Napoleon had been holding in his hand rolled out of reach. The noise was immediately drowned out by the roar of the electrified crowd, chanting '*Vive la République! Vive la Commune!*' as they rushed past the stewards to collect trophies from the rubble. Speeches followed, and more music, as the crowd 'buzzed around' the fallen column. To mark the occasion, the square was renamed Place Internationale.

Lissagaray was one of the tens of thousands participating in this moment of joyful collective catharsis:

> The extremity of the column slowly displaced itself, the shaft little by little gave way, then, suddenly reeling to and fro, broke and fell with a low moan. The head of Bonaparte rolled on the ground, and his parricidal arm lay detached from the trunk. An immense acclamation, as that of a people freed from a yoke, burst forth. The ruins were climbed upon and saluted by enthusiastic cries, and the red flag floated from the purified Pedestal, which on that day had become the altar of the human race.[2]

A week after the Vendôme Column was brought crashing to earth, the French army finally pushed back into the city, to destroy the Commune in what would become known as *la semaine sanglante* – 'the bloody week'. As the army surged into Paris, breaking through the city walls, the pro-Commune National Guards began to set fire to buildings that symbolised the French government and the old regime. On 23 May, the vast and imposing royal palace on the banks of the Seine, the Tuileries, was set ablaze. Oil, liquid tar and turpentine were spread around the walls, floors and curtains across the palace, and barrels of gunpowder placed at the foot of the grand staircase. Jules Bergeret, the National Guard commander who had given the order to the group of twelve guards who set the fire, sent a message to the Hôtel de Ville: 'The last vestiges of royalty have just disappeared. I hope that the same will happen to all the monuments of Paris.'

And the Tuileries fire was just the beginning. While the Versailles army reduced residential parts of Paris to rubble, firing shells, iron balls and bullets into the city's working-class districts, demolishing barricades as they went, their opponents, in rage and desperation, sought to destroy the physical fabric of the *ancien régime*. By the next day, the sky above Paris was filled with black smoke from the burning palaces and government ministries, the rising flames taking on blue, greenish and violet tones.

The fires spread to the library of the Louvre, the Hôtel de Ville, the Cour des Comptes, the Ministry of Finance, the tapestry factory of Gobelins, the Palace of Justice and the home of the Legion of Honour. 'As long as there are walls there is a monument / And we've had enough of that filth . . . As long as the nest is still there / The bird expects to return', wrote the contemporary (pseudonymous) character Père Duchêne in *Burn Down the Tuileries*. The French royal palace burned for forty-eight hours before the fire was brought under control, leaving only a charcoal husk. It was never rebuilt.

'Flames, now slow, now rapid as darts, flashed from a hundred windows,' wrote Lissagaray.

> The red tide of the Seine reflected the monuments, thus redoubling the conflagration. Fanned by an eastern wind, the blazing flames rose up against Versailles, and cried to the conqueror of Paris that he will no longer find his place there, and that these monarchical monuments will not again shelter a monarchy . . . the Rue Royale to St-Sulpice seemed a wall of fire divided by the Seine. Eddies of smoke clouded all the west of Paris, and the spiral flames shooting forth from these furnaces emitted showers of sparks that fell upon the neighbouring districts.[3]

Watching aghast from the sidelines as the Tuileries burned was a recently discharged military doctor called Gustave Le Bon. Aged just twenty-nine, Le Bon had been in charge of military ambulances in the Franco–Prussian War, and had seen the French army suffer crushing defeats in all their horrific gristle, gore and agony. He then returned to Paris to recover, only to witness his fellow countrymen reducing the architectural bastions of the old France he loved to ashes and rubble. Everything he believed in was in disarray. The flickering images of Paris on fire haunted him for the rest of his life, and threw permanent shadows across his illustrious and prolific writing career. It was a traumatic experience, one which shaped not only Le Bon's epochal, phenomenally influential 1895 book *The Crowd*, but over also a century of our thinking about crowd psychology and behaviour.

The young Le Bon had seen the revolutionary masses in action that spring, and was convinced they would 'pitilessly extirpate by fire and sword whoever [was] opposed to the establishment of the new faith'.[4] Of the many errors he made in formulating his crowd theory, his experience of the Paris Commune was its original sin: he determined that this complex, dynamic mass uprising (with its myriad competing political factions, goals and contradictions) was being driven by the 'crowd' (*la foule*) as he understood it: a homogeneous mass of brainwashed, dangerous savages, a ragged-trousered army happily carrying out terrorist atrocities against civilised France.

This paranoid version of events found its clearest expression in the lurid myth of the *pétroleuses*: cadres of deranged revolutionary women, hell-bent on wanton destruction, numbering as many as 8,000. They supposedly hurled Molotov cocktails into aristocratic palaces, and were identifiable by the gunpowder on their hands. It was all complete nonsense. But even while the Commune was still going, and the Versaillais army was sweeping through the city, the fiction of the *pétroleuses* took hold in Paris – and all working-class women came under intense suspicion from the troops. There are shades of the Salem witch trials underscoring the whole narrative. According to Lissagaray, 'every woman who was badly dressed, or carrying a milk-can, a pail, an empty bottle, was pointed out as a *pétroleuse*, her clothes torn to tatters, she was pushed against the nearest wall, and killed with revolver-shots.'[5]

Alongside these baseless conspiracy theories, the French establishment proceeded to launch a very real and protracted period of violent revenge. *La semaine sanglante* – and the Commune – concluded with mass executions on the street. Tens of thousands of unarmed Parisian civilians were arrested, exiled, or summarily shot by the French army. Some of those executed were avowed supporters of the revolutionary ideals of the Commune, but many were not. The authorities took the crowd to be a homogeneous bloc, and adopted a brutal policy of collective punishment without any shred of evidence or due process.

The truth of the infamous fires that set Paris ablaze is that they were not started by the swarming subaltern masses, or by cultish groups of nihilistically violent women. Many began by accident, the consequence of artillery fire in hot, dry weather. In the case of the Tuileries fire, it was methodically set by barely a dozen National Guard soldiers under specific orders, for tactical military reasons as much as for its symbolic anti-royalist resonance. There was no massed barbarian mob behind the arson, and there were no civilian bystanders who got 'swept up in the moment' or 'carried away by the crowd'.

But Le Bon was certain of the contrary. And he was sure that the sky-blackening orgy of destruction he had witnessed could happen again. The crowd's influence was growing all the time, in his view, and 1871 did not signal the climax, but merely another spike on the crowd's tyrannical journey to power. As far as Le Bon was concerned, society's natural leaders had capitulated to the mob in the French Revolution of 1789, and remained weak enough that they might do so again. The violence of France's long, bloody century had risen from the bottom up.

In his book *The Psychology of Socialism*, written twenty-eight years later, Le Bon attacked the utopian naivety of socialism, its willingness to rip down the old world, and its blind faith in 'new dogmas'. 'It is evident' to socialists, he suggested, 'that a society may be disorganised by violence, just as a building, laboriously constructed, may be destroyed in an hour by fire.'[6] He was still thinking about the Tuileries, decades later. In his reflections in *The Psychology of Revolution*, a full fifty years after the Commune, he wrote that 'the people may kill, burn, ravage, commit the most frightful cruelties,' and yet this 'mysterious fetish' for 'the people' had persisted among a naive political class.[7] Socialism and mass democracy were on the rise everywhere in the world, setting the moral, natural order of things ablaze, and even his beloved elites seemed powerless to intervene. All politicians could do was capitulate to the whims of the masses, and let the flames rise higher.

Gustave Le Bon was a unique and highly eccentric character in the public life of *fin-de-siècle* France. He was an intellectually gregarious and ambitious polymath – *Homo multiplex*, one friend called him – who conducted research into physics, medicine, anthropology, biology, education, sexual reproduction, warfare, psychology, and more. He travelled to and documented some of the ways and cultures of India, Arabia and Nepal. He was interested in the world, and contemptuous of large parts of it – an advocate of the pseudoscientific racism of phrenology, as well as a heterodox thinker who 'irritated the academic hierarchy'.[8] He investigated tobacco smoke, skulls and socialism. He carried out chemical experiments in a laboratory in his home with instruments he built himself. He conducted an extensive study into the psychology of horses, complete with 200 photographs – a project that began after one of them had rudely thrown him to the ground. Le Bon was curious to the point of obsession – and all because he wanted his research to propel him into France's intellectual elite, to become a member of the Academy of Sciences, and to receive a university posting.

These two last goals eluded him, to his great resentment. He was excluded from the gilded halls of the Parisian institutions, and yet he achieved an impact on public life that was almost unparalleled amongst his peers. As 'a precocious and enduring pessimist', even before the Commune he was publishing work 'decrying the signs of French decadence', Susan Barrows observed – fretting especially about alcoholism and the country's declining birth rate.[9] He was a renowned opinion-former in his own lifetime, even while the Parisian academic elite rejected him. His books were translated countless times; he bent the ears of dukes, presidents, princes and dictators. However, it was *The Crowd* that truly made his name, not just in France, but around the world. His idea of the crowd – his sense of its vital importance to world-historical events, and desperate warnings of its reckless, destructive potential – would resonate into the age of extremes in the early twentieth century, and on into our own.

For Le Bon, the decades that followed the burning of the Tuileries Palace marked the age of the crowd as a phenomenon. He was not alone in this perspective: the crowd was a key protagonist of the period, and the invention and blossoming of crowd theory in the late nineteenth century was an attempt to address 'the problem of the crowd'. It is not just in retrospect that the period broadly encompassing 1870–1918 appears as a turning point in human history, a transition from the industrial age into the modern age of mass culture and democracy: it felt that way at the time too. The masses who had been packed ever more uncomfortably into the slums of the world's cities during the previous century of ferocious industrialisation were becoming increasingly sophisticated in their thought and action, and increasingly effective in influencing the political life of nations. For those who had historically held the levers of power, the new urban crowd was to be feared, to be militantly guarded against, and its psychology and behaviour became the subject of fierce intellectual and scientific – frequently pseudoscientific – debate. Were the masses inherently criminal? Was it in their blood? Were they predisposed to violence? Could their reckless and amoral behaviour be read in their faces, or their skull shape? What implications did the psychology of the crowd have for politics, and for established power?

Le Bon felt certain he knew the answers, and he was terrified by them. With poverty and squalor endemic, and liberty and justice for all still distant dreams, the French Revolution of 1789 was unfinished business – and the urban crowd continually threatened to finish it. The mass uprisings of 1830, 1848 and 1871 were painful reminders of this. For the European conservative establishment in this period, the mob was permanently gathered outside, hammering on the palace gates. Revolution was not an abstract idea, but a clear and present danger, immanent in every assembly of society's poorest. Their very congregation suggested change, and violent upheaval. In *The Crowd*, Le Bon summoned the spectre that haunted his ranging intellectual career, and which loomed as a warning to the world: the 'howling, swarming, ragged crowd which invaded the Tuileries'.[10]

So what were Le Bon's theories of the crowd? Firstly, that a hugely significant psychological transformation occurs when an individual joins a crowd. Out of singular thought and consciousness, 'a collective mind is formed' – a process that was later labelled 'deindividuation', where the rational self diminishes and is replaced by a childlike, credulous mass consciousness. The individual will is submerged into the group-mind, and the cloak of anonymity replaces personal accountability. At the moment of becoming part of the crowd, individuals begin to think, act, and feel differently, and become abruptly afflicted by 'extreme mental inferiority'.

Secondly, Le Bon declared 'contagion' to be an inevitable consequence of crowd formation – not just in feeling, but also in action. If the man next to you throws a brick, the chances are that you will then do so too. Finally, an animal derangement of righteous (Christian) human morality ensues: madness, violence, irrationality, barbarism and the 'savage' pursuit of unconscious desire take over. Fundamental to Le Bon's thesis was his idea that a crowd is always likely to become a mob – contained within the former is the intrinsic anarchy and bestiality of the latter.

It is in the nature of crowds, Le Bon believed, that they have an automatic tendency towards social dysfunction and violence, that they are wildly emotional and impulsive. A person's intelligence and moral stature before they entered the crowd offers no protection: even good, upstanding citizens are swept along in the collective madness, falling under the hypnotic influence of agitators and demagogues. 'By the mere fact that he forms part of an organised crowd,' Le Bon wrote, 'a man descends several rungs in the ladder of civilisation. Isolated, he may be a cultivated individual; in a crowd, he is a barbarian.'[11]

He pointed, not for the first or last time, to the French Revolution of 1789, where, he asserted, 'the most savage' members of the revolutionary parliament during the Reign of Terror had previously been 'inoffensive citizens . . . peaceable notaries or virtuous magistrates'; and yet, whipped up by the fervour of the crowd they had joined, they happily sent innocent men to the guillotine.[12]

Le Bon argues that crowd members rarely act in their *individual* self-interest, even when they exhibit debased violence and dangerous assertiveness: instead, under the influence of demagogues and one another, crowd members fight pointless battles, embracing conflict and even death on behalf of causes, ideologies and belief systems which they have 'scarcely understood'. This is an extremely common allegation made about crowds of protesters to this day, that they 'don't even understand' the issue they are shouting about. Crowd members undergo deep psychological transformations because they become fundamentally gullible, Le Bon asserts. Rendered weak and emotional, they are moved by the fiery words of a leader, by all-encompassing ideologies (whether Christianity or Islam, nationalism or socialism); they are also extremely susceptible to the influence of 'theatrical representations', as they have been since the days of Rome, when bread and circuses kept the plebs happy.

We are told that crowd members are so taken in by fake representations of the real world that they have been moved to try and kill the actor playing a traitor in a popular play; in this incident (of which Le Bon gives no specifics), the theatre manager had to provide protection for the actor when leaving the building. 'The unreal has almost as much influence on them as the real. [The crowd] have an evident tendency not to distinguish between the two.'[13] Le Bon could almost be writing a hand-wringing modern-day newspaper op-ed about the exponential rise of 'fake news' and conspiracy theories among the credulous, uneducated masses – contemporary moral panics which are often as overheated as Le Bon's own tall tales.

While he concedes one small positive effect – that crowd members can sometimes be moved by those around them to acts of enthusiastic heroism – Le Bon assures us that these conversions are always accompanied by violence. The frequency with which human beings gather in their thousands without a hint of animosity, either within the crowd or to out-group members, surely gives the lie to the idea that crowds are inherently predisposed to aggression. As we will see later, statistically the remarkable thing is the *absence* of violence, social dysfunction and criminality that characterises vast carnival, sporting and protest crowds. Something much more interesting, and peaceable, is going on. And this is why we keep coming back to them: because they make us feel secure, inspired and happy; because we want to sing songs, chant slogans and dance with total strangers, not just our friends and family.

Where members of a crowd *are* involved in violence, they are always a tiny minority of those present, rare exceptions to the rule. Of course, they are the ones who make the headlines and the front-page photos, and prompt fresh 'crackdowns' from the authorities. To Le Bon, crowd members are all alike, nothing more than hypnotised, 'primitive beings . . . the slave of the unconscious activities of the spinal cord', their feelings and thoughts directed entirely by the hypnotiser.[14] This is one of many areas – though perhaps the most important one – where modern crowd psychology has roundly, soundly, repeatedly debunked Le Bon's thesis. He believed that in a crowd, individual agency simply ceases to exist: all individuals become just 'a grain of sand amid other grains of sand, which the wind stirs up at will'.[15]

Most modern public order policing still enthusiastically works to Le Bon's theories of the crowd, just like the press and political class do. There is no other way to interpret the mentality behind police kettling, for example, than as the idea that all protesters are the same, and all are liable to violence: a homogeneous bloc who are all equally culpable for any single small act of antisocial behaviour committed by one individual. It is collective punishment in response to what Le Bon called the 'collective mind'. As we will see later in this book, even some police forces are finally changing their public order tactics to adapt to the demonstrable fact that not everyone in a crowd thinks and acts the same, and that violence is never inevitable; indeed, it is almost always avoidable. These pioneering forces have ensured calmer, safer outcomes for the public whenever they have decided to hang back, rather than tar everyone in a group with the same brush, and steam in with truncheons raised at the slightest hint of tension.

For all its dire warnings about the descent of humanity into savagery, there are moments in *The Crowd* that appear inadvertently optimistic to twenty-first-century eyes. Le Bon uses a hypothetical example of a great mathematician and his humble bootmaker, two men who have 'an abyss' between them intellectually and materially, but nevertheless share many unconscious traits, including a similar emotional and moral core. These similarities, normally dormant, are awakened and brought out into the open once the 'collective mind' has formed in a crowd. Far from being disastrous, to a modern liberal this sequence of events sounds positively utopian.

It is a truism of contemporary political discourse that if we would only put in the work to locate the things we have in common, then society would be less hateful. This may often be presented in a way that is glib or disingenuous, but in modern politics it is common sense that you should at least pay lip service to the idea that we are 'stronger together' or have a shared identity or social purpose. It highlights how different things were in the late nineteenth century. Because for Le Bon, the story of the bootmaker and the mathematician is not an inspiring ideal, but a warning: the great mathematician's naturally superior intellect will be dragged down by associating with his bootmaker. His individuality, his social standing, knowledge and good manners are all diminished – indeed, completely erased – thanks to his participation in activities alongside the bootmaker. This mixing is not a positive development, but a danger to the natural, hierarchical order of things. Le Bon would have scorned the idea that we are all 'better together' as a toxic communist myth. Universal suffrage, free mass education and equality before the law might place the mathematician and the bootmaker on the same level, which would be a catastrophe. This fear of the potential levelling effects of democracy itself still applies today: hostility to 'the mob' is usually hostility to democracy, dressed up in a phoney concern for propriety and order.

There are other such moments in the origins of crowd theory which strike a discordant note today. Le Bon observed with dismay that those joining a crowd enjoy 'a sentiment of invincible power'.[16] An optimist might frame this as the cornerstone of the many *benefits* of crowd membership: the growth in feelings of empowerment, self-confidence, vindication, empathy, comradeship and belonging. It is precisely what I find appealing about joining a crowd of like-minded strangers (while still being keenly aware that I am, of course, *vincible*). For Le Bon, this empowerment is highly dangerous – because the base instincts it unleashes override our sense of decorum and our humility in our social position. When we walk down the street alone, rather than flanked by 500 like-minded souls, we are naturally inhibited – and this inhibition is good for us, Le Bon reckons, because our unconscious instincts are not to be trusted. Walking alone, the individual's rational brain overcomes the 'reflex' impulses of the animal within, whereas the crowd encourages these impulses to run riot.

According to Le Bon's thesis, we feel empowered precisely as we become more stupid and open to conspiracy theories: 'the most improbable legends and stories' are created, he writes, lapped up and given resounding echoes by the crowd.[17] Suspicion and exaggeration all flourish, swamping any attempt at sensible, evidence-based reasoning. One passionate cry of condemnation goes up from the front of the crowd: it is repeated and amplified, moving through like a wave, rapidly spreading but also growing, building to a crescendo of furious, unanimous hatred . . . *Let's get him! Act first, ask questions later!* The notion that we all turn into zombie-like morons, arms flailing in front of us, the moment we join a large group of strangers is pervasive in modern society. But how many of us have ever actually felt that way in a crowd? How many of us have truly *lost it*? How can it be – and how convenient is it – that crowd madness is only ever an affliction ascribed to other people?

All of this matters a great deal because, in spite of its deeply flawed, wild-eyed, ideologically slanted exposition of this new discipline, Le Bon's *The Crowd* is one of the most widely read and influential non-fiction books of all time, not just at the turn of the century, but throughout 'the age of extremes'. *The Crowd* was an immediate best-seller in France, and within a year of its 1895 publication had been translated into no fewer than nineteen languages. It became central to the period's overlapping conversations about democracy, mass politics, racial and class biology and hierarchies, psychology, criminality, and social and moral decay. It was a great influence not only on twentieth-century dictators – as we will see in Chapter 2 – but also on Sigmund Freud, while the former US president Theodore Roosevelt asked to meet Gustave Le Bon when he visited Paris in 1914. He was read by politicians and princes around the world. Japan's foreign minister from 1916 to 1918, Baron Motono, personally translated *The Crowd* into Japanese. Lenin, regularly depicted in propaganda declaiming to a massed crowd, seems to have read some of Le Bon's work despite its consistently anti-socialist character. Le Bon's theories directly informed colonial police manuals, before these violent, aggravating tactics returned to the European metropole in the second half of the twentieth century. There are academic papers enumerating his influence on subjects as varied as political elites in twenty-first-century China and the US military during the Second World War.[18] *The Crowd*, one scholar claims, was 'one of the best-selling scientific books in history', and, another suggests, 'perhaps the most influential book ever written on social psychology'.[19]

Le Bon was in no doubt about how critical a historical period of transformation he was living through, not just in terms of political and cultural change, but with regard to 'the thought of mankind'.[20] The French government responded to the urban crowd and the shock of the Paris Commune by fleeing the capital and occupying the gilded seat of the *ancien régime* in Versailles until 1879. Mass socialist organisation of workers in the 1880s and 1890s, along with anarchist bomb attacks, gave the bourgeoisie more reasons to fear the near future. Over 100,000 Parisians gathered for 1890's May Day demonstration – in London, three times that number did the same. Strike waves swept across France, quadrupling in the two decades after the Commune, culminating in a staggering 634 strikes nationwide in 1893.[21] Workers' demands were moving beyond economic or workplace bargaining, and broadening out to a wider call for an end to exploitation and a new world built on socialism and democracy. The gathering crowd prefigured a new way of ordering society. This era was, Le Bon wrote in *The Crowd*, 'a period of transition and anarchy', an upheaval he compared to the fall of the Roman Empire.[22]

Indeed, it is true that the largest and most powerful crowds are often generated specifically by great changes in popular thought and feeling: at hinge points, or breaking points, in human history. From the 1381 Peasants' Revolt to the 1992 LA Riots or the global uprisings of 2011, crowd formation and action is sparked by a widespread sense that what had hitherto always been tolerated by individuals is no longer acceptable. A crowd emerges at the point when those who have been suffering more and more finally reach their limit and come together to say 'Enough!' Even historic crowd eruptions that are ostensibly cultural rather than political – like the late 1980s rave scene in Britain – usually follow this pattern; in that example, the rave crowd emerges from the atomising individualism, social conservatism and economic inequalities that had accumulated over eight years of Thatcherism.

Crowds often appear as a surprise, in that respect, because the suffering experienced alone by its constituent members was not visible to those meting it out. Everything would remain the same, always and forever – until it no longer could. 'The moment that one deserts his or her couch', wrote the Greek students occupying the Athens School of Business in 2008, as the global economy collapsed around them, 'and the passive contemplation of his or her own life, and takes to the streets to talk and to listen, leaving behind anything private, carries in the field of social relations the destabilising force of a nuclear bomb.' This is the moment of crowd formation: leaving behind anything private, abandoning introspection in favour of comradeship and solidarity – and in doing so, reconfiguring who we are at an atomic level.

There is great continuity across the centuries, and across the globe, in why crowds form to begin with, what happens when they do, and how elites respond to those formations. And yet, all periods are not alike. There are special moments of world-historical intensity which draw people out of their homes and bring them together. A wave rippling through the social and political order, a rupture in one 'structure of feeling' and its simultaneous replacement with another, a mass reconfiguration of people's subconscious, these are liable to propel everyone into the town square at once. Le Bon was wrong about many things. But he was right that something notable happened in the spring of 1871, something that outlasted the dying embers of the Tuileries fire.

The modern age was dawning, and the masses were reducing the old ways to rubble. Traditional authority, traditional morality, traditional power and class hierarchies were all threatened by the latent power of the crowd, and by the incomplete revolutions of 1789, 1848 and 1871. The ghost of the crowd that stormed the Bastille in 1789 was haunting not just France but all of Europe, the academic J. S. McClelland wrote: '[It] became the mob that had been at all revolutions, failed and successful, past, present and future. The French Revolution showed how permanent and far-reaching the effects of a bread riot allowed to get out of hand could be.'[23] Ruling-class politicians and thinkers saw these phantom mobs lurking everywhere. They were sure that what followed each gathering of the poor and disenfranchised was – with an awful, relentless inevitability – the return of the brutality of the Terror which followed the 1789 revolution.

Even with the guillotine wheeled awkwardly offstage, Le Bon spied the glint of its blade behind every strike and peaceful demonstration, and behind the gradual bourgeois political and social reforms that were nudging Western nations towards becoming more egalitarian and democratic. 'While all our ancient beliefs are tottering and disappearing,' he wrote, 'while the old pillars of society are giving way one by one, the power of the crowd is the only force that nothing menaces, and of which the prestige is continually on the increase. The age we are about to enter will in truth be the era of crowds.' The violence and destruction of the Paris Commune, he wrote, was just the beginning: 'we are destined to witness many others of a like nature.'[24]

And here's the rub. Here's where, notwithstanding his trauma-addled misunderstandings, analytical biases, failure to present any actual evidence, and at times hysterical fear and loathing of the French working classes, Gustave Le Bon does in fact arrive at broadly the correct conclusion about the shifting tectonic plates beneath his feet.

'The destinies of nations', he lamented in *The Crowd*, 'are elaborated at present in the heart of the masses, and no longer in the councils of princes.'[25]

The age of the crowd had begun.

2

The Nuremberg Spectacle:
Authoritarian Crowds

*I believe in the born leader, the natural despot, the master, not
the man who is chosen but the man who elects himself to be ruler
over the masses. I believe in and hope for one thing, and that is
the return of the great terrorist, the living essence of human
power, the Caesar.*

– Knut Hamsun, 'At the Gates of the Kingdom' (1895)

It was a bright, cold day in January, and a ragged steampunk
militia were heaving their flags up towards the gleaming white US
Capitol building. Most were decked out in black, or in camou-
flage gear, with flashes of red, white and blue, and a number wore
bullet-proof vests, goggles and beards. One man was wearing a
black sweatshirt bearing the words 'Camp Auschwitz' above a
skull and crossbones. Others had erected a wooden gallows and
hung a noose from it. 'We, the people!' they bellowed in unison.
Then they bellowed it again. It was an abrupt declaration, a fragment of a thought, still unfinished – cribbed, of course, from the
opening of the US Constitution.

They were certainly *some* people – about 20–30,000 altogether –
but the definite article makes it an important claim: that this
bleak parade of Trump-supporting militants was definitively representative of *the* people. *All* the people. America in its totality,
and at its most authentic. Casting our eyes around this neo-
fascist fancy dress party – the 'QAnon Shaman' in his horned

headdress and Norse tattoos, holding a spear, the man in an Abraham Lincoln costume, the man who had come as a bald eagle, the men in capes, or animal skins, or head-to-toe army fatigues, the biker goons and gun fanatics, the adult human beings wearing stars-and-stripes face paint – suggests maybe the claim was a little overcooked.

If the crowd is the physical, flesh-and-blood expression of democracy, or at least some significant part of a population, we have to reckon with the fact that democracies not infrequently produce outrageous or repressive results – in elections or otherwise. Not all crowds are seeking a more egalitarian society through political change. Several significant modern crowds have sought to deploy their symbolic power and tangible force to install or bolster a fascist or otherwise authoritarian leader.

On 6 January 2021, the people who marched on and invaded the US Capitol were essentially hoping to bring about a coup d'état, following Trump's election defeat to Joe Biden two months earlier. Many carried placards bearing the Trump slogan, 'Stop the Steal'. The crowd included armed, uniformed militiamen, demobilised soldiers and nearly thirty off-duty police officers from a dozen different departments.[1] They were led from President Trump's rally 1.5 miles away to the Capitol by a cadre of the Proud Boys, a de facto paramilitary fascist group who have taken to triumphantly burning Black Lives Matter banners and flags. They marched in a sloppy kind of unison, with more baseball caps and beanies on display than the average military unit – but in unison nonetheless. 'It looks like soldiers because we are soldiers,' boasted one Proud Boy as he began filming, warning his comrades to mask up to protect their identity. 'We're the new police around here,' said another, before they proceeded to overwhelm the small handful of actual police who had been stationed to protect the US government.

When the reinforcements followed them, from the main body of the crowd attending Trump's rally, they did so armed with baseball bats, hammers, spears, guns and flagpoles, and wearing everything from helmets to full body armour. They dismantled bits of scaffolding that had been erected for Joe Biden's imminent inauguration as president and used the physical fabric of the state as weapons to continue mass, unruly fighting with the outnumbered local cops. At least 2,000 people succeeded in invading the Capitol, nine people died in the process and its aftermath, and it was generally agreed that both the political consequences and the death toll could have been considerably worse. Congresswoman Alexandria Ocasio-Cortez called it a 'terror attack', and you could see her point. The 6 January crowd was not so much a representative sample of *the people* at large as a messy combination of some relatively peaceable Trump supporters and elements constituting a bloodthirsty, anti-democratic vanguard, focused on, prepared for and predisposed to violence.

What makes a fascist crowd like this different from a revolutionary one?

Both types of crowd are liable to attack property and sometimes their opponents or the police, to propel each other along with fiery rhetoric, to believe that the political ends are justified by their collective, often somewhat improvised, means. But there are qualitative differences.

Fascist and authoritarian crowds are convened and directed from the top, and work obsequiously for their masters. They rely on fierce identification with a charismatic leader figure, rather than revelling in the horizontal solidarity and shared identity of the rest of the crowd. 'I am your voice,' Trump told the crowd in his acceptance speech at the Republican National Convention in 2016. Seven years later, speaking at the Conservative Political Action Conference (CPAC), he offered his adoring listeners a new form of embodiment, a distillation of any grievance they might have in their life: 'I am your warrior. I am your justice. And for those who have been wronged and betrayed: I am your retribution.'

Another significant difference concerns the two crowd types' relationships with power elites and the institutions responsible for state violence – mostly the police and the army, but also magistrates, landowners, wealthy industrialists and right-wing politicians – in short, anyone with a vested interest in the status quo. A revolutionary crowd usually seeks to overthrow the existing order in the name of a more egalitarian society, whereas a fascist crowd weaponises the state's existing authoritarian tendencies, and then seeks to remake society in the image of the new leader. Having some people on the inside is a critical part of the fascist coup crowd, even if the goal is ultimately to replace the status quo with a supercharged new form of power hierarchy, backed by unabashed and arbitrary violence.

While media coverage of 6 January focused on the startling, unprecedented spectacle of the crowd clad in red, white and blue swarming around the hallowed white Capitol buildings, the coup also had powerful allies inside, wearing suits and ties, with lanyards and security clearance, working simultaneously towards the exact same goal: to reject the result of the 2020 US presidential election in favour of its loser, Donald Trump. This so-called 'sedition caucus' in Congress comprised no fewer than 139 Republican members of the House of Representatives – more than half of Republicans – and eight Republican senators, all of whom voted to invalidate the 2020 electoral college vote count. The joint effort to overturn a democratic election result was undertaken in the name of, and at the direct incitement of, a despotic leader who was fighting against his own removal. The irony was that the only man who could stop them – and did, just about – was no pinko commie, but a former Tea Party Caucus ultra-conservative and Trump's own vice president, Mike Pence.

The 6 January insurrection was not a spontaneous, organic outpouring of mass popular resistance, but something instigated from the very top of American political life. The campaign to 'Stop the Steal' had been ongoing for many weeks, via the flagrant incitement, legal challenges and madcap conspiracies of Trump, his lieutenants and his media outriders. At the rally itself on the morning of 6 January, the intention was unmistakable. 'You

44

have an opportunity today,' Donald Trump Jr told the crowd: 'you can be a hero.' Rudy Giuliani chimed in that now was 'a time for action', and declaimed: 'Let's have trial by combat!' President Trump himself rounded off the proceedings with a characteristic lack of subtlety: 'We will never concede . . . we're going to walk down to the Capitol . . . you'll never take back our country with weakness. You have to show strength, and you have to be strong. And we fight, we fight like hell.'

Not just the messaging but even the physical congregation was coordinated from the top, and through official channels. Subsequent congressional hearings found that in the days leading up to 6 January, Trump and his team had discussed a march on the Capitol following the end of the rally. The insurrection's vanguard, the neo-fascist Proud Boys, had received not just approval from the Trump camp ('Stand back and stand by', he told them in a presidential debate in 2020), but the support of his former chief strategist Steve Bannon, who also fundraised for their bail money. Rioters were brought into Washington, DC, that day on chartered buses, organised by Trump-supporting Republican politicians like state senator Doug Mastriano, and by county-level party organisations. Charlie Kirk, the founder of the right-wing youth group Turning Point USA (TPUSA) wrote on 4 January that he was 'honored to help make this happen, sending 80+ buses full of patriots to DC to fight for this president'. TPUSA even seems to have offered to cover the cost of hotel rooms for people willing to make the trip to the Capitol.[2] After the riot, Kirk deleted the tweet.

The riots and siege of Brazil's presidential palace, Congress and Supreme Court on 8 January 2023, two years and two days after Capitol Hill, bore remarkable similarities: there were conspiratorial myths about a rigged election dispensed from the very top, a refusal to accept the end of an authoritarian presidency ('Don't throw in the towel', said Jair Bolsonaro, a week before the coup), growing incitement online, a sea of national flags, and repeated appeals to the army and the police to demonstrate their 'patriotism' by joining the insurrection. On the day itself, the Brazilian military police present appeared very relaxed about the prospect of a far-right coup – several groups of officers stood around idly, even pointing the crowd towards the government buildings, while others chatted and took selfies with the rioters.[3] While the military police made their allegiances clear and effectively stood down, the small number of legislative police tasked with protecting the state buildings were overwhelmed. Two separate requests for police backup were refused, until it was too late to stop the rioters from invading the government buildings. This is another common trope from far-right insurrections: suspicious levels of passivity and tolerance from cops and soldiers who normally do not need to be asked twice, or even once, to draw their weapons against a crowd of protesters.

In the US case, it seems pretty reasonably counterfactual to suggest, as many have, that had a hypothetical armed, angry, thousands-strong crowd of Black Lives Matter protesters reached the gates of the US Congress instead of the Proud Boys, brandishing the same weapons, attacking cops and vociferously demanding an election be overturned in their favour, their blood would have been pouring down the Capitol Hill steps before they could have finished saying 'We, the people'.

An obsequious flock, marching in lockstep in support of a despotic leader, is worlds away from an elastic, sometimes anarchic, democratic congregation of the people. A crowd that has assembled on the street, by itself, is fundamentally different in composition, movement and collective psychology from an institutional collective like an army regiment or militia, a church, a corporation or a police force. If this second set of formal, organised groups can be described as 'crowds' at all, they are usually a 'closed shop' to the outside world, and are characterised by hierarchy, discipline, organisation, strict codes of behaviour, and a degree of permanence. For the conservative-minded, the latter type is often the answer to the former. The underclass is rioting?

46

Well, send in the army. Young people are being dissolute? Send them to church, or bring back national service.

At a time of population explosion and rapid, industrialised militarisation in Europe, questions of national character and collective behaviour were suddenly of great interest, especially in the run-up to the 1914–18 war. Could the multiplying, unruly urban masses be channelled towards a cohesive infantry with a unified spirit and morale, with the help of the new science of psychology? Could the discipline and hierarchy of the factory floor help produce a similarly obedient soldiery, a proletariat in military fatigues? The British surgeon Wilfred Trotter, in his 1916 book *Instincts of the Herd in Peace and War*, built on Le Bon's ideas to argue that a 'herd mentality' emerged from each individual's subconscious instincts, from 'the "lower" and more obviously brutal qualities of man. It is irrational, imitative, credulous, cowardly, cruel, and lacks all individuality, will, and self-control. This personality takes the place of the normal personality during hypnosis and when the individual is one of an active crowd.' Trotter argued that for all these weaknesses, the herd acquires its strength through the production of homogeneity. As a result, all war efforts must contribute to the fostering of 'national unity' and to 'keeping their souls full of a burning passion of service'.

Perhaps the most useful label that can be applied to these generally disciplined, militaristic, armed, conservative, deferential, hierarchical crowds is 'reactionary', in that they often emerge in direct reaction to larger crowds which are more chaotic, open, mass-participatory and democratic. When conservative-inclined people feel the ground shifting beneath their feet, and widespread social and political change seems to be gaining mass support, small vanguardist crowds like the Proud Boys often gather and lash out pre-emptively – citing the urgent need for 'patriotic' resistance to a progressive 'enemy within' (or without), in the name of maintaining the status quo.

The Capitol Hill Riot was an immediate reaction to a democratic defeat – with the recent Black Lives Matter uprising very much in the background – and while Joe Biden's proposed policy programme was hardly a communist threat, it evidently felt that way to many who came to Washington DC on 6 January 2021. One of the flags brandished that day read 'Revolt Against Socialism'. Likewise, the events in Brasilia followed the electoral victory of left-wing presidential candidate Lula over Jair Bolsonaro. Lula was perceived as a grave threat to the dominance of the Brazilian military, the wealthy, agribusiness and the Church, and so their foot soldiers responded.

These attempted insurrections are reminiscent of Mussolini's March on Rome with his Blackshirts in 1922, and Hitler's Beer Hall Putsch and attempt to march on Berlin in 1923. There are several similarities between the would-be putsches of the 1920s and the two described in the 2020s: smallish cohorts containing many demobilised soldiers, already pretty comfortable with extreme violence and skilled with weaponry (not to mention scarred by their experiences of war), inspired to acts of collective violence by fascist leaders leaning on tenuous conspiracism, narratives of unfairness (for Trump's 'Stop the Steal', replace with Hitler's 'stab in the back' myth), and fiery rhetoric about the threat posed to the nation's 'traditional way of life', masculinity and national greatness by some form of democracy or socialism.

In each example, the arrival of the reactionary vanguard crowd offers a violent counterweight to a rising mass progressive movement, and it is allowed into the corridors of power with suspicious ease by the uniformed authorities working on the day. The crowd's violence is then usually regarded with telling ambivalence, if not tacit support, by some wings of the establishment, and punished lightly if at all by judiciaries with right-wing sympathies.

Hitler and the Nazis first acquired national prominence with just such a crowd in Munich in 1923, and street violence continued to be vital to the party's rise to power. This included coordinated attacks and other actions that were planned from the top and carried out by small, aggressive, ragged crowds of true believers, but were also spectacles in which civilian participants were invited to join. Book burnings in Germany in May 1933 were accompanied by speeches, bands playing, and 'fire oaths' – carefully designed to inflame the senses as theatrically as possible, to bind the totalitarian crowd together through hatred of Jews, democrats, Bolsheviks and foreigners, coupled with dedication to a Germany they were told was desperately imperilled, and had already been betrayed by the same constellation of national enemies.

There is some overlap here in crowd type between what J. S. McClelland called 'institutional crowds' – army regiments, police forces, formal religious congregations – and these far-right groupings. The Nazi groups the SA and later the SS were essentially politicised armies, a crowd whose level of coordination, hierarchy and solidarity had been trained into them through the deep adhesive regimentation of drilling, and often by frontline military experience. They present a very different scene to the seething, dynamic mass that stormed the Bastille, or which attempted to build a socialist society in Paris in 1871. 'The choice between the left and the Nazis was a choice between two different versions of crowd politics', McClelland writes, and viewing it as exactly that – a choice – Germany's elites opted for what they viewed as the safer of the two, as the Weimar Republic collapsed in slow motion.[4] Building on analysis by Herbert Marcuse, Angela Davis once observed that 'fascism is the preventive counter-revolution to the socialist transformation of society.' The fascism of the 1920s and '30s was a militarised bulwark against the socialist crowd.

The vanguard crowd, a relatively small, quasi-militarised group of ideological fanatics, was, of course, not the only type of fascist crowd. The second, the supine totalitarian crowd, is the kind assembled by the charismatic leader once he is in power – as a piece of theatre, a grandiose human mosaic and monument to the greatness of the leader: a flesh-and-blood propaganda spectacle, to be consumed, and to inspire awe in both participants and external observers. Before long, what had begun with the ragtag army of insurgent fascists in Rome in 1922 and Munich in 1923 took on an even more melodramatic historical form: the gargantuan menace of Hitler's Nuremberg rallies.

At this point it is necessary to pick up where we left off in the last chapter, to consider the role of traditional crowd theory in shaping actual physical crowds. We have already seen just how widely the work of Gustave Le Bon was read around the turn of the century, but what is too little understood is just how profound a bearing *The Crowd* had on the mass fascist crowds of the twentieth century. Indeed, it is no exaggeration at all to say that Le Bon's most famous book contributed directly to the rise of totalitarianism in Europe.

To understand how we got from *The Crowd* in 1895 to Hitler declaiming to hundreds of thousands of people at Nuremberg in the 1930s, we need to revisit the imagined enemy they held in common, the conspiracies and rising tides of social change they both felt it was essential to hold back. The surge in interest in democracy and socialism in Europe around the turn of the twentieth century induced panic in the ruling classes. These ideas were seen as a pathogen, an unnatural disorder spreading among the minds of the working classes. Reformist legislation – gradual expansions of the electoral franchise, for example – failed to quell discontent, and the clamour for change continued to grow louder.

The masses' assault on the West's *anciens régimes* was being conducted on numerous fronts. Trade unions were growing rapidly and beginning to effect change in working conditions, hours and wages. Nationalisation of mines, railways, factories and land were being discussed. Secularisation had been surging throughout the nineteenth century, dragging down the good Christians of Europe into an amoral mire. The gradual extension of the vote and the call for universal suffrage, even including women, threatened to replace the traditional dispensation of power by tiny elites of upper-class men with what would surely be woefully inept new parliamentary representatives. The era of mass literacy, mass education and mass democracy had arrived, and threatened to do irreparable damage.

This was an age of burgeoning mass cultural life, of crowds united by ever more shared experiences, as well as physical congregations. Cheap books, pamphlets and newspapers exploded in number, as did public libraries, along with the wider late-Victorian expansion of civic and cultural life, from public parks and swimming baths to theatres and then cinemas. Mass communication and mass culture was becoming the norm, in tandem with the political crowds gathering in the town square. As John Carey's punchy polemic *The Intellectuals and the Masses* records, these developments were greeted with grave concern and down-right animosity by many modernist intellectuals: T. S. Eliot, for example, wrote that newspapers were fostering 'a complacent, prejudiced and unthinking mass', illustrated in the homogeneous crowd of zombie commuters that 'flowed over London Bridge' in 'The Waste Land'.

The new urban masses – with their vulgar tastes and growing demands for socialism and democracy – appeared to Britain's elites as a coarse, ignorant pack of undifferentiated morons. 'Universal education', wrote Aldous Huxley, 'has created an immense class of what I may call the New Stupid.' Thomas Hardy wrote of his contempt for the guileless 'crowds parading and gaily traipsing around the mummies' which he witnessed in the British Museum, reflecting that 'when these people are our masters it will . . . possibly be the utter ruin of art and literature.' The crowd were here to trash all that was civilised.

This root-and-branch transformation of European civic life in the final decades of the nineteenth century did not amount to a step forward for Western society but a step back, Gustave Le Bon argued: a step back to the 'primitive communism' of pre-feudal societies, a reversion to life 'before the dawn of civilisation'. The rise of crowds was 'tantamount to a barbarian phase', he wrote, surveying the mass squalor, hunger and disease which the

51

industrial revolution and the proletarianisation of western Europe had brought to its cities.

For Le Bon, this new barbarism was the fault of its massed ranks of workers, rather than of their masters and landlords. He worried that socialist and anarchist teachers were creating a generation of even more dangerous youth in the new schools springing up across Europe. The frantic pace of urbanisation, alongside advances in technology, industry, transport and science, left no one in any doubt that humanity was entering a truly 'modern' era, and that everything was in flux – and up for grabs. But because Le Bon and his allies believed that modernity was being shaped by the subaltern crowd, by the politics of the mindless masses and not of the enlightened elites, it heralded nothing less than a regression to the Dark Ages.

There was a substantial amount of social Darwinism underlying nineteenth-century discussions of the working-class urban crowd, which was often characterised as inherently criminal, or at least susceptible to the influence of 'the criminal mind'. It is notable that two of the most prominent European intellectuals exploring crowd theory in the nineteenth century, Scipio Sighele and Gabriel Tarde, were criminologists. Related to this was a grave concern about the sheer scale of population expansion in the great cities of Europe. Some of the great thinkers of this age, men like Friedrich Nietzsche, delivered dire warnings about the vertiginous growth of the urban masses, and suggested that a war needed to be waged to subdue them by Caesar-like authority figures, men of means and power.

Bluntly, crowd theory emerged at the end of the nineteenth century because many medieval European cities were suddenly *heaving*, unable to adequately house, feed and heal their new arrivals. Within two generations, streets and squares which had been relatively calm for centuries were now desperately overcrowded. The population of London rose from 2.29 million people in 1851 to 6.23 million in 1901. Berlin grew from 426,000 to 1.88 million people in the same period, while the populations of Paris and Manchester more than doubled. In the US, Chicago's population grew from 30,000 to 1.7 million in the second half of the nineteenth century, and New York from 590,000 to 3.43 million. London, thought Thomas Hardy, peeking out from behind the curtain of his suburban home, was 'a monster whose body had four million heads and eight million eyes'.

If the Enlightenment and Western civilisation had created the rational, free-thinking individual, nineteenth-century intellectuals presented the age of the crowd as an alarming retreat to an under-developed, less than human condition. With the right upbringing, moral guidance and education, individuals can become enlightened, but masses never will be. After the crushing of the Paris Commune, some of the Communards who weren't simply shot dead in the street by the French army were put on display, as if in a zoo, or characterised as monkeys in satirical cartoons: the same grotesque humiliation frequently meted out to European colonial subjects. The barbarian hordes were not only in distant colonies, not merely at the gates, but literally inside them, crammed like animals in overcrowded cages, threatening to bring down Western civilisation.

For Gustave Le Bon, a dreadful and dystopian twentieth century loomed ahead, which was unquestionably to be defined by the crowd. What could be done about this? How could elite power be protected, and the 'mob rule' of democracy and socialism be smothered at birth? The only option, Le Bon argued, was to try and canalise the rabid energies of the crowd towards the maintenance of civilised order and the natural hierarchy of men. Crowds, with their childlike, feminine and suggestible sensibilities, always responded to the incitement of demagogues, he reasoned, so it would be wise to put the right demagogues in front of them. 'The multitude is always ready to listen to the strong-willed man, who knows how to impose himself upon it,' Le Bon wrote. 'Men gathered in a crowd lose all force of will, and turn instinctively to the person who possesses the quality they lack.'[5]

He proceeded to offer explicit instructions in *The Crowd* on how an upstanding, 'civilised' and authoritative leader might best dazzle the crowd, through clear, simple speech and actions. Indeed, he noted that the most astute crowd psychologists of all were in fact 'the world's masters': the kings, emperors, apostles, chiefs and religious leaders. Because it was they, with their good breeding and natural predisposition to leadership, who best understood the masses' base desires, and so could most successfully play them like puppets, and keep their anarchic power channelled in the right direction.

The Crowd is a book with an almost unparalleled influence on 'the age of extremes', the rise of dictatorships in Europe in the 1920s, '30s and '40s. It played a critical role in guiding those who were constructing totalitarian mass party politics and propaganda and in cultivating the relationship between a dictator and his worshipful crowd. It is no coincidence that Le Bon was also one of the most vehement advocates of the racial pseudoscience that underscored twentieth-century fascism, believing in a strict hierarchy of intelligence between races that could be determined by skull measurements.[6]

Benito Mussolini admired *The Crowd* so much that he and Le Bon would become correspondents, and then friends. 'I don't know how many times I have re-read his *Psychologie des foules*,' Mussolini said publicly in 1927, already Italy's prime minister at this point. 'It is an excellent work to which I frequently refer.' He subsequently told the French writer Pierre Chanlaine that his general understanding of crowd psychology and behaviour, and even specific techniques for addressing audiences and whipping them into a frenzy, were lifted directly from Le Bon's book. 'Mussolini related his satisfaction with Le Bon's principle of "affirmation",' Chanlaine recalled.[7] 'He laughed as he told of how he could vigorously state a principle to the crowd, then ask them "Isn't that so?" to which they would reply "*Sì, Duce, sì, Duce*".'

The Crowd was also cited by Joseph Goebbels as an influence on Nazi propaganda – he considered it a masterpiece, and it's not hard to spot the connections between Le Bon's theory and Nazi praxis. 'The convictions of crowds assume [the] characteristics of blind submission, fierce intolerance, and the need of violent propaganda,' Le Bon wrote. 'The hero acclaimed by a crowd is a veritable god for that crowd. Napoleon was such a god for fifteen years, and a divinity never had more fervent worshippers or sent men to their death with greater ease.'[8]

Violent propaganda, militarised public life and unquestioning submission to authority were all central to the Nazi regime, of course. The Nazis met the threat of the Bolshevik masses by summoning their own marshalled, hierarchical crowds in response. While propaganda in one form or another has been used for as long as politics has existed, the form it took in the Third Reich can only be understood as an attempt to 'play the crowd' – a top-down exercise in manufacturing group psychology. The German government, Goebbels announced in March 1933, upon taking charge of the Ministry of National Enlightenment and Propaganda, intended 'no longer to leave the people to their own devices'. The writer Joachim Fest observed that the expression 'man the beast' occurs repeatedly in Goebbels' private notes – it is an anti-humanist ideology built on a deep-rooted contempt for ordinary people, much like Le Bon's.[9] When you believe the masses, the crowd, to be bestial, fascism and genocide follow with great ease.

There is even a persuasive case that Germany's 'Caesar' was himself heavily influenced by *The Crowd*. There was certainly a German translation of it in the Vienna library where Adolf Hitler spent time writing *Mein Kampf*. One German academic, Alfred Stein, conducted a close study of *Mein Kampf* which claimed that many substantial passages were plagiarised, or at least paraphrased, from *The Crowd*.[10] The theoretical connections are unnervingly clear. The pseudo-biological colonial racism underpinning Le Bon's work, combined with his class hatred of both universal suffrage and revolutionary communism, were grounded in a deeply stratified, hierarchical view of humanity. He believed that an all-consuming clash was brewing within Western civilisation. In response to the latent depravity he was sure lay just below the surface of the primitive masses, came the new theories of 'group mind' and group behaviour – and the possibility of their manipulation through fiery rhetoric and symbolic imagery.

When the massed Nazi crowd was gathered in a physical space in Nuremberg, nothing was left to chance. The party rallies there ran from 1927 until 1938 (after which the war took precedence), and up to 1 million people attended at their peak in the mid-1930s. By that time the rallies were no longer the assemblies of an insurgent party, but a huge national event lasting over a week, the result of the fascist government putting Goebbels's propaganda theories into practice.

Under the guidance of Hitler's architect, Albert Speer, the principles of mass psychology were deployed to luridly theatrical effect, to generate 'an almost phantasmal sense of mass fascination and awe'.[11] This featured innovative and atmospheric illumination, using a ring of 150 searchlights borrowed from the Luftwaffe to create a breathtaking 'cathedral of light', as well as spotlights and torches, stirring martial music, and an oversized version of the quasi-regal pageantry, flags and parades of a medieval fair. Everything was meticulously programmed for maximum emotional impact – both there 'in the room', for the people present, and also externally, through photography and cinema, as a spectacle intended to communicate the vast scale, unwavering oneness and militarised potency of the Nazi populace. The rallies' function as film propaganda was so integral that Leni Riefenstahl was permitted to commission her preferred backdrops – even new bridges were built in Nuremberg – as set dressing for *Triumph of the Will*. Even though its freedom to move, shout, or do anything remotely participatory was extremely limited, the crowd itself had become a central part of the spectacle.

Watching footage of the rallies now, what is striking, beyond their extraordinary scale, is how conventional they are in content:

like supercharged modern versions of ancient military parades, with endless rows of troops marching in lockstep, cavalry processions, tank parades and flyovers, the soldiers and civilian audiences alike reverentially saluting the Führer. Everywhere you look is uniformity, clean lines, right angles and pattern repetition, from the colonnaded backdrops and rows of swastika drapes to the Roman-style, perfect-square formations of infantrymen. It is a vast, horrifying testimony to the power of military drilling and discipline, as much as anything; the relentless symmetry of marching soldiers, outstretched right arms Sieg-Heiling, seem to have turned these individual men into identical components on a production line.

One of the propaganda effects Riefenstahl seems to be striving for in *Triumph of the Will* is to show off the Nazi mechanisation of the crowd; the asphalt ribbon of the Nuremberg parade grounds turned into a human factory churning out Aryan soldier-bots. A populace which is uniformed, and uniform. Individuals have been abolished in favour of the unified, homogeneous Nazi crowd – itself intended as a message of the strength of the Third Reich. Where there is disorder, it seems to declaim, we are bringing industrialised, militarised discipline. The messy reality of the crowd on the ground in Nuremberg was very different. Drunken party officials, widespread public urination, rubbish strewn everywhere, and the fact that large parts of the parade grounds were a permanent building site throughout the 1930s: all of this was, of course, concealed from view.

Behind Speer's theatrical and technological innovations, the Nuremberg rallies were a revanchist project to crush the democratic anarchy of the proletarian crowd, and replace it with a totalitarian caricature of a confected, rose-tinted history. The two-kilometre-long, eighty-metre-wide Great Road that formed the parade path for the Nazi rallies was pointed towards Nuremberg Castle, an emblem of bygone German imperial strength, to invoke the stability and permanence of traditional hierarchical power in an age of upheaval. It was an attempt to elevate Nazism to the status of a pseudo-religion, via symbolism, pageantry and mass ritualistic participation. It was 'more than a gorgeous show,' wrote the American journalist William L. Shirer in his diary, after attending the rally in 1934: 'it also had something of the mysticism and religious fervour of an Easter or Christmas Mass in a great Gothic cathedral.'

The aim was to lift this unique and revolutionary Nazi moment out of a conventional present and suggest a permanence stretching back to Germany's medieval past, and forwards to a utopian future. Nuremberg's historic medieval centre and city walls were also carefully restored, to provide another propaganda link between the Nazis and German heritage. The architecture at Nuremberg was intended to convey the 'enduring grandeur' of the Nazi movement, Speer said. Following this logic, the display of its crowd as that purportedly homogeneous bloc, 'the German people', can be read as the human embodiment of the thousand-year Reich.

Everything about the Nuremberg rallies was built around architectural and human gigantism, to render the crowd an implacable bastion of Aryan unity – as if the totalitarian nation is only as strong as its crowd is big. The full site was a vast 16.5 square kilometres, large enough to require two dedicated railway stations, with multiple distinct but connected spaces, halls and grounds. The Zeppelin Field and Luitpold Arena, where the main action took place, were flanked by a 370-metre-long colonnaded stone grandstand (the Zeppelin Tribune) with Hitler's podium at the centre, along with seating for the party elites, giant stairways, ramparts, flagpoles and huge swastika banners and reliefs.[12] Hitler had plans for even larger rallies in the future: incomplete when war broke out was the military parade ground Märzfeld, with tribunes alongside intended to hold 160,000 people, and the Deutsches Stadion, a horseshoe-shaped stadium with seating for 405,000.[13] The greater the crowd, the greater the show of national unity. The idea was to keep inflating the Nazi crowd until 'the crowd' and 'the German people' were not two overlapping circles in a Venn diagram, but had fused into one whole.

'The entrance pylons, portals and galleries of all of the facilities were typically far larger than life – the better to diminish those who passed through them,' write Joshua Hagen and Robert Ostegren.[14] The parade grounds were consciously designed to negate the crowd's individual humanity and heterogeneity, to humble and intimidate its feeble-minded participants, and to affirm the absolute power of the Caesar-like figure at the top. Gustave Le Bon died in 1931, before the Nuremberg rallies reached their peak – but it is hard to think that he would not have greatly approved of this translation of his crowd theory into practice.

For its creators, the Nazi built environment and the human beings populating it were not separate enterprises, but part of the same artistic endeavour: indeed, the party leadership let Speer have input into the human choreography of drilling and marching.[15] Speer's 'monumental liturgy', wrote Joachim Fest, saw him arrange 'human masses' and non-human structures so that the spectacle 'perfectly mirrored the psychology of the movement'.[16] These human masses were not simply witnesses to the events, not merely an audience, but a key part of the show – to be manipulated, choreographed and framed by the director like any of its other components.

Their presence on the stage, as part of the twentieth century's explosion of mass culture and media, meant that crowds could be arranged and publicised for mass consumption with an ease which had never existed before – and from this process of 'massifying' emerged a great deal of political capital. This process, the use of crowds for propaganda – on the radio, on television, in newspapers, or cited in the abstract as 'ordinary folk' or 'the public' or 'normal people' – has always been highly suspect, not least for the dishonesty with which it presents complexity and dynamism as homogeneity.

The crowd, when assembled from above, is always a convenient construct. 'The masses are always the others, whom we don't know, and can't know,' wrote Raymond Williams by way of critique of this phenomenon in *Culture and Society*. 'To other people, we also are masses. Masses are other people. There are in fact no masses; there are only ways of seeing people as masses.'[17]

Those ways of seeing were developed at a phenomenal rate in the twentieth century. For the first time, how the crowd was presented in political communication and reproduced in the mass media became a vital part of the propaganda process. The sense created by film and photography of the Nuremberg rallies is of an irresistible collective demand, forged in the unconscious mind of the *volkisch* Nazi subject, multiplied and shared equally by an uncountable number of peers. This crowd forms the base level of the *Führerprinzip* or 'Führer principle', with Hitler as its pinnacle. It is the organic product of the Nazi crowd-nation displayed at Nuremberg and, as such, places his legitimacy beyond question. The ideology of national socialism could not have existed in the same way without the confected, massified, *made-to-be-seen* crowd at its base.

If the joy of crowd membership is partly in the very real experience of freedom it affords (and partly in that it often hungrily demands freedom for others), then the question imposes itself: why do people join totalitarian crowds? Why do people join crowds which strive not for freedom, but its opposite: for submission and subjugation to an autocratic leader? What do they get out of that subjugation, and can the answers be found in psychology, as much as in an adherence to a political ideology? It is not good enough, as Wilhelm Reich observed in *The Mass Psychology of Fascism*, to point to 'the befogging of the masses', 'Nazi psychosis', or deception via demagoguery, to try and explain away the movement's success; you need to understand how sentient, rational adults could be in agreement with Nazi propaganda, or ready to be persuaded by it. 'Why would millions upon millions affirm to their own suppression?' he asks.[18]

In addition to theories of sexual repression, one of Reich's answers to that question is that members of the German petty bourgeoisie were susceptible to the appeals of Nazism because they had become deeply alienated, under threat from a growing proletarian power and the rising tide of communism. Even before the Wall Street crash and the Depression, the petty bourgeoisie were becoming drastically poorer in an age of global industrial capitalism: shopkeepers and artisans were losing out to large department stores (a frequent target of Nazi propaganda) and were in search of a saviour. Reich argues that lower-middle-class Germans' 'passive and servile attitude to the father-Führer figure' created a party base of willing supplicants. In the vast 1950 sociological study, *The Authoritarian Personality* – surveying those who were susceptible to following fascism, rather than leading it – Theodor Adorno and his colleagues theorised that such personalities were forged in childhood experiences of very strict, especially religious, parenting, which produced adults with few close or loving attachments. The result was a dysfunctional relationship both with the nature of authority and with the person dispensing it. What emerged from this was an ambivalent mixture of reverent worship for their stern dictator-parent, and resentment of their need for submission.

Rigid and disciplined totalitarian mass crowds such as those at Nuremberg are constructed around fervent identification with the charismatic leader, rather than, as would normally be the case, the rest of the crowd. The participants empty themselves out and replace their desires with those of the leader. In the Soviet Union, the leadership cult of Stalin became as spectacular and overblown as Hitler's, while the Bolshevik promise of a 'radiant' egalitarian future was increasingly filtered only through the beneficence of Stalin himself. This relationship was also presented through a parent-child lens in state propaganda. 'Thank you Comrade Stalin for our happy childhood!' was a ubiquitous slogan that appeared on posters, in newspapers, and in nurseries, orphanages and schools across the USSR.[19]

In Hannah Arendt's analysis, in order to shift the revolutionary legacy of 1917 towards totalitarian rule, Stalin had to 'fabricate an atomized and structureless mass' in the place of what had been Russian society. He liquidated all pre-existing class formations and groupings with extreme violence – whether it be the peasantry, the party bureaucracy, the workers' soviets, the myriad national and regional identities, or even the solidarity of the proletariat, dismantled through Stakhanovism – in order to foster widespread alienation and atomisation, an empty vessel that only the leadership cult could fill.

'Totalitarian movements are mass organisations of atomised, isolated individuals,' Arendt wrote in *The Origins of Totalitarianism*:

> Compared with all other parties and movements, their most conspicuous external characteristic is their demand for total, unrestricted, unconditional, and unalterable loyalty of the individual member ... Such loyalty can be expected only from the completely isolated human being who, without any other social ties to family, friends, comrades, or even mere acquaintances, derives his sense of having a place in the world only from his belonging to a movement, his membership in the party.[20]

In this sense, the totalitarian crowd never looks sideways, and does not draw its strength from the solidarity to be found in the crowd, but gazes only upwards, to the podium – the reason it has been summoned there in the first place.

Authoritarian personalities are, Adorno et al. concluded, markedly conformist – and more than ready to have their feelings of impotence, of being cheated by the world at large, transplanted onto the first available scapegoat. The cynical nurturing of grievances against an out-group, in order to foster greater cohesion and a more robust identity in the in-group, is not unique to twentieth-century totalitarian dictatorships – but rarely had misery and hatred been stoked as ferociously as at this moment in Germany, or organised and marshalled with such efficiency. Fear and hatred of the other – Jews, Bolsheviks, Freemasons, intellectuals – was integral to Germany's rightward drift in the

1930s, and the spectre of the communist crowd was frequently raised as an inducement to join the fascist one. Wilhelm Reich cites a nationalist leaflet from 1932 which warned of the 'ruthless annihilation' of the German middle classes at the hands of communists: 'This is the issue. Whether we shall all sink into the great grey bleakness of proletarianism . . . or whether energy and diligence shall again put the individual in a position to acquire property by hard work. Middle class or proletarian! That is the issue!'[21]

For another key Nazi demographic, the willingness to join the disciplined fascist crowd spoke to their existing sense of their place in the world: clerks and public officials, soldiers and bureaucrats, people who admired authority figures and identified with the power of the state, employer, nation, Church or army – whichever hierarchical structures they inhabited. This submission to and sense of solidarity with authority was at odds with the more horizontal solidarity being discovered, practised and cultivated by the ever-more-organised and politicised German working classes. Their burgeoning strength was presented by fascist parties and regimes as a Bolshevik tide that would submerge the unique creativity, genius and personality of the individual – the ideological cornerstones of middle-class self-image. Which was all tragically ironic, of course, given the uniformity demanded at gunpoint by the fascist crowd-master.

Reich was not alone in thinking about the mental state of the crowd. In the 1920s he worked in the outpatient section of the surgery run by Sigmund Freud. They would soon fall out on these very questions of the 'herd instincts' of the group – the notion popularised in Wilfred Trotter's best-selling 1916 book – and their relationship to the unconscious mind. Even though Freud's influential work in this period was steered towards developing theories of the *individual* unconscious, and its expression through dreams, he drew directly on Le Bon's work and greatly admired it. In *Group Psychology and the Analysis of the Ego* (1921), Freud devoted an entire chapter to praising and paraphrasing Le Bon's 'deservedly famous' book *The Crowd*.[22]

Le Bon's work on the 'group mind', Freud writes, 'shows not a single feature which a psycho-analyst would find any difficulty in placing or in deriving from its source. A group is impulsive, changeable and irritable. It is led almost exclusively by the unconscious.'[23] The group mind, he affirms, is similar to that of primitive peoples or children, in their credulity and lack of logic or reason; the crowd, in defiance of all the lessons of human history – not to mention the world he was living in – is inherently conservative. Crowds provide a channel whereby small traces of antipathy can be 'turned into furious hatred'.

Freud arrived at the same conclusion as Le Bon but took it further, arguing that the crowd desires its own oppression: its unconscious desire is to be obedient and to live in fear and deference towards its master. Tragically, given the fate of his fellow central European Jews, Freud ends up agreeing with both Le Bon and Goebbels – that the crowd, in its guileless stupidity, is ripe for totalitarian exploitation. 'Anyone who wishes to produce an effect upon [a group] needs no logical adjustment in his arguments; he must paint in the most forcible colours, he must exaggerate, and he must repeat the same thing again and again.'

This last quotation describes something else illuminating about the crowd theories of the early twentieth century: the role that hypnotism and hallucination were thought to play in winning over the crowd. Exaggeration, painting in 'forcible colours' and sheer repetition were hardly new inventions in the art of oratory, but here Freud does inadvertently describe the speeches of Hitler as early as 1922 – and this is no coincidence, given they were drawing on the same ideas about the crowd's susceptibility. Le Bon and his acolytes believed that through the right kind of totalitarian rhetoric, a docile and compliant state can be induced in a crowd, such that even if an individual enters a mass event with some scepticism towards its political message, their free-thinking can be overcome through the sensory and rhetorical inducement of a quasi-religious crowd trance. This is more than just deindivid-uation, or the submergence of the self into the crowd: it is a transformation and altered consciousness sometimes called 'crowd magic'. Hypnotism, wrote J. S. McClelland, was dragged 'out of the music hall . . . to account for the remarkable goings-on of the crowd'.[24]

Le Bon himself was unequivocal about the 'magnetic influence' the crowd can have on an individual in its midst:

> The activity of the brain being paralysed in the case of the hypno-tised subject, the latter becomes the slave of all the unconscious activities of his spinal cord, which the hypnotiser directs at will. The conscious personality has entirely vanished; will and discern-ment are lost. All feelings and thoughts are bent in the direction determined by the hypnotiser.[25]

Like all his theories, this is entertaining, lurid, and completely without scientific basis.

The notion that human beings are innately susceptible to such easy and harmful influences is depressing, because it is so anti-humanistic. A similar conclusion is often drawn from the Milgram Experiment, conducted some decades later in 1961, sug-gesting that totalitarianism derives from the weakness of ordinary people in the face of authority figures telling them what to do, backed by the threat of violence. It is a narrative which, apart from anything else, provides a useful 'get out of jail free' card to the participant, whether this be a member of a lynch mob, a foot-ball hooligan beating up an innocent opposition fan, or an attendee at a Nazi rally.

When groups of religious fanatics round on someone they see as a heathen or a heretic and murder them in cold blood – as with Catholics killing Huguenots in sixteenth-century France, or Hindu nationalist fundamentalists killing Muslims in India today – they do so driven by a powerful assurance of their own ideology and group identity. They have become convinced by

MULTITUDES

their religious or racially supremacist politics to see their victims as less than human. To pathologise such atrocities, blaming them on a moment of 'crowd madness' or 'mob mentality', not only lacks the slightest basis in evidence, it also exonerates both the individual wielding the blade and the destructive, hateful ideology they adhere to.

Millions of Germans attended the Nuremberg rallies because they wished to do so. They went because they enjoyed the experience, or wanted to be part of something historic and spectacular, however it made them feel. They were not under hypnosis, nor were they drugged or kidnapped. As Wilhelm Reich's account implies, the will to submit to the fascist crowd can also have a banal, material basis: it was in the class interests of many Germans to attend, while party members gained prestige and better work opportunities.

Yet the idea that human beings joining crowds become helpless, childlike and suggestible persisted, and still persists. It informed the mid-twentieth century's third major growth industry, after psychology and fascism: public relations. PR's great pioneer Edward Bernays was Sigmund Freud's nephew – and his work built directly on that of Le Bon and Freud in theorising the unconscious desires and caprices of the public, and how they might be successfully manipulated to buy things they did not want or need, for the good of capitalism.[26] The result was the mid-century explosion of the PR, marketing and advertising industries, the driving forces of modern consumer capitalism, especially during its American postwar boom. Granted, the spectacle of mass consumption as represented by, say, a 1950s Lucky Strike advert, was of a rather different hue to what Hitler was selling at Nuremberg. Yet these two bulwarks of twentieth-century tyranny – Nazism and PR – are built on the same foundations in Le Bon's crowd theory: contempt for the general population, a belief that they unwittingly desire conformity and to be herded around by their betters, and the determined and relentless use of deception in order to achieve that compliance.

66

'The conscious and intelligent manipulation of the organised habits and opinions of the masses is an important element in democratic society,' wrote Bernays – because the little people who comprised the masses were not capable of making rational choices for themselves.

If the general population were indeed guileless and eminently persuadable, as Le Bon and Freud had theorised, then Bernays reasoned that there was a great deal of money to be made in telling the providers of goods and services how to persuade them: through appealing to consumers' unconscious fears, whims and desires, just as Hitler had done from the podium. Fickleness was one of the key characteristics of Le Bon's crowd, a perspective founded on ideological bias and an elitist contempt for the masses, rather than on evidence. The masses couldn't *possibly* harbour deeply held beliefs or serious political and class allegiances. Instead, they are easily swayed by loud noises, bright colours and shallow incentives, like small children, or puppies in obedience class. This prejudice shaped the age of dictators, and the mass-participation propaganda spectacles they constructed, but much else besides as the twentieth century progressed.

While it reached its peak in the 1930s, the authoritarian crowd, the crowd as a vast propaganda spectacle, emboldening the egos and public image of dictators, was not entirely new in the twentieth century. Nor was the use of military drills and parades to instil a feeling of solidarity and unity, even joy, in those participating or waving their hankies from the sidelines. But the military rally and crowd spectacle created for mass media, cinema and newspapers *was* new, and persisted after the Second World War in nominally Communist countries, as it does today.

Soviet parades commemorating the October Revolution – dominated by displays of military hardware, fly-pasts and marching soldiers – became a huge part of USSR propaganda efforts during the Cold War, as did China's National Day Parade. The most recent iteration of the latter, in 2019, featured 100,000 performers, 15,000 soldiers and a new ICBM, among other attractions. These events offer spectacular exhibitions of collective athletic prowess and awe-inspiring choreography, movement and colour, and rely on vast reservoirs of dedicated rehearsal time and central state planning. The message is not a subtle one: not only are we militarily strong, but we can boast a singular group-mind and ideological unity among what you might otherwise suspect was a huge, disparate population with diffuse regional, cultural and ethnic identities, priorities and political beliefs.

North Korea's 'mass games', centred on vast gymnastic dis-plays but using many outdoor theatrical techniques similar to those deployed at Nuremberg, are the most vivid and grandiose contemporary version of the human crowd as a state propaganda spectacle. The human participants become flecks of paint on a giant canvas, seen from enough of a distance that their fluctua-tions and coordinated movement make the painting 'come alive' and transform into animation. The attendees fall into two groups: firstly, the gymnasts are the ostensible centre of attention, having practised endlessly, exhaustingly, for months on end. Secondly, the tens of thousands of spectators in the stands are themselves enlisted to create highly detailed 'tifos', as they are called in foot-ball stadiums: complex images, words and changing colour swatches, composed pixel-style, by giving each spectator a spe-cific piece of coloured card to hold up at just the right moment. Everyone participates, including the spectators, because everyone participates in the life of the totalitarian nation – or else. The mass games are the physical, human manifestation of the DPRK ideology of 'the single-hearted unity of the leader, the Party and the masses', as Kim Il Sung described it.

The dictators who have propagated the idea of single-hearted unity since *The Crowd* was published in 1895 have done so moti-vated by a mixture of wish-fulfilment, domestic and foreign propaganda, and straightforward contempt for their subjects as 'little people'. In exchange for their submission to the great leader, members of the authoritarian crowd are granted access to what

Hannah Arendt called an 'entirely fictitious world' of fantastical conspiracies and impossible promises – one far superior to the grim and aggrieving world they had hitherto inhabited. The fundamental reason for the superiority of totalitarian propaganda, Arendt continued, is that 'its content, for the members of the movement at any rate, is no longer an objective issue about which people may have opinions, but has become as real and untouchable an element in their lives as the rules of arithmetic.'

The line from Le Bon's book to the Nazis' manipulation of the crowd at Nuremberg was direct, and any resemblances were entirely uncoincidental. Quite simply, in the late nineteenth century Le Bon and his peers persuaded the world that the twentieth-century crowd would undoubtedly be democratic and socialist in character, and those same theories directly inspired their fascist opposite. It is not a stretch to suggest that contemporary political elites often follow this same pattern, even in electoral democracies: delegitimising the crowd as 'the mob' almost always goes hand in hand with the ratcheting up of state power and hierarchical authority. American Democrats (and democrats) should heed this warning: it doesn't help the battle against Proud Boys and alt-right militiamen to describe them as a rampaging, brainless mob, in place of trying to understand their various motives and ideological positions.

There are in fact no masses, Raymond Williams reminds us: but the common fin-de-siècle *way of seeing people as masses* – as a homogeneous, scary blob of mindless proles and drones, ingenuous child-men who were easily susceptible to influence – helped in no small part to construct the actual, flesh-and-blood authoritarian crowd.

3

'Feral Thugs': Protest and Riot Crowds

The excitement of that day still lies in my bones. It was the closest thing to a revolution that I had physically experienced. A hundred pages would not suffice to describe what I saw. Since then, I have known very precisely that I need not read a single word about what happened during the storming of the Bastille. I became part of the crowd, I dissolved into it fully, I did not feel the least resistance to what it did.

– Elias Canetti, *The Conscience of Words*

It is an experience as exhilarating as it is rare, but sometimes you can actually feel the electric crackle of history being made in the air around you. On 7 June 2020, amid the tumult of the global Black Lives Matter uprising, a long-hated statue of the seventeenth-century slave trader Edward Colston was lassoed with ropes and pulled off its pedestal in Bristol by a crowd of hundreds of mostly young protesters. The action made headlines around the world, but it mattered most of all to those people who were right there, in the midst of it: chanting for racial justice and then screaming with elation, exulting at the metallic CLONK of the bronze statue finally hitting the ground, jeering as it was rolled along the ground, before the final giant SPLOSH as it was dumped into the river Avon, where Colston's slave ships used to dock.

There was 'a rain of cheers' as the statue came down, 'a standing ovation on the platform of [his] neck', wrote Bristolian poet Vanessa Kisuule the next day, in a poem titled 'Hollow'. She was dazzled by the astonishing power of the crowd to achieve something they had been told repeatedly by the authorities should not and could not be done. It was a moment of pure catharsis, generated by the righteous anger and action of the protesters, who had pulled off that magical trick of transmuting rage into joy, changing the physical fabric of Bristol and, with it, themselves, and the world they moved in. This is crowd alchemy, and you know it when you experience it. 'The air', wrote Kisuule, 'is gently throbbing with newness. Can you feel it?'

The previous day in central London, along with squads of riot-suited, armed Territorial Support Group (TSG) officers, the Metropolitan Police had deployed the perversely antiquated military tactic of cavalry charges against the crowd of BLM protesters. The Met's mounted division select their horses for size and strength, and they can weigh up to a tonne each. They were spurred into the throng without warning – a cavalry unleashed during heavy rain, on the slippery Whitehall asphalt, against a crowd composed largely of teenagers attending their first-ever protest.[1] At one terrifying moment, a police horse that had unseated its rider bolted, confused, through the delicate human figures that scattered beneath it.

One protester, nineteen-year-old nursing student Jessie Tieti Mawutu, was knocked unconscious and then trampled by the horse.[2] She was lucky to survive. The police did not offer any medical support to Mawutu, leaving that to the crowd. The Met subsequently told her that they could not be held responsible, and issued a statement blithely saying that 'the horse, which was uninjured, made its way back to the nearby stables.' A subsequent Netpol report into the policing of the BLM protests that summer found that 'excessive use of force, including baton charges, horse charges, pepper spray and violent arrest were commonly reported and well-evidenced.'[3]

It was June 2020 in an uncanny Britain: the Covid-19 transmission rate was still very high, a vaccine was still six months away, and hundreds of people were still dying from the disease every day. Britain was still officially locked down – pubs and restaurants were closed, households were not allowed to mix, and offices, non-essential shops and city centres were all deserted, as they had been for three months. And yet here were tens of thousands of young people on the streets of central London, bristling with righteous anger, protesting in solidarity with the murdered African American George Floyd, and denouncing Britain's own colonial history. Meanwhile far-right groups of self-appointed 'statue defenders' gathered in equally fractious counter-demos, rucking with the police.

More often than the 'great men' of statuary like Edward Colston, it is crowds of ordinary people who make history, although ordinary people are rarely represented on plinths in the public squares that are their natural home. The toppling of Colston's statue was a moment of intense relief that followed decades of patient local campaigning for the statue's removal, or at least its recontextualisation. *What about going through the official channels?!* screamed the defenders of propriety and order in the aftermath of 7 June 2020. Wearied by this prevailing stupidity, campaigners explained that they had tried these official channels for years, and found them to be unyielding. What they discovered instead was – and there's no way this won't sound corny, but it is undeniably true – their own collective power to effect political change. Barely a handful of people actively pulled down the statue, but they were able to do it with the support of the assembled crowd of thousands roaring them on. Over the following six months, almost seventy public tributes to slave owners and other traffickers in human misery, including plaques, statues and street names, were modified or had explanatory plaques added.

Not everyone shared the giddy joy and pride of the Bristol BLM crowd and their supporters. In response to the Colston action, anyone with any power seemed to be reading – as they always do – directly from Gustave Le Bon's *The Crowd*. What the Bristol protesters had done was 'sheer vandalism and disorder,' said Home Secretary Priti Patel; 'mob rule, completely out of kilter with the rule of law'. Policing Minister Kit Malthouse also called it 'mob rule'. Prime Minister Boris Johnson declared the protests had been 'hijacked by extremists'. Keir Starmer condemned the action as 'completely wrong'. In a rare but commendable outbreak of good sense from someone in his position, Avon and Somerset's (white) police chief, Andy Bennett, risked opprobrium from his paymasters and refrained from sending officers to intervene, saying he understood why it had happened: the statue had 'caused the black community quite a lot of angst'. The local paper got it too – the *Bristol Post* editor Mike Norton wrote that the city had 'been in denial for decades', and 'brought upon itself' the drama. In a poll of the paper's readers, 61 per cent backed the protesters, with only 20 per cent saying the statue should have stayed in place.

For the majority of the British press, however, this was undemocratic, unthinking thuggery. Even if you agreed with the (seemingly contentious) point that our cities should not uncritically glorify slave owners, *this was the wrong way to go about it*: 'LAWLESS & RECKLESS' screamed the front page of the *Daily Mail*. When the four Colston protesters charged with criminal damage were eventually cleared by a jury of their peers, Transport Minister Grant Shapps described this due legal process as, you guessed it, 'mob rule'. Boris Johnson said that statue topplers should not 'change our history'. To Colston's heirs in the British establishment, the statue-toppling was sinister, violent and Stalinist in character, and even, apparently, a threat to freedom of speech, despite the fact it seemed to be bringing to the fore Bristolian voices that had never been heard before. 'You can't just cut history off at the mains. History is history. You can't edit or censor it,' said former Conservative MP Nicholas Soames, the grandson of Winston Churchill, a man whose voice has never been in want of a microphone.

Colston's statue was sent to the bottom of the river Avon, just as tens of thousands of African people had ended up at the bottom of the Atlantic, dumped over the side of his boats. His company transported more than 100,000 people as slaves from West Africa to the Caribbean and the Americas, and more than 20,000 died along the way. Cities like Bristol, Liverpool, London and Glasgow are garlanded with beautiful buildings, homes and churches that were built with money made on the backs of enslaved people. The 2020 Bristol crowd had done more than any reverential statue to educate the general public about Edward Colston's life, and about how the Britain we live in now came to be the way it is. I don't mind telling you I'd never heard of Colston or his crimes until the Bristol crowd intervened; all of their efforts were generating 'more history, not less', as a friend put it to me.

The actions of protest crowds have a tendency to draw out revealing opinions from pundits and politicians. What appears as an expression of 'people power' to crowd members and supporters will be dismissed as shallow groupthink and thuggery by their enemies. To be a protester is to be smug and self-righteous, and uninterested in the serious business of political power. Indeed, the pejorative label ascribed to the Labour Party under Jeremy Corbyn by his detractors, notably Keir Starmer and Tony Blair, is that it consigned itself to being merely 'a party of protest', more interested in 'virtue signalling' than realpolitik, and thus remained outside the norms of effective politics. The crowd-politics of public protest on the one hand, and the formal politics of bureaucracies and committee meetings on the other, are held to be in direct opposition to each other, and only the latter carries any legitimacy with the establishment.

Political crowds are still regarded by those in power in the same way as they were in the nineteenth century. Le Bon's formative explanations of their behaviour have persisted into our own age. The only real change to the narrative over time is that every politician, police commander, right-wing broadcaster or newspaper will now pay lip service to the idea that, *of course, peaceful protest is a legitimate part of any functioning democracy. I've got no problem with peaceful protest!* It is a desultory caveat issued before the inevitable 'but' screeches into the sentence like a van of riot police. Condemnation is never far away. To the enemies of the crowd, every peaceful protest crowd is liable to become a violent mob, composed of naive rubes who don't understand the issue at hand, particularly if the perennial folk devils of 'outside agitators', 'a minority of extremists', 'anarchists', 'vandals', 'yobs' or 'criminals' 'hell-bent on violence' infiltrate the crowd, 'masquerading' as peaceful protesters and corrupting the guileless masses from within.

There are threads linking the Bristol BLM protest all the way back to Gustave Le Bon – and not only that Colston's statue was erected in 1895, the very year *The Crowd* was published. Le Bon believed in the same hierarchy of races – Europeans at the top, of course – that informed the transatlantic slave trade. He developed this into a racial hierarchy of crowds. Latin crowds, for example, were more 'feminine', more emotional and susceptible to influence. Le Bon reflected the spirit of his age in the colonial manner of his thinking: the crowd was like 'a savage', he wrote, irrational and fixated only on the realisation of its base desires. The 'Oriental crowd' is effectively a tautology in Le Bon's writing – the crowd is violent, irrational and uncivilised, just like individuals from non-European races.[4] Arabs, he wrote in *The Psychology of Revolution* (1912), 'shout because there are men shouting, revolt because there is a revolt, without having the vaguest idea of the cause of shouting or revolution'.[5] It's not unlike the way people rebelling in the global south are orientalised in our own day, depicted as wild-eyed and subhuman. Following the Hamas terror attacks in October 2023, the Israeli defence minister Yoav Gallant announced: 'We are fighting human animals and we act accordingly', as the occupying regime cut off electricity, food, water and fuel to the 2.2 million citizens of Gaza.

Since pseudoscientific racism and fear of the other lie at the centre of his crowd theory, it is no wonder Le Bon exercised a unique intellectual influence on the rise of European fascism. But these same racist readings of crowd behaviour also informed violent, military-style policing by the colonial powers of Western Europe. There is a feedback loop in operation across the twentieth century. First, Le Bon's work was directly influential on colonial policing, and then those same ideas, tactics and toolkits were imported *back* to the West in the postwar period. Indeed, they were, and are, most often used to repress crowds comprising the descendants of those colonised peoples who had combated and eventually overthrown British, French, Spanish, Portuguese, Belgian or Dutch rule. For example, documents acquired via FOI by Liberty in 2023 revealed that the only events since 2017 for which Metropolitan police chiefs authorised the use of baton rounds, aka plastic bullets, were majority-Black events: the Notting Hill Carnival and Black Lives Matter protests.[6] Such exceptional methods are reserved for the policing of crowds drawn from 'suspect communities', wherever they are in the world: this is what is called the 'boomerang effect' of colonial policies and elite ideology, dispensed from the European metropole to the periphery, and then returning to their homeland.[7] Traditional crowd theory is at the very heart of this process.

The associations made by Le Bon and other nineteenth-century crowd theorists 'between criminality and crowd behaviour, between collective psychology and urban disorder, would influence lawmakers and law-enforcers for decades to come,' writes Martin Thomas in his study of colonial military policing, *Violence and Colonial Order*.[8] With dissenting crowds gaining in strength and indignation in the colonies and the metropole alike in the first decades of the twentieth century, those in power were desperate to find ways to disperse them. They had one key text to lean upon. Thomas surmises that most colonial politicians with responsibilities for security and policing 'had some acquaintance with Gustave Le Bon's ideas . . . Even those who had never encountered [his] writings directly were bound to do so indirectly when reading the police manuals and individual colonial government instructions that dealt with police responses to public protest and crowd violence.'[9]

Well before Le Bon's time, the colonial boomerang underlay Western policing. Robert Peel's original vision for a national police service in the 1820s, immediately following his years as chief secretary for Ireland, was to be a re-creation of the Royal Irish Constabulary, Britain's occupying colonial force – in other words, a paramilitary force, controlled by politicians. When this was rejected on grounds of both cost and principle, Peel reluctantly created a more civilian force, which is where the convenient myth that British officers are simply 'civilians in uniform' comes from.[10]

The link between British paramilitary policing and the North of Ireland remains strong today. Sir Hugh Orde of the Police Service of Northern Ireland, speaking to the Home Affairs Committee in 2009, recounted the lessons he had learned there before taking up the role of president of the Association of Chief Police Officers (ACPO): 'In Northern Ireland it would be right to say we have, sadly, what we call "rent-a-mob", who actually do try to encourage my officers into areas and then attack them.' This paranoid notion of a suspect, hostile community, an enemy within, which poses a danger to the state whenever it assembles in public, is at the heart of quasi-militarised crowd policing – whether in Bogside in Derry, Amritsar in India, or Broadwater Farm in London.

Some useful indications of the impact of Le Bon's theories on modern British policing can be found in an obscure little volume written by a senior training officer with Greater Manchester Police, Kenneth Sloan, called *Public Order and the Police*. Published by the Police Review Press in 1979, it was designed as a manual for serving officers – but should also be read by members of the public, Willie Whitelaw insists in the book's foreword, when he was mere months away from becoming Margaret Thatcher's first home secretary. Whitelaw commends Sloan's 'very lucid analysis' and expresses sympathy with how hard it is for the police to control the 'extremists' who are 'frankly conspiring to overthrow our society'. The enemies within had been identified before the Conservatives even took office. Establishment paranoia about insurgency is a constant background noise in the Sloan manual. Intriguingly, this pocket-sized, 144-page manual on public order policing finds space for individual chapters dedicated to Marxism, Trotskyism, anarchism and fascism respectively. Sloan suggests proscribing the National Front and Socialist Workers Party as terrorist organisations. Even more bizarrely, the manual contains information on the party structure of the (tiny) Communist Party of Great Britain, and short biographies of both Marx and Engels – something every riot cop should have access to in case of emergency.

With a medley of communists (and a few neo-Nazis) apparently lurking everywhere, and the recent experience of militarised policing of the conflict in Northern Ireland in mind, Sloan has no hesitancy in recommending greater militarisation of policing in Britain too. 'Training methods require some fresh thought,' he writes.

> One obvious requirement for all officers who may be called upon to do battle is that they should be physically fit and practised in working as a team. Great experience in controlling civil disorder has been obtained by the Army in recent years and their methods could doubtless be adopted for police use.

Attributing a rise in marches and mass meetings after the Second World War to 'increased freedom and greater opportunity for leisure', Sloan's view of the crowd is almost a direct lift from Le Bon: 'There is bound to be an accompanying increase in crime and violence wherever crowds gather, as even the most inoffensive persons will do things in a group that they would never do as individuals.' This is the view of the policing establishment on the very cusp of the Thatcher period, endorsed by the home secretary-to-be: a force preparing itself to 'do battle' against the crowd.

'Every large crowd is a potential source of disorder,' begins a chapter titled 'Crowd Control', proceeding to recommend 'long staves', firearms and whatever other weapon is needed to ensure 'the police must always win against any violent rabble.' The chapter concludes with a tongue-in-cheek 'last word' from an anonymised officer 'who offered an alternative solution for the control of rioting mobs. He said simply, "All you have to do is spray them – spray them with machine-guns."'[11] Policing by consent at its best. Sloan continued to write public order law and police manuals into the 1990s.

The paramilitary-style policing of crowds, deploying larger numbers of specially trained riot cops with more armour and more weapons, and more aggressive tactics, escalated significantly under Thatcher, with support from Whitelaw, who continued to see extremists and revolutionaries everywhere. They soon found opportunities to put the Sloan manual into practice: in response to the riots in St Paul's in Bristol in 1980, and in Brixton, Handsworth, Chapeltown, Moss Side and Toxteth in 1981; against striking workers in Wapping, Orgreave and other hot spots of the miners' strike in the mid-'80s; against football fans across the decade; as well as the 1985 Broadwater Farm riots, and finally the poll tax riots in 1990. Thatcher's crusading antagonism towards working-class collectivity made a backlash inevitable. And those pulling the levers of the state understood this all too well, girding themselves for 'periods of serious disorder' on the streets of Britain.[12]

The new assault on the crowd was ordered from the very top. Thatcher's government secretly granted draconian new public order policing powers, including the use of dogs, CS gas, plastic bullets or 'baton rounds', attacks with short shields and truncheons, 'snatch squads', and the tactic of riding police horses or even vehicles into the middle of a crowd.[13] Integral to this process was a secret manual called the *ACPO Public Order Manual of Tactical Options and Related Matters* (1983), an even more pernicious follow-up to the 1979 Sloan manual, compiled by a select working group of senior police officers and Home Office officials. Parliament was neither consulted nor aware of the manual's existence. The ACPO manual amounted to an unprecedented act of covert political interference in the police's supposed operational independence. The epitome of how the establishment works together to subdue crowds, and thereby democracy, is to give police chiefs permission to violently attack crowds of unarmed civilians.

The secret manual was launched by Willie Whitelaw at a celebratory drinks party in the Home Office in January 1983 and was immediately classified, available only to senior police officers – that is, members of ACPO. In order to control crowds in an age of class war, 'there has to be a departure from the traditional image of the British policeman,' the ACPO manual declared gravely – 'normal policing', as Whitelaw described it at the drinks party, would no longer be sufficient. Instead, the colonial boomerang was welcomed back to the UK, and lessons in aggressive crowd policing were learned not just from the Royal Ulster Constabulary, but from the paramilitary Hong Kong police. The ACPO manual section on the use of 'snatch squads', officers trained to rapidly and aggressively enter a crowd and seize individual members, 'was a direct lift of that used by the British colonial police', wrote Matt Foot and Morag Livingstone in *Charged*.[14]

Perhaps the most shocking and historic test case for this new manual was the infamous escalation in the miners' strike on 18 June 1984 at Orgreave in South Yorkshire. As many as 6,000 officers were sent to police a miners' protest against scab labour. This was to be no ordinary operation, and no pretence was made of 'keeping the peace'. After a few skirmishes early in the day – miners in shorts and t-shirts facing thousands of officers in full riot gear – the vast squadrons of police were dispatched to wage an explicitly offensive war on the picket lines. Cavalry charges were led by a mounted division of forty-two officers, fifty-eight police dogs were used, and thousands of fully armoured riot cops steamed in, chasing the fleeing miners and beating them on the ground where they lay, often truncheoning them in the head, and then pursuing them as they ran for safety into the nearby village.

What occurred that day wasn't even as demure as 'crowd control', let alone 'crowd management' – it was an all-out attack. 'I wouldn't have been worried in the slightest if people were trampled' by the horses, the senior officer on duty at Orgreave, Asst Chief Clements, freely admitted. 'The concepts and terminology have become those of the military,' miners' solicitor Gareth Peirce wrote in the *Guardian* in 1985, when it came to trial. 'Senior officers at Orgreave spoke of "incapacitating" demonstrators, "flushing out" pickets, and leaving "strike zones" as they advanced,' he continued, describing the extraordinary events, still rarely acknowledged in histories of modern Britain.[15] Peirce further describes the scene, corroborated by the police's own videos of the day's events:

> Suddenly the ranks of the long-shield officers, thirteen deep, open up and horses gallop through the densely-packed crowd. This manoeuvre repeats itself. In one of those charges you see a man being trampled by a police horse and brought back through the lines as a captive, to be charged with riot. You see squadrons of officers dressed in strange medieval battle dress with helmets and visors, round shields and overalls, ensuring anonymity and invulnerability, run after the cavalry and begin truncheoning pickets who have been slow to escape.

John Picken, the area secretary for Doncaster NUM, later reflected that the police assault was reminiscent of the Battle of Rorke's Drift, the famous Anglo-Boer War battle depicted in the film *Zulu*, with the vast, intimidating ranks of the enemy ranged across the horizon.[16] The invocation of British military adventures abroad is apt. 'They practised in Ireland, and in Brixton and Toxteth – and when it were our turn, they'd perfected their techniques – and they used them to great effect,' reflected another picket, Jimmy Rae, in the documentary *The Battle for Orgreave* (1984). The availability of film footage made it different from many previous historic clashes of this kind, although the BBC still helped to distort the narrative in the establishment's favour, as they often do at times of crisis. They were later found to have switched the timeline of the footage to make it look like the miners had 'started it' by throwing things at the police, before the riot police and horses moved in to control their spontaneous violence. The reality was the other way around.

This explosion of paramilitary police violence had been authorised, via the ACPO manual, by senior Conservative ministers and civil servants, in a pattern that would become familiar: disperse with extreme force, and then defame and prosecute the victims as they tend to their wounds in the cells. The crown prosecutor's opening speech at the Orgreave trial declared of the pickets: 'their aim was force and violence . . . The rule of the mob prevailed.'[17] In spite of the best efforts of the state to follow up its all-out attack with vexatious prosecutions, every one of the ninety-five picketing miners who had been charged with riot-related offences saw their case collapse. South Yorkshire Police were later forced to award £425,000 to thirty-nine men in compensation.

There is no question those in power knew what they were doing, and what the consequences were. It was, as one picketing miner said, understood to be class war on both sides. The ACPO manual itself acknowledges the impact of their new public order toolkit on several occasions. A section on the use of armoured vehicles warns police chiefs that their presence 'can antagonise the general public and invite increased hostility and the throwing of missiles. They may also attract adverse publicity.'

The ACPO manual also offers thoughts on how to prevent crowds from forming in the first place. For example, the 'saturation policing' strategy deploys a large number of uniformed police officers on foot and on mobile (car) patrols to pre-empt riots 'by discouraging bands of unruly persons from associating together in large groups'. Alongside the collective punishment that is a recurring feature of paramilitary-style policing, this seems to be a conscious attempt to prevent freedom of assembly – dispersing the crowd before it has even had a chance to gather.

It grants the police discretion to determine who is 'unruly' and therefore may not associate in public.

This kind of 'pre-dispersal' appears to fall well outside the bounds of what the police should be permitted to do if they are indeed only there to 'keep the peace' and 'facilitate peaceful protest' – yet preventing crowds from gathering is a common police practice. Ahead of the 2011 royal wedding and the 2012 London Olympics, the Met pre-emptively arrested numerous people on their way to attend peaceful gatherings, and others who were planning a protest.[18] Their justification for these draconian 'pre-crime' arrests was 'suspicion of intent to cause a breach of the peace', and the individuals concerned were kept out of commission for the duration of the events. And so, in that sense, it was 'mission accomplished' for the Met. More broadly, a growing array of police surveillance tactics, equipment and officers are dedicated to stopping political crowds from forming, including police spotters at tube stations looking out for particular activists on their way to a demo. Police negotiation with protest organisers can achieve similar results, especially if these organisers are more modest in their ambitions than the crowd at large, as is often the case. Police objections can be raised against protesters' desired routes and locations – permission is sometimes only allowed for a static protest, rather than a march, and sometimes denied entirely. Our right to political assembly and protest isn't nearly as fundamental as most of us would like to think.

It is worth adding that the deployment of colonial-style paramilitary crowd policing in the 1980s was not really an innovation. What changed significantly in the Thatcher era was that these tactics were formalised, written down and signed off from the very top. Throughout the history of the British police, similar tactics have been used on unarmed civilians. The use of offensive police violence against the anti-war, anti-nuclear group the Committee of 100 when they staged a modest, peaceful sit-down in Trafalgar Square on 17 September 1961, included the dragging of women and girls by their feet, up and down concrete steps, over curbs, and even the use of moving cars as weapons against the crowd. 'On no less than four occasions I witnessed policemen compelling motor car drivers to drive into and through a mass of people', recalled James Tye, chairman of the British Safety Council, an eyewitness, in a subsequent report by the National Council for Civil Liberties.[19] As well as the broken noses and sadistic humiliations meted out by the police, several of these peacenik protesters reported the unique experience of being thrown into the Trafalgar Square fountains by the police, fished out and then thrown back in again.

The other 'way in' to a political crowd for a state that is suspicious of that crowd is undercover infiltration. From 1968 onwards, the Metropolitan Police's Special Demonstration Squad (SDS) and its heirs sent around 140 officers to spy on over 1,000 political groups, across four decades. In a period of intense neo-Nazi street violence and murder in the 1970s, the authorities focused on infiltrating anti-racist groups instead. One SDS manager responsible for sending spy cops undercover, Detective Inspector Angus McIntosh, said in 2020 that it was 'a high-level policy decision' to not have a single officer in a right-wing organisation during his time running the operation.[20] From spy cops targeting anti-racist groups in the 1970s, '80s and '90s, to the draconian response to BLM protests in 2020, the asymmetry in policing reveals the Le Bonian assumption of the establishment: that crowds drawn from marginalised communities will always be suspect.

One of the many benefits of joining a crowd of protesters is that it illustrates certain truths to you about the politics of power in pulsating colour, truths you may have nodded along to before, but which felt remote and intangible. One of the major revelations to me at the 2010 UK student protests was an understanding of just how arbitrary, bewildering and shocking state violence is up close, something I (as a white, middle-class man) had previously grasped largely in the abstract. Experiencing it for myself was a whole different matter, and further radicalised me and many others. There were young people in the Parliament Square kettle who had voted Liberal Democrat in the general election six months earlier, only to be turned into anarchists by their betrayal by that same party, and the experience of the protests and university occupations which followed.

One of the main reasons that these protests amounted to a political epiphany for me was a tactic used by the Metropolitan Police, and used to a wholly unprecedented degree: kettling. It is such a British verb; a darkly comic inversion of the national obsession with the serenity to be found in a nice cup of tea. Kettling is a public order tactic whereby a crowd of protesters are corralled – surrounded by riot police with shields, truncheons and body armour – in a confined space without food, water, or toilet facilities, without warrant, interview or caution, for an indeterminate period of time. Amounting to de facto imprisonment without charge, this is an especially devious form of crowd control. The inevitable result was the fictive creation of 'feral thugs . . . hell-bent on violence', as Prime Minister David Cameron described the overwhelmingly sweet, serious young people I interviewed on those protests, some of whom had bunked off school and risked suspension to be there. These *feral thugs*, belying the prevailing wisdom of the time about 'apathetic youth', had taken to the streets to oppose a tripling of university tuition fees, abolition of the Education Maintenance Allowance that kept many poor sixteen to eighteen-year-olds in further education, and swingeing cuts to public services.

The climactic day of these protests, Thursday 9 December 2010, began brightly, that rare northern European treat of freezing cold temperatures and dazzling winter sunshine. It was the fourth demonstration of its size in a month, numbering about 40,000 people, timed to coincide with the decisive vote on tuition fees in the House of Commons. By early afternoon the march had arrived in Parliament Square, the small green space outside, framed by the imposing edifices of the Supreme Court, HM

Treasury and Westminster Abbey, and populated by the statues of Winston Churchill, Nelson Mandela and Abraham Lincoln. Students of all ages, races and social backgrounds lifted aside the temporary police fencing blocking off the grass and occupied the square, squinting at the low sun and still smiling from the conviviality of the march. Around 4 p.m., as a blazing orange sunset descended on what was at this point an almost entirely peaceful crowd, the riot police lines closed in, blocking all the exits to the square, and the lid was put on the kettle.

Having no choice in the matter, trapped as we were, my friends and I wandered repeatedly from one edge of the cage to another, stopping to graze on biscuits and hip-flask whisky, laugh at homemade protest signs, talk politics, make new friends and swap flyers for future protests, as the temperature fell rapidly towards freezing. In an incredible turn of events, several hundred teenagers managed to start an impromptu grime rave inside the kettle, keeping warm to the sound of a battery-powered sound system, making the best of a bad situation, basking in the solidarity of the moment. Two lads even removed their shirts, climbed onto adjacent rubbish bins and held a dance-off, the crowd beneath cheering them on, even as some of their peers tried to fight their way free through the police lines, barely 200 metres away. For a short while, the kettle's barbed-wire edges were blunted, and Parliament Square was turned into a celebratory occupied space, with Lethal Bizzle's 'Pow!' and Tempa T's 'Next Hype' as the soundtrack.

But it got dark, and it was freezing, and after an hour or so more people started to ask police officers on the kettle perimeter if they could leave or, at the very least, *when* they might be able to leave. The convivial warmth of democratic participation was beginning to cool – and in any case we'd made our point, and wanted to go home: to eat, to drink, to use toilets, to sit down, to reduce the risk of hypothermia. With their black snoods up and their thick plastic visors down, the postmodern storm troopers of the Metropolitan Police's Territorial Support Group were

86

unrelenting and unmoved. *None shall pass!* Half of the officers blankly ignored any pleas for freedom or requests for basic information – play-acting like they were the Queen's Guard, faces carved in granite – while others told us to shut up, it was 'all your fault' that the kettle had been closed. A few officers playing 'good cop' would smile, and reassure protesters who they could see were tired, cold and peaceable: 'Head over to that exit, they'll let you out over there', or 'Give it half an hour, then you can all go home.' Each of these promises turned out to be bogus, designed merely to deflect our attention.

Eventually, after five hours of icy captivity, just before 9 p.m. the kettle appeared to open, towards the golden Georgian lamp-lights framing Westminster Bridge. The relief was immense. For about sixty seconds we walked south from Parliament Square towards the bridge, thinking it was over. But this was the most crushing of false dawns: we were, it quickly became clear, merely being herded onto Westminster Bridge (the Germans call this kind of forced march a *wanderkessel*). With fresh lines of riot cops already positioned halfway across the bridge, waiting for us, the others aggressively chased up the rear, trapping us in a dangerously confined space. We were already exhausted, and increasingly angry and confused, and this was when things got potentially life-threatening.

The forced march to the bridge marked the transition from a kind of open-air pigpen to what was suddenly, terrifyingly, a battery cage. Hemmed in, to the point of significant psychological (and, for many, physical) discomfort, it was so tight you could not lift your arms without hitting the person next to you, or in front of you. 'This!' shouted one earnest adolescent from somewhere in the darkness, his voice cracking with emotion, 'is not what democracy looks like!' We were held in such a tight space by the Metropolitan Police that some protesters suffered respiratory problems, chest pains and the symptoms of severe crushing. It felt 'like I'd been in a car accident', one female student told the *Observer*. 'It is a miracle', commented a doctor who was present, 'that no one was killed from crowd panic and surges similar to those at Hillsborough.' With the walls on either side of Westminster Bridge barely waist-high, it is also tremendously lucky no one was squeezed out into the still, icy depths of the Thames below, where death would have been both inevitable and horrific.

During the strange, interminable hours that followed (the last people were released at 1 a.m.), the mood swung from defiant rage to black humour and back again. At several points, over 1,000 people stood on Westminster Bridge with both arms thrust upwards to the sky, palms open in a show of ostentatious compliance, chanting 'This is not a riot! This is not a riot!' over and over, doing so in the direction of the police, and yet into the void. As we stood there, confused and powerless, the crowd occasionally surging one way or the other, chanting felt like the only thing we could do. But who were we chanting for? There were no TV cameras present, and the only reporters had, like myself, consciously and unapologetically crossed the line from observation into participation. Kettled in the middle of a bridge by hundreds of riot police, with traffic diverted for several streets around the area, there were no passers-by to persuade, or reach out to. It was a moment of affirmation, a crowd reminding each other that we were in the right. In contrast to the panic, anger and desperation inside the kettle, the only aerial photo of the event – taken by an amateur from a high-rise block on the south bank of the Thames – displays a scene of breathtaking tranquillity.

The Met claim that kettling 'prevents disorder', but this is pure Newspeak. On 9 December 2010, police kettling alone created the disorder. Some students lit fires, fought with riot cops, smashed windows and, in one startling moment, very nearly succeeded in crashing through the double doors of the Treasury using the Met's own metal fencing as a battering ram. All of this took place after 4 p.m., after the kettle was closed, and all of it because protesters had been trapped, illegitimately. That loss of any sense of police legitimacy or proportionality enraged the students, and changed the boundaries. Why should protesters engage on the terms established by the state, by the police, when these were their terms? In terms of crowd psychology, the moment the students were encircled and illegally detained by rows of armoured riot police, apropos of nothing, was the moment when the group were bonded much more tightly together – even before they started performing other bonding rituals, dancing to grime bangers and passing around hip flasks.

Dr Hannah Awcock, an academic working on the geographies of historic protests, observed to me that many sustained protest campaigns subsequently develop their own 'defend the right to protest' movement as an adjunct. It was something that happened after the student and anti-cuts demos were suffocated by aggressive policing and vexatious mass arrests – in the case of UK Uncut, mass arrests that saw 146 peaceful sit-in protesters, including a fifteen-year-old girl, kept in the cells overnight, and thirty of them dragged through the courts for a year, before finally ten were convicted of 'aggravated trespass'. 'There are a lot of protest movements that start off being about something completely unrelated to public space and the right to protest, but they end up taking on these issues, in addition to the immediate concrete demand,' Awcock told me. 'People experience having those rights to protest and to gather denied, and the experience of protesting can change the way you see things. Protests can create a new kind of shared identity.'

Crowd membership forces epiphanies on us, whether we anticipate them or not. My righteous anger at what I experienced in the Westminster Bridge kettle and at the absurd lies told about it by the Met, the government and the press is still with me now, and still makes my neck bristle to think about – in a sense, there is no going back to the person I was before.

In the parliamentary debate that followed, Labour MP David Lammy asked the Conservative home secretary Theresa May a pointed question: 'Is not the point of a kettle that it brings things to the boil?' She replied, as she had done several times already, that 'the police ensure[d] that it was possible for peaceful protesters to

leave Parliament Square.' By suggesting that individual agency –
the choice of non-violence – would have allowed freedom, she was
essentially denying that a kettle had even existed. It was a flat-out
lie. We must have asked over twenty police officers, across four
hours, at four different exits, whether we could leave. Theresa
May's non-answer was also an ingenious logical construction:
peaceful protesters were allowed to leave, she said.[21] The corollary
of this logic was that anyone who remained was not peaceful – and
therefore deserved everything they got. It is another recurring
trope of the way the crowd's enemies speak about it: homogenising
a wide and dynamic range of people and behaviours into two categories, 'legitimate' and 'illegitimate' protesters.

A year earlier, during the 2009 G20 protests in central London,
similar Met Police tactics had had fatal consequences. Ian Tomlinson, a middle-aged homeless man who was walking through
central London, hands in pockets, trying to get back to his shelter
through the lines of riot cops, was attacked from behind with a
truncheon and 'unlawfully killed' by TSG officer Simon Harwood. At his trial, Harwood's long record of disciplinary
misconduct was not disclosed, and he was cleared of manslaughter and allowed to keep his police pension. Ian Tomlinson was
not a G20 protester, he was not a crowd member; he was a passer-
by quietly trying to get home.

In the aftermath, the force revealed its hand. Peter Smyth,
chairman of the Metropolitan Police Federation, told BBC Radio
4's *Today* programme: 'On a day like that, where there are some
protesters who are quite clearly hell-bent on causing as much
trouble as they can, there is inevitably going to be some physical
confrontation. Sometimes it isn't clear, as a police officer, who is
a protester and who is not. I know it's a generalisation but any-
body in that part of the town at that time, the assumption would
be that they are part of the protest. I accept that's perhaps not a
clever assumption but it's a natural one.'

Guilt by association – or in Smyth's words, guilt by *assumption* –
along with collective responsibility and collective punishment,

are the cornerstone of protest policing, not to mention media coverage. If you are in the crowd, you are taken to have endorsed all its worst behaviours, spoken its most sinister words and enacted its most violent deeds yourself. Fleeting moments and isolated individuals are plucked out of everything that has happened, and presented as natural representations of the whole. When three people among 300,000 protesters were photographed carrying antisemitic signs to a 'Stop bombing Palestine' demo I attended in October 2023, for some mainstream pundits that was enough to deem the other 299,997 present antisemitic too – Jews like myself included. What I experienced as an entirely peaceful, poignant anti-war march was in fact a 'hate march', in the words of Home Secretary Suella Braverman.

A week later, I walked over Waterloo Bridge on another Palestine demo, this time in a crowd of around 500,000, and looked out over the Thames as a British Muslim girl about eight years old led the chants through a loudhailer: 'Gaza, Gaza, don't you cry / we will never let you die'. Later that afternoon, I attended a peaceful sit-in in Waterloo Station: the central demand was for a ceasefire, and for long-term peace. In the week that followed, TV presenters Simon Schama and Rachel Riley responded to videos of these same protests, telling their hundreds of thousands of social media followers how appalled they were that the crowd were chanting 'intifada' and 'jihad now'. Except that, clearly and for all to hear, they were doing no such thing – they were chanting 'ceasefire now'. Members of the establishment hear what they want to hear, and some of them are lucky that a crowd cannot sue for defamation.

Similarly, media coverage of the climactic day of the 2010 student protests ignored the kettling outrage in Parliament Square and on Westminster Bridge, focusing instead on a bizarre incident elsewhere in central London. On Regent Street, Charles and Camilla's Rolls Royce had run into traffic, and was met with a handful of student protesters who had avoided being kettled, whereupon Camilla was 'poked with a stick' through the car's open window (she was fine, the royals continued to the theatre as planned). A striking photo of the royal couple, mouths open in shock in the back of their car, appeared as a front-page splash on papers in Britain and around the world. 'Assault on the capital', thundered the *Times*: 'Charles and Camilla caught up in violence after student fees vote'. The crowd does not appear in any of these photos, but is implicated nonetheless. The *Sunday Times* later reported that Met commissioner Sir Paul Stephenson had told Prince Charles he would be prepared to resign over the poking-with-a-stick matter. Stephenson had managed no such offer after his force killed Ian Tomlinson in cold blood only a year before; indeed, he had hailed the policing of the G20 protest as 'a remarkable operation'.

One of the most distressing things about the Westminster Bridge kettle was the realisation that no one knew about it. Rumours went around during that strange, terrifying hour or two, as people tried to eke final text messages and tweets from the last of their phones' battery power, that the *BBC News at Ten* had not even mentioned that people were still being kettled, directly outside Parliament, while the MPs and lobby correspondents were presumably happily getting pissed in the subsidised bars. When I called my mother two days later, she was astonished to hear about the kettling – and she'd read the *Guardian*, watched the TV news, and listened to Radio 4's *Today* programme, like she always does. The crowd experience that had filled thousands of us with clear-eyed rage had simply been erased from the record.

This is the paradox of kettling: it both invigorates the crowd and silences it. It forges greater solidarity and in-group strength, but also prevents the crowd from speaking to their fellow citizens about the injustice they left their homes to shout about. The aptly nicknamed Peter 'Tank' Waddington, a former senior officer, public order policing adviser and professor – author of *The Strong Arm of the Law* – has written about his role in bringing kettling into regular use by British police. After the 1990 poll tax riots had seen the police unleash chaos and terror in the name of dispersal – driving cars into the crowd, trampling a woman with a police horse – Waddington wrote a memo to the assistant commissioner for Territorial Operations, calling on him to use kettling in future instead. 'I argued that it would have been better to have contained the protesters in Trafalgar Square until they calmed down and then allowed to disperse under controlled conditions.' Alas, the idea that kettling is somehow less brutal, or less likely to lead to injuries or an escalation in tensions than aggressive crowd dispersal, is patently false. By the time of the BLM protests in 2020, the Met were using both, simultaneously: kettling the young protesters, and then charging at them on horseback and with batons raised.

In 2011, Britain's high court ruled that the Met's use of kettling during the G20 protests had been illegal. The Met were completely untroubled by this judicial smackdown: 'At the heart of this case', they responded, 'lies a vital public order policing tactic that prevents disorder and protects the public.' The wording is telling: in the eyes of the police, protesters are not a part of 'the public': they constitute a crowd that has elected to separate itself from the public, and its freedoms can therefore be curtailed, even if no crime has been committed. A year later, in 2012, the high court ruling was overturned; Lord Neuberger, the Master of the Rolls, backed the Met's appeal – if a commanding officer believed there might be 'imminent and serious breaches of the peace', that was justification enough.

The police refuse to even acknowledge the verb 'to kettle' – it is too active, too honest about the likelihood it will incite violence. Instead, they call the tactic 'containment': merely an attempt to mop the brow of the hot-headed in the interests of everyone else's 'public safety', like 'time out' for children who have had too many sweets. When challenged on the use of kettling at the G20 protests, PC Simon Harwood's commanding officer that day, Inspector Timothy Williams, chose an even more outrageous euphemism, telling the inquest that he disliked the term 'kettle', and preferred 'peace bubble'. Sir Paul Stephenson's response to his force attacking from behind and killing a random passer-by was to suggest a review of public order tactics, including the possible introduction of 'distance weapons' such as water cannons and tasers. They are always looking for more sophisticated weapons to use on the crowd.

It took a social psychologist, Professor Clifford Stott, to point out to me this rather elemental observation: police almost always conduct their public order policing from *outside* the crowd. Stott has seen how the police operate up close, from a number of angles; his interest in crowd psychology and social conflict emerged when he was an 'anti-authoritarian' young man in the 1980s, on the dole and involved in Anti-Nazi League protests, getting beaten up by skinheads, and his PhD was built around being a participant-observer in the poll tax riots. 'The police almost never go into crowds, and if they go into crowds they generally do that in force, in number,' Stott told me. 'They think, "we wouldn't go into crowds on our own, crowds are dangerous – you can't go in there, because you'll become the next PC Blakelock".' This reference is to the killing of Met officer Keith Blakelock in the 1985 Broadwater Farm riots in Tottenham, where he was effectively ambushed on the Broadwater Farm Estate and murdered.[22] The unrest was triggered by the death of forty-nine-year-old resident Cynthia Jarrett of a heart attack 'following contact with police', when they stormed into her flat unannounced, after falsely arresting her son. A week earlier the Met had shot another Black woman, Cherry Groce, in her home.

Riots are treated differently from protests in a number of ways, even if the line between the two is sometimes blurred; when does a high-octane protest become a riot? Is it simply a case of a once-coherent protest crowd putting down their placards and scattering in many different directions? Is the level of violence the only determinant? Once a window is smashed, your protest has usually become a riot. Or is the difference the extent of pre-planning and organisation, and a consensus on one or more clear demands, before a crowd gathers to make its point?

One distinction that usually holds true is that when it is generally agreed that a riot has occurred, it will be framed as a more 'mindless' form of public disorder, or 'anarchy', and the press will not concede any political motivation or agency to those involved. English law makes an amusingly precise distinction based on the number of participants: in order to be charged with the offence of riot under the Public Order Act 1986 – and face up to a ten-year sentence – twelve or more people must be involved, using or threatening to use unlawful violence for a 'common purpose'. (The offence of violent disorder, by comparison, only requires three participants.) So a football team of eleven cannot riot, unless they have a sub available. Incredibly, this specific number of twelve goes all the way back to the original Riot Act of 1714 – the one that literally had to be read out loud by a magistrate to take force, and gave us the idiom used about stern headteachers today.

Compared to protest crowds, rioters are often not at all crowd-like in their physical composition, behaviours or movements. In riots, people tend to move as individuals or in pairs or small 'affinity groups' of say, three to twenty people, which ebb and flow, join and part ways with other small groups, scatter and reassemble, argue, debate, moralise, drift, and push in direct directions, towards different focal points. Riot crowds are bolder in their actions, but also tend to be more furtive because of this, aware of their own transgression of laws and social norms. A riot rarely involves a surging mass of hundreds, let alone thousands of people moving in lockstep and speaking with one voice.

I have seen this kind of incoherent, messy crowd up close. A quarter of a century after the tragic and unnecessary death of Cynthia Jarrett, in 2011 the police shot Mark Duggan, another Black Tottenham local, and then lied and obfuscated about it, and refused to acknowledge a peaceful protest outside the police station demanding information about his death. Within hours, Tottenham was on fire again.

I arrived on Tottenham High Street on the first night of four days of rioting, across numerous English cities, involving many thousands of people, after seeing a post on social media from Cynthia Jarrett's grandson, the grime MC Scorcher: '25 years ago police killed my grandma in her house in Tottenham and the whole ends rioted, 25 years on and they're still keepin up fuckry'. It was about 10:30 p.m., things had barely kicked off, but even so early in the proceedings, the atmosphere was noticeably febrile as soon as I got off at Seven Sisters tube and walked down the High Street. I ignored a riot cop's warning to stay away from the police station, which was guarded by lines of officers on horseback, and instead followed a few teenagers around the back of the block, re-emerging on the High Street again, where one man was trying to break a plate-glass shop window, but doing so alone, neither helped nor hindered by the other people drifting around in a daze, in a mixture of anxiety, simmering anger and (least documented of all) fascination at this dreamlike spectacle.

One local man in his thirties I spoke to had brought out a teenage nephew, visiting from out of town, so he could see the historic commotion and aggro firsthand – a mixture of education and entertainment, as the odd glass bottle arced over the police lines and smashed on the asphalt a few metres away. Ostensibly, the events were too incoherent and dispersed to be called the work of a crowd; I don't think I saw a group of twelve or more acting together all night. Across the four days of the 2011 riots, most incidences of looting, robbery, attacks on individuals, shops or cars involved a small handful of people, presumably friends already. When a double-decker bus was abandoned by its driver in this strange no man's land on Tottenham High Road, it was set on fire, and we watched in awed horror and fascination as the giant red icon went up in flames – but this was not carried out by anything approaching a crowd. It does not, as the small group of soldiers tasked with burning the Tuileries discovered, take many people to start a fire – in fact, a crowd is rather a hindrance.

Media coverage of the riots in the days that followed reproduced the same framing that the nineteenth-century pioneers of
crowd psychology had fashioned: the unrest amounted to a
pathological intrusion into civilised society, a contagious infec-
tion of the normally stable and contented body politic, which, of
course, couldn't possibly have anything to complain about. There
was a special focus on some ominously described but ill-defined
'criminal gangs' stirring things up, agitators preying on the weak-
willed crowd, puppet-masters coordinating their mayhem via the
dark arts of BlackBerry Messenger, a service primarily used by
young people.

The 30,000 rioters were, the British press declared, less than
human. Scum. Chavs. Animals. The frontpage headlines were
clear: 'Rule of the mob', 'Yob rule', 'Flaming morons', accompanied by repeated references to 'anarchy' and 'war zones' and 'the
mob'. One business owner whose shop had been looted described
the rioters as 'feral rats'. A Tory MEP called on the government
to 'shoot looters and arsonists on sight'. Kit Malthouse, then
deputy mayor of London and chair of the Metropolitan Police
Authority, compartmentalised the rioters into three groups:
anarchists, organised gangs and 'feral youth . . . who fancy a new
pair of trainers'. For PM David Cameron, no discussion could
be envisaged that permitted the slightest analysis or complexity:
the entire thing was just 'criminality, pure and simple'.

It was not just right-wing politicians and tabloids that aired the
idea of an innately criminal underclass which could only be dealt
with via a military response. 'It's time to send in the army and
water cannons,' left-wing Labour MP Glenda Jackson told her
local newspaper. Prominent liberal newspaper columnists like
Caitlin Moran did the same. There were clear racist overtones to
much of the response from commentators – dog-whistle comments about deviant Black youth culture and rap music, as well
as sweeping references to the influence of 'gangs', themselves
often tenuous, racialised constructions meaning 'a group of
young Black friends'. As Adam Elliott-Cooper has noted, this

contemporary categorisation has followed the same boomerang process originally employed to lump together, racialise and demonise suspect communities in Britain's colonies: 'It is a term that has been used for the so-called communist "gangsters" of Malaya [and] the so-called terror "gangs" of the Kenya Land and Freedom Party,' Elliot-Cooper said.[23] 'The so-called "gangs" in all of these different colonial contexts [were] a way of rationalising a form of collective punishment imposed upon a colonised population which was seen to be inherently violent, inherently dangerous, and therefore requiring a different form of policing and prison control.'

In the left-leaning *Daily Mirror*, former punk Tony Parsons decided subtext was a waste of everyone's time and offered the words Gustave Le Bon would surely have written about the 2011 riots:

> Without the gang culture of black London, none of the riots would have happened – including the riots in other cities like Manchester and Birmingham where most rioters were white. The snarling, amoral pack mentality of gangs that are too often a substitute for family, school and work made the riots possible. These youths were the shock troops of the riots, and its inspiration.[24]

Historian David Starkey, extending this astonishingly racist piece of Le Bonian crowd construction, declared on the BBC that many thousands of white people rioting could be simply explained by the fact that 'the whites have become black.'

Once again, Raymond Williams's epigram is pertinent. Where there is a writhing jumble of incoherent complexity, dynamism and myriad competing desires, aims and behaviours on the ground, the establishment will find a way of seeing and describing a coherent mass: sketching its contours and filling in the outline in bold colours. Those in power chose to read the 2011 riots as the singular action of a singular crowd, and could therefore deal with it as Le Bon would have done, with blanket condemnation and fierce repression. *Criminality, pure and simple.*

The function of this language was twofold: to legitimise the unprecedented legal overreach that followed, and disqualify any serious thought or discussion of the diverse and varied motives and behaviours at play. Almost no one in the media or political establishment was willing to countenance the possibility that for many thousands of rioters there might have been some genuine motivating grievances, that there might have been *meaning* to the events. Professor Stephen Reicher has made the point that the government response and prevailing discourse was positioned firmly against any attempt to understand what had happened – because to seek explanations is to 'make excuses', and endorse the disorder. Rejecting calls for a public inquiry, David Cameron made the establishment's position clear: 'This was not a political protest or a riot about politics. It was common or garden thieving, robbing and looting. And we don't need an inquiry to tell us that.' Exploring context is itself framed as suspect behaviour, because it throws up subjects some don't wish to see discussed: police racism, violence, poverty, inequality, alienation and anomie.

In 2015, Oxford University sociologists presented their findings after mapping the home addresses of more than 1,600 people charged with rioting, cross-referencing them with surveys of attitudes towards the police conducted before the riots. They found that rioters tended to come from areas where the locals did not feel they were treated with respect by the police.[25] Some participants reported a truce between 'gangs' in Tottenham and Hackney, given the opportunity to lash out at a common enemy:

DAN: So even though there was beef [vendettas] between the gangs, they wanted to unite against something which was repressing them collectively.

PAUL: Yeah, BB messages were sent out to cool it, saying like 'it's not about a postcode war, it is "us" against "them"' and 'forget our beef with each other and let's get the police.'[26]

Some of the instant-commentary rap and grime music released about the riots pointed to exactly that sense of collectivity. 'They Will Not Control Us', a track by little-known rapper 2KOlderz uploaded to YouTube on 10 August, while the rioting was still going on, lamented a nation of nefarious tabloids, unfair taxation and excess CCTV, and addressed David Cameron directly:

> How about you go and pay rent to the landlord,
> earn shit money doing a labouring job?
> We're living like shit in this country,
> while you've got your feet up living nice and comfy
> Well we know where the problem is,
> the people acknowledge this:
> stand up to the politics.

The 2011 riots arguably represented the crowd's 'post-political' moment. Across three decades of neoliberalism, marked by growing voter apathy during the New Labour years, followed by the Conservative–Lib Dem coalition's punishing austerity regime, the primary job of party politics was to dismantle postwar forms of collectivity: the youth club, the community centre, the trade union, the NHS and social care system.[27] In its place arrived the politics of the riot – in its own way, no less a form of collective politics – a challenge, albeit a nihilistic one, by the powerless to the class who hold a monopoly on power. 'Let's turn on them now, let's stick together and stand our ground . . . let's reclaim the United Kingdom,' 2KOlderz concludes.

While some of this yearning for lost collectivity is discernible in the 2011 riots, a vital truth, obscured by the 'mob mentality' myth, is that rioters' motives varied extensively: not just between cities but between groups, and between friends and neighbours. In the interviews subsequently conducted with rioters by researchers, there emerges a wide array of social, economic, or police-related motives given by participants, ranging from unemployment, alienation and boredom, to resentment over a lifetime of racist police stop-and-search or elite political corruption. Some were drawn in by all the media coverage, and 'going down to see what was happening' gave them the opportunity to switch from being observers to participant-observers. A few saw money-making opportunities from looting, though that did not seem to be a prominent motive. One sixteen-year-old dad told Sky News he had looted to provide for his family, stealing clothes, nappies and toiletries for his infant son.[28] Some took part simply because they could, because they had been waiting for something to happen: because in a world without stimulation or reward, *what else is there to do*, when something like this happens?

Another interesting aspect of riot crowd dynamics, which perhaps disproves the idea of 'crowd contagion' more than any other, is that riot crowds throughout history always seem to contain people who are actively trying to limit the rioting – either trying to keep it laser-focused on what are understood to be legitimate targets, or dissuading people altogether. In 2011, the story of 'the Hackney Heroine' Pauline Pearce stands out. With cars on fire and glass breaking in the background, Pearce, clutching her walking stick, was depicted berating the rioters in a viral video clip: 'Get it real, Black people, get real! Do it for a cause. If we're fighting for a cause let's fight for a fucking cause. You lot piss me off. We're not all gathering together and fighting for a cause, we're running down Foot Locker and stealing shoes!' Unaware she had been filmed, Pearce continued on her mission to calm some of the rioters, and ran into others doing the same thing: people 'trying to keep it less than it could have been,' she told the *Guardian*. 'They were trying to stop scuffles. People were charging around burning vehicles, and they would step in and say: "Well, why are you burning it? What's the point?"'

As the historian E. P. Thompson wrote in his highly influential survey of eighteenth-century food riots in England: 'It is the restraint, rather than the disorder, which is remarkable; and there can be no doubt that the [collective] actions were supported by an overwhelming popular consensus.'[29] Thompson gives several examples of what contemporary crowd psychologists call 'self-policing', where pro-social behaviours – like that of the Hackney Heroine – emerge in the midst of crowd disorder, butt up against more chaotic behaviours, and, on occasion, win the argument. For example, the Honiton lace workers of 1766, 'who, having taken corn from the farmers and sold it at the popular price in the market, brought back to the farmers not only the money but also the sacks'.

The gap between the dynamic and complicated reality on the ground and the official, sweeping version of events has always been a yawning chasm. In *Barnaby Rudge*, Charles Dickens describes at length and in vibrant colour 'the rabble's unappeasable and maniac rage', attributing the 1780 anti-Catholic Gordon Riots in England to a mob of desperate, drink-addled animals, 'the weakest, meanest, and most miserable' of people, most of them bribed to take part, gullible rubes with no understanding at all of their purported cause.

The prevailing premodern syntax is telling: a 'mob' was usually something that was 'raised' by men of means and power, rather than a crowd self-assembling under their own agency; the mob's constituent parts were poor, stupid, mercenary men, paid or bribed with drink or 'favour' of some other kind. Contrary to Dickens's lurid version, the historical reality of the Gordon Riots, Dr Hannah Awcock told me, was a collection of mostly serious, petty bourgeois people carrying out a brutal but targeted campaign of religious violence. 'Although they did violent things, they were quite careful about not allowing any violence against people,' Awcock explained. 'There's very clear evidence that they weren't mindless, and they were actually restrained and capable of organising amongst each other.' In some instances of arson, the rioters were so wary of fire spreading to the neighbours of their prominent Catholic targets that they removed all the furniture from the house, even the staircases, and burned them in the street. Abhorrent and vicious the violence may have been, but it was the polar opposite of 'indiscriminate violence' – it was highly discriminating, that was the point.

One perhaps unpalatable truth is that where most see only misery, nihilism and dysfunction, people often experience great joy in the midst of a riot. 'It was really enjoyable, actually,' one respondent to the 2011 Reading the Riots project said. 'At one stage, it was like a street party.' The St Pauls riot in Bristol in 1980 left one participant 'elated', he told the BBC years later – buoyed by the community togetherness that had fought back a racist police force.[30] 'I can't deny it was very exciting for a fifteen-year-old,' reflected another. As the bottles rained down on the police lines, someone cried 'Freedom!' Crowd membership grants people the agency they are denied as individuals, especially in unequal societies, where rights and a decent standard of living are granted to some and not others. This empowerment, joy and sense of kinship with others can be as profound where cars are ablaze as in any more sanitised, or universally welcome, crowd.

While the Thatcher government and the ACPO manual were ramping up the militarisation of British policing in the 1980s, a new generation of social scientists were developing a fresh approach to crowd psychology and behaviour – by studying the same incidents of urban unrest. Just one mile away from where the Edward Colston statue stood, in St Pauls, Bristol on 2 April 1980, a prolonged period of police racism and malpractice against a working-class Black community already enduring poor housing and infrastructure culminated in a raid on a beloved community hub, the Black and White Café. It had happened numerous times before, but this raid was the last straw. What followed was a night of mostly young, multiracial locals fighting with the police, torching police cars and injuring a number of officers.

A seminal study of the St Pauls riot published in 1984 by a young Stephen Reicher tested the Le Bonian view against the evidence, and found crowd members' behaviour to be character-ised above all by 'restraint and selectivity', just as E. P. Thompson had done. Building on work by Henri Tajfel and John Turner in the late 1970s, Reicher's study helped raise the profile of a new framework, which has become known as the Social Identity Model (SIM) – a paradigm-shifting and far more sophisticated version of the bogus idea of 'crowd contagion':

> The social influence process operating in the crowd depends on social identification. Thus the basis of behavioural homogeneity is a common social identification and, conversely, only those who have identified with the relevant category will be subject to crowd influence ('contagion'). In other words, the limits of participation will be the limits of identification . . . while crowds may show a range of behaviours, that range will be limited by those attrib-utes which define the social category to which they belong. The socialist crowds of which Le Bon wrote may have done many things but they would never have attacked the poor, or crossed a picket line.

In other words, we do not simply do as the person next to us is doing, just because they happen to be standing next to us. Our behaviour *can* be conditioned by the social norms of crowds or groups we belong to, but only when we identify with our fellow group members. We are social animals, and find solace and soli-darity in being around others we identify with – and it is only because we respect these people that they can help shape our behaviour. One of Reicher's St Pauls interviewees told a story of kids shaping up to throw stones at a private car, rather than a police car, and being first told off, and then 'forcibly stopped from doing it'. The target, they were reminded, was the police: 'direct your antagonism that way'. Even within a riot crowd, social relations are complex and negotiable – very far from the myth of 'anarchy'. Other St Pauls rioters recounted the conviviality of the atmosphere – a greater sense of community unity emerged amid the broken glass, rather than being destroyed. 'People were so warm,' recalled another witness. 'They said, "glad to be with you, brother", and put their arm around you.'

When the 2011 English riots erupted in Tottenham, the police did not enter the crowd, and were lambasted by the right-wing press and political class for 'hanging back' and letting the disorder happen. Even the *Guardian*'s front page headline on Thursday 11 August echoed this critique: 'Tories on riot policing: too few, too slow, too timid'. While analysis of the rioters' motives was beyond the pale, analysis of the failure of police to stop them was the subject of a great deal of public discussion. The consensus was clear: there had not been enough officers on duty, and they had not moved aggressively or quickly enough to bash heads and arrest people. At no point during the aftermath did anyone suggest the difficult truth: that the only way to be certain of stopping a riot is to build a society where people have enough at stake that they would never choose to riot in the first place. In a democracy, no police force should ever be so vast (which it would need to be), no legal deterrent should ever be so extreme, that they could instantly stop a riot.

In fact, once the burning cars had been quenched, and the Crown Prosecution Service, under Keir Starmer, had gone to work dispensing 'exemplary' sentences at the behest of Cameron's government (four years in jail for posting an incitement to riot on Facebook that no one took up; six months for stealing a case of bottled water), what happened was that the police both stepped back from the crowd and found new ways into it. As Hannah Awcock explained: 'What you've seen more in the last few years are techniques like increased surveillance and intelligence gathering, using specially trained liaison officers to gather intelligence from the crowds, to make more strategic arrests.'

For Chief Inspector Melita Worswick of Greater Manchester Police, the relatively novel array of community mediators, the PCSOs (police community support officers, who are volunteers) and police liaison officers (PLOs) have been essential to bridging gaps with communities and making detailed contact before any crowd event takes place. 'It's really important to have the right people communicating with crowds. In the old days we would have said, "Well, we're the police, and we say you need to move there, so we're going to move you there regardless",' Worswick told me. 'But this is about building on "policing with consent", and knowing that if we don't manage that right, it could result in disorder. We have to be part of the community that we're policing. I think we have come a long way since the 2011 riots.'

The role of PLOs at protests remains contentious. The police argue they are a progressive new presence, wearing calming baby-blue bibs over regular 'beat officer' black-and-white uniforms, sent into crowds in pairs for a casual chat: a victory for dialogue and de-escalation over phalanxes of riot cops circling the perimeter. The Network for Police Monitoring, on the other hand, argue that PLOs are Trojan horses for intelligence gathering, and have distributed placards for protests that read: 'WARNING: Talking to the "friendly" officer in the blue bib is a quick way to ensure you end up on a police intelligence database'.[31]

What is uncontentious is that some senior members of the British police are now listening to progressive crowd psychologists for the first time. In addition to her Manchester role, Melita Worswick is also the policing standards manager for the professional development body, the College of Policing, overseeing the teaching of new approaches to public order policing, including the latest academic research into crowd psychology. One of the major changes of the last few years is a shift in emphasis to 'public safety' in tandem with public order, Worswick said. 'It's to redress that balance a bit. When people hear "public order" they think about that traditional riot scenario with running lines of officers with shields and batons. But actually, event policing isn't about that – that's the worst-case scenario. Sometimes the police have to learn to step back, and that's what we train now: sometimes taking no action is the right way. As long as you've got experienced event organisers, by removing the police you can remove the potential for disorder, because sometimes we become the catalyst and the focus – and actually, it's not the police's job to enforce those event rules. Have your private security do that. So we're removing ourselves from a lot of things.'

The G20 protests, and the killing of Ian Tomlinson, were a catalyst for this historic, if inconsistent and incomplete shift in public order policing. In the aftermath of his death in 2009, Her Majesty's Inspectorate of Constabulary (HMIC) asked Clifford Stott to provide an overview of the literature on crowd psychology, including its latest findings, and advise them on how they should move forward.

'What we began to understand,' Stott recalled, 'is that the training they were receiving was still teaching them this outdated nineteenth-century mob psychology, when the science was showing very, very clearly that that wasn't just incorrect, it was also counterproductive, and indeed dangerous, because it was leading them to make decisions and act in ways that were creating violence and confrontation.'[32] The result was *Adapting to Protest – Nurturing the British Model of Policing* (2009), a 220-page report which for the first time openly acknowledged the influence of Gustave Le Bon on British policing, discussed his ideas, and then roundly rejected them as 'outdated and unsustainable scientifically'.

Adapting to Protest (ATP) became the new national guidance, asserting that the 'Elaborated Social Identity Model of crowd behaviour' (ESIM) should 'serve as the conceptual basis for crowd policing in the UK'.[33] It is now down in black and white, on HMIC-headed paper, that collective action is informed by a shared social identity, rather than the contagion of mob mentality; that crowds' behaviour is complex and changeable; and that it will be heavily influenced by how draconian the policing is.

This, in theory at least, was a huge leap forward in the campaign of Stott, Reicher and their peers to shake the institutions of the state out of their ideologically ingrained Le Bonism.

Alas, the extent to which the experts who understand the realities of crowd behaviour have 'won the argument' with any finality can be seen in the policing of numerous events since the report was published: the kettling and brutal attacks on student protesters in 2010; the vexatious mass arrest of hundreds of UK Uncut protesters doing a sit-in against tax evasion in Fortnum & Mason in 2011; the de facto criminalisation of all protest during the 2012 London Olympics; the use of both kettling and horse charges against young BLM protesters in 2020; and the violent dispersal of a peaceful, overwhelmingly female vigil for Sarah Everard, after she was kidnapped, raped and murdered by a serving Met officer in 2021.

On the other hand, the conversations are at least taking place, and the argument is there, for police chiefs to adopt or ignore – but they can no longer claim ignorance about what more draconian and aggressive methods of protest policing will bring about. It is also becoming more common for other European police forces to restrain their use of force in favour of greater dialogue and hanging back. As the political scientists Olivier Fillieule and Fabien Jobard write in their analysis of Germany's development of a so-called 'de-escalation' policy:

> Far from being unique to Germany, this policy has . . . participated in a new model of policing in Europe – a model that is now found in the system of Dialog Police Officers and the Special Police Tactics in Sweden, the Event Police in Denmark, the Peace Units in the Netherlands, the Liaison Officers in the UK, as well as the so-called 3-Ds model (dialogue, defuse, defend) in French-speaking Switzerland.[34]

This new crowd policing model, they write, is based on four key principles.[35] And the first of these four key principles? A rejection of the long-standing theory of crowd behaviour popularised by Gustave Le Bon.

There are several recurring themes and motifs to the way that the police, political class and media tend to respond to protest crowds.

They will significantly lowball the size of a protest, because the greater the numbers on the streets, the greater the potential legitimacy of the argument.[36] For all that the establishment now pays lip service to *the vital role peaceful protest plays in a democracy* (yadda yadda), their ideal would be a world without any protests at all, because that would vindicate the status quo over which they preside.

They will exaggerate the danger posed by the crowd, often inventing things out of whole cloth to do so. 'It is no exaggeration to say the sky was black with missiles', said the senior commanding officer at Orgreave, Asst Chief Clements – exaggerating, and wildly, to justify sending horses charging into the crowd. As part of his defamation of the 2010 student protesters, David Cameron told the public that police officers had been 'dragged off horses and beaten' in Parliament Square. This was a flagrant lie, originating with the Met, who were later forced to pay £50,000 in compensation to the two protesters they had accused of doing so, after it was finally disproved in court. Cameron has never retracted or apologised.

They will slander, hound and maliciously prosecute the very protesters who have been hurt by wanton police violence – to muddy the waters, to troll and demoralise their victims, or some combination of the above. Take Eric Newbiggin, who was photographed with blood pouring down his face after the police assaulted him at Orgreave in 1984, before they charged him with rioting. He was later acquitted. In the Parliament Square kettle in 2010 was a twenty-year-old student, Alfie Meadows: he was truncheoned in the head by a riot police officer and very nearly killed, and then, as he lay in hospital with brain damage, charged with violent disorder. He was prosecuted, tried, re-tried, and found not guilty in 2013. Finally, a full twelve years after the near-fatal assault, in 2023 the Met were forced to apologise and pay him substantial damages. The force informed Meadows that 'despite extensive inquiries', they just could not work out which officer had assaulted him, so none could be held accountable.

It is a process which repeats itself over and over. Six women who attended the 2021 candlelit vigil for Sarah Everard were aggressively arrested, handcuffed on the ground and then charged; these charges were finally dropped a year later. Two of the women, Patsy Stevenson and Dania Al-Obeid, pursued counterclaims and were awarded substantial damages by the Met. It happens so often, and the charges are so frequently and transparently vexatious, that one can only assume such prosecutions are not a systemic failure by the police and Crown Prosecution Service, but in fact a conscious tactic and a key part of the propaganda battle against protesters. 'There's no smoke without fire' is very far from being a central tenet of the English legal system, but if you are an institution like the Met, capable of fanning smoke around everywhere, having your obfuscations and lies taken up with zeal and repeated uncritically by large swathes of the media, it certainly makes the truth harder to discern.

As part of this, the police will also use what Professor Paul Gilroy has called 'the golden hour' after an outrage of their own making, the short window available to fix the narrative in aspic and in their favour – a moment when credulous journalists will happily print whatever allegations they are fed, thanks to an excess of trust and an absence of time and energy to corroborate the police line. Any debunking in the weeks, months or years that follow the event inevitably reaches far fewer people, so this approach always constitutes a net gain for the state, reputationally speaking. Lie first, have the record corrected months later, and shrug, because the press have stopped paying attention and the public has forgotten.

One final theme, regarding more militant protests or riots, is the establishment's refusal to accept that those involved might have had a legitimate reason – or any reason – to leave the house in the first place. Stephen Reicher has observed that opinion-formers are almost always willing to concede, and perhaps even applaud, the 'meaningful' political motivations that explain *historic* rioting. Those motives could include racism, poverty, or gender inequality, but the event has to have taken place at least a few decades ago: anything similar but recent is mindless thuggery, which must be condemned completely and immediately.

In the past, goes the received wisdom, people protested against injustice with clear-eyed, righteous indignation, but not anymore. *This time it's different* – this time it's invalid, without context, without reason or morality. See, for example, the suffragettes – now sanitised in their behaviour and held up as sweet, pious heroes in children's books and on coffee mugs. Both their misogynistic demonisation at the time as deranged harpies, and their extensive campaign of targeted arson and attacks on property, have been forgotten.

The same goes for the sanitisation and sanctification of the heroes and history of the American civil rights movement – now celebrated from a safe-enough distance, with any militancy or socialist principles airbrushed from the picture. This historic lag in the understanding of riots is no accident, and has a clear political imperative. In order to maintain the legitimacy of the established order it is vital that the Le Bon version of events is repeated loud and clear, and no attempt is made to understand the motivations of rioters until the dust has long since settled, and the government ministers, newspaper editors and police chiefs are dozing gently in the House of Lords.

For someone who was present on the first night of the 2011 riots in Tottenham, it is really very easy to disprove the central, somewhat mystical Le Bonian concept of crowd contagion – in that there were far more people watching the riots unfold on

Tottenham High Street than were drawn to participate in them. For several hours I milled about talking to people scattered along the cordoned-off road, spectators watching in shock, some saddened, some laughing, many murmuring that this had been coming. There were groups of teenage girls gossiping about which local boys they knew were or were not involved; Orthodox Jews handing out bread rolls from open baskets as a gesture of community spirit; lads spilling tipsily out of the pub, confused by the scene that greeted them; members of the Socialist Workers Party wandering out from a fundraising party next door to pronounce, with satisfaction, that the working-class uprising they had been predicting had finally arrived, before heading back inside.

Ultimately, even when individuals strongly 'socially identify' with their fellow crowd members, and feel bolstered by that sense of solidarity, they still operate within their pre-existing set of behavioural limits. Even when I was brimming with anger and consternation at the police's aggression, cynicism and kettling in Parliament Square, doing the bidding of the ruinous Conservative–Lib Dem government in the Gothic palace behind them, the most illegal or violent thing I did in those nine hours was take a piss on a tree; I'm just not the sort of person who throws a placard, or a brick. Individuals in crowds can certainly become disinhibited from doing things they would like to do, but wouldn't risk doing alone – but that is not the same as being 'infected' by the behaviour of others.

What *can* feel contagious is something more abstract and emotional, and long-lasting: the thrilling energy generated by a political crowd. Canetti's words at the opening of this chapter, describing the Days of Horror in Vienna in 1927, evoke the same feeling I experienced in Parliament Square when the doors of the Treasury were burst open in 2010 – the same feeling Vanessa Kisuule described in Bristol in 2020 – the crackle of history in the air. It follows the realisation that your elected leaders will always fail you, to one degree or another, whether by accident or by design, and flows from the refusal to accept those failings, taking democracy into your own hands, indeed your own body, and letting it guide you out into the town square.

The sensation of this kind of crowd power is almost one of weightlessness – a giddy feeling that time is not passing in the normal fashion. You are lifted out of the present and commune with the eternal crowd, the Bastille crowd. Sometimes the means can feel as vital as the ends, for the journey to achieve change together, the sharing of tactics, ideas and perspectives, is itself catalysing, invigorating and transformative. You can leave the protest crowd, as I did from the Westminster Bridge kettle at midnight on 9 December 2010, exhausted, freezing, aching, numb, angry and scared, and with your eyes *bulging*, livid with the sheer sensory assault of it all but, in spite of everything, tingling with possibility, desperate for revenge and determined to continue the fight. This feeling, Michael Walzer wrote of Occupy Wall Street, 'is socialism-in-the-making, and that is the only socialism we will ever know.'

4

Don't Take Me Home: Football Crowds

This book began to take shape during the first Covid lockdown, when I became suddenly obsessed with a football anthem for a team located 400 miles away. I had read a news story about Edinburgh residents opening their windows to sing a Proclaimers song called 'Sunshine on Leith' together. Even without knowing the song, I found this incredibly poignant – a yearning for the crowd in its absence, and the proscribed magic of choral singing, a whole flock of caged birds looking for solace and reassurance in a scary time.

Intrigued, I looked up 'Sunshine on Leith', and found a breathtaking video of 26,000 fans of the Leith-based club Hibernian singing it in a sun-drenched stadium, after a forever-deferred Scottish Cup win in 2016. The match was long over, both teams had left the pitch, and the Rangers' half of the stadium was completely empty, but the Hibs fans stayed behind, revelling in their moment and belting out their anthem. It was like a concert in which the 26,000 fans were simultaneously the performer and the audience.

I was entranced. I watched it again, and again. The sight and sound of this collective joy is transcendent: tens of thousands of green-and-white scarves held aloft, everyone wailing the song at the top of their lungs; and when the crowd hits the chorus, the volume levels on the shaky smartphone video blow up into a delirious warble of noise. In the YouTube comments, fans of other clubs, from Millwall to Lyon – even the defeated Rangers, even their arch-rivals Hearts – congratulate the Hibbies, not on their rare Cup victory, not on the performance of the team, but the performance of the crowd. 'Even the riot police horses shedding tears there,' observes one.

'Sunshine on Leith' is ostensibly a love song, but in this instance it wasn't being sung to a lover, or to the victorious Hibs players, or to the football club, or even to Leith. The 26,000 singers seemed to be addressing each other. 'While I'm worth my room on this earth, I will be with you / While the chief puts sunshine on Leith, I'll thank him for his work, and your birth and my birth.' In their many and varied voices, they had transformed it into a love song to the crowd: a collective homage to their fellow fans, who had suffered all these long years together.

'Football without fans is nothing' has become an oft-repeated truism in football's age of hyper-capitalist excess. Never has it been better illustrated than during the pandemic: when professional sport returned in June 2020, after a three-month hiatus, it did so for many months without fans, behind closed doors. The Germans had a term for this unnerving sight: *geisterspiele*, ghost games. The normally raucous spectacle of a match played in front of 70,000 people bellowing their passions and fury in unison was reduced to a barren, near-silent TV ballet. It reminded me of the disconcerting Lars von Trier film *Dogville*, where the setting of a small town is reduced to chalk outlines on a black floor where walls would normally be, like an especially spartan local theatre production.

Broadcasters plunged viewers even further into the uncanny valley by piping in fake crowd noises. You could turn off this artificial soundtrack, but then you were left with the emptiness of it all, occasional thwacks of the ball or distant shouts from the players echoing around the Premier League's vast, glossy arenas. It felt wrong, an unwelcome reminder that the pandemic was still roaring on and people were still dying in large numbers, just out of shot. It was also a surprise just how dreary it became, like you had tuned in to a training session in the local park by mistake.

Most football fans I know could not bear the eerie silence, and did not watch the games at all.

The *Economist* commissioned a consultancy to look at 1,534 of these matches played without fans, and found that the lack of crowds not only reduced teams' usual home advantage in terms of the final scores, it even made the refereeing more even-handed.[1] In every one of the sixteen European leagues they studied, the proportion of yellow and red cards given to away teams fell to parity, reducing the share from 54 to 50 per cent. For the first time in history there was a sizeable body of evidence to prove what had always been suspected: the intensity of a home crowd roaring them on makes the home team play better and win more games, and intimidates supposedly neutral officials into a degree of favouritism, whether they realise it or not.[2]

Every now and then, a chant sung by fans points to the true meaning of football crowd membership: that it really has very little to do with what happens on the pitch. People don't go to games so they can *see* their teams better – the view will always be better on TV; they go in order to be part of the collective experience of watching them with their fellow fans. In parts of the Spanish-speaking world, you might hear a crowd belt out the following: 'Alcohol alcohol alcohol alcohol alcohol / Hemos venido a emborracharnos y el resultado nos da igual'. The first line should be fairly clear; the second translates as: 'We don't care about the result, we just came to get drunk.'

Another chant along these lines, from the UK, is given a beautiful rendition in the documentary series *Sunderland Till I Die*. I have seen it claimed as a north-eastern anthem, but it is also popular with England and Wales fans when following their national teams abroad. In the documentary, it is sung by an exuberant, arms-aloft crowd of Sunderland fans, in the enclosed area underneath the terraces, after a game. It runs, to the tune of 'Achy Breaky Heart': 'Don't take me home, please don't take me home / I just don't want to go to work / I want to stay here, drink all the beer / Please don't, please don't take me home'.

As with the Hibs fans' rendition of 'Sunshine on Leith', the handsomely paid footballers that have ostensibly brought these Sunderland fans together are nowhere to be seen at this point: the match is over, and the crowd is singing only to each other. It is a beautiful ode to crowd membership, and testament to the crowd's anxiety that the drudgery of work under capitalism is the countervailing force that threatens to disperse them, and smother their capacity for joy. *Please don't take me home, I just don't want to go to work* – because this? This is what life is about.

There is an afterglow to being in a large, raucous, celebratory crowd: a halo of energy that stays with you and refuses to budge. After watching my lower league team narrowly lose – yes, lose – to Chelsea at their substantially larger and more famous ground recently, I struggled to get to sleep for hours: not because I was upset, but because I could not shake off that collective adrenaline. There is something particularly thrilling and transgressive about an evening cup match, played under floodlights: an oasis of crowd intensity, a chorus of collective angst and joy illuminated in the darkness, while people in the houses all around quietly eat their dinner, and ask each other about their day.

My team, AFC Wimbledon, is a fan-owned club, started in 2002 by its fans, the 'Phoenix club' which emerged from the ashes of a Premier League team, Wimbledon FC, that was moved to Milton Keynes by cynical money men in spite of years of protests. We were facing a local rival who, even after the departure of Roman Abramovich, was absolutely luxuriating in dodgy money. All of which is why, many hours later, our songs, the self-righteous songs of the underdogs, the 4,200 away fans, were still ringing around my head. 'Two times out of non-league, we're never going to stop / The franchise to the FA, we beat the fucking lot'; 'You're only here for the Wombles, here for the Wombles'; 'You're just a Tube stop in Fulham, a Tube stop in Fulham'.

They look daft written down, they feel amazing sung together: from one, self-contained stand full of people in one shade of blue nylon football shirt, towards another, wearing a slightly different shade of blue nylon football shirt. Fan partisanship is to some extent artificial, a theatrical affair, and it should be treated lightly, of course. But the collective partisanship is very much the point, and the source of joy: mocking opposition players for slipping on wet grass, singing songs about excessive pie consumption to the tune of 'Any Dream Will Do', calling into question the parentage and professional integrity of every single referee, suggesting that fans of any club from outside the M25 have travelled to the game by tractor, and – as every fan base up and down the country does – asserting in musical form that your own *empirically rubbish* side are 'by far the greatest team the world has ever seen'.

Into the safer but also more sedate, gentrified and surveilled football stadiums of the twenty-first century, we are now seeing an attempt to restore some of the vivacity and energy that has been lost from the terraces. This is taking the form of an enhanced kind of crowd theatrics, attuned to the age of Instagram and online bragging rights – and copied directly from Ultras (hardcore, semi-organised fan groups) on the continent, in particular Italy, where the concept originates. Pyrotechnics, in particular, have surged in popularity in British football recently: coloured flares and smoke bombs, as well as 'tifos', 'choreos', flags, surfing banners, North Korean–style crowd mosaics, and vast fan banners which can cover almost an entire stand.

These trends can feel a little forced at times, like a slightly desperate lunge for some of the lost libidinal chaos of yore, all that repressed crowd energy sublimated into a massive flag – not least because it takes a lot of work to make these vast, colourful displays happen. To achieve the desired effect of a crowd mosaic at the 2021 Scottish Cup final, hardcore Hibernian fan group Block Seven laid out 18,000 green, white and black foil sheets on the plastic seats before the game. It took thirty dedicated fans over four hours, on a damp, foggy morning in December, in Glasgow, to lay them out (and then they lost the match).[3]

In 2015 Dynamo Dresden fans raised an orange and black banner hailing the greatness of their club; it went around virtually the entire stadium: 450 metres long, two years in the making, and at a cost of about €20,000. (The following year, the same fans received fewer plaudits and more opprobrium for throwing a severed bull's head onto the pitch, in protest at their opponents Red Bull Leipzig 'buying their way' into the top flight.)

The crowd-as-performer – 'the twelfth man', as they are often known, for the added power they are supposed to lend to the eleven on the pitch – has entered a bold new era of self-conscious choreography. Groups of fans know they are being judged, that they too are in competition with their rivals, in the age of YouTube and Instagram, and have to put on a good show. Even if it *is* all a little forced, new traditions and rituals have to start somewhere – and if it helps make the corporate circus of modern football more participatory, it can only be a good thing.

One peculiar example of the football crowd's mirror stage of self-reflexivity, a key element of a modern fan culture which is at its most ferocious and partisan online, is the peculiar world of 'limbs'. The word has become a social media shorthand for the eruption of crowd joy greeting a goal, or a victory – arms everywhere, and sometimes, if the setting is a 'fan park' where beer is permitted, then beer everywhere too. A good 'limbs' video, one that will secure approval from observers, should be as chaotic as possible, like Kermit the Frog dancing. A weak display of limbs by a crowd after a goal suggests the crowd is a bad crowd, and a bad set of fans. Rival fans derided the crowd celebrations in one recent AFC Wimbledon Instagram post with the comments, 'Shocking limbs and fan base' and 'More limbs in a care home' – both cutting blows. It is not enough, in the age of social media, to be a loyal, committed crowd of supporters, or even to prove it at the game by chanting often and loudly – you now have to perform your devotion for the multiple camera angles, lest ye be judged tepid.

Sports crowds' performances have become the subject of extensive scrutiny for YouTube content creators. Should you wish to watch a fifteen-minute video titled something like 'American Reacts to Basketball Fans and Atmosphere USA vs Europe' (698k views), I can assure you there are literally scores of them for you to choose between. These reaction-video narratives all seem to contain the same two halves: 1) American college basketball fans do some mild, cringeworthy, colour-coordinated dancing to a melty pop-rap song playing through the stadium speakers; 2) cut to a Greek or Serbian basketball crowd – deafening chanting, flares, clouds of smoke, huge flags flying everywhere, tops off – which looks a bit like Paris must have done during the Commune. The same reaction always follows from the American YouTuber: wow, those European basketball crowds are lit, bro.

This chapter is about football crowds, rather than sports crowds in general, because football crowds have never been treated like other sports crowds. I have seen no riot cops at Lord's for the cricket, nor at Citi Field for the baseball. Professional cycling fans don't get kettled, and tennis fans don't routinely have their intelligence questioned. Football crowds are usually larger in size, they are composed differently, they behave differently, they are policed differently, and they are discussed differently, in the media and elsewhere. There is an irksome saying which speaks to the historic snobbery around football, since it was, until fairly recently, an overwhelmingly working-class sport: 'Football is a gentleman's game played by thugs, and rugby is a thug's game played by gentlemen'.

Elites have whined about football since the fourteenth century, when Edward II banned the sport, with a proclamation lamenting that 'there is great noise in the city caused by hustling over large balls from which many evils may arise.' Maligning football fans as violent oiks or guileless sheep – the Le Bon klaxon should be deafening at this point – is still one of the easiest and most frequently hit targets in modern life, because that is what working-class collectivity looks like from above. It is the Carnival crowd crammed into a large steel and concrete box every week.

The paradox is that to be a football fan in the 2020s is simply normative for most adults – and the game's gentrification in the last three decades has been accompanied by a long overdue, growing openness to fans who aren't straight white men. Given modern football's globe-bestriding hegemony, it seems extraordinary that as recently as the 1980s, the *Sunday Times* published an editorial describing the game as 'a slum sport played in slum stadiums, and increasingly watched by slum people who deter decent folk from turning up'. It's a verdict all the more jarring when you realise it was issued in the aftermath of the horrendous fire at Bradford City's Valley Parade stadium in 1985, where fifty-six fans lost their lives.

Football fans, like all groups of people, are not uniformly good, moral or wise, because, like all groups of people, they are not uniformly anything. Even while watching my small, broadly liberal-minded, 'family' club, I have heard racist abuse (not since the 1990s, but still), sexist abuse, homophobic abuse and sectarian abuse (a rather more niche form, given the south London context). When this has occurred, it has always come from one or another isolated person, and that person has usually been shouted down by other fans around them, a good example of a crowd self-policing. But it still happened, and it's still mortifying. Such incidents, and an accompanying possibility of violence at or after games, used to be far more common. Football crowds, football stadiums, and the experience of attending a football match in general, were all so wildly different just forty years ago, it is hard to compute.

In 1983, things had gotten so bad that sports ministers from the Council of Europe met to discuss how to stop what one of them termed 'soccer terrorism'.[4] The crisis football was in by this point had been brewing for a while, tied in with wider moral panics over juvenile delinquency and male youth violence. Stuart Hall warned in the late 1970s of an 'amplification spiral', whereby exaggerated media reports exacerbated fears of trouble, which fed calls for police and judicial crackdowns, which fed greater confrontation with fans, and so on.[5]

In some cases, forecasts of violence in the press seemed to add to the real-world likelihood of it. 'Scandal of Soccer's Savages – Warming Up for the New Season' ran one such headline in the *Daily Mirror* in August 1973. Vociferous, dehumanising language has been used about football crowds for decades, to the point that headlines like this just feel routine: 'RIOT! United's Fans Are Animals' (*Sunday People*, 1975); 'SAVAGES! ANIMALS!' (*Daily Mirror*, 1975); 'Smash These Thugs' (the *Sun*, 1976). 'Cage the Animals', urged the *Daily Mirror* in 1976 – a morbid foretaste of the tragedies that would soon follow, as trouble on the terraces was met with harsher policing and higher fencing. The same newspaper made the following suggestion in 1977:

> Another idea might be to put these people in 'hooligan compounds' every Saturday afternoon . . . They should be herded together preferably in a public place. That way they could be held up to ridicule and exposed for what they are – mindless morons with no respect for other people's property or wellbeing. We should make sure we treat them like animals – for their behaviour proves that's what they are.

In Bill Buford's seminal piece of 1980s hooligan reportage, *Among the Thugs*, the American writer spends a heroic amount of time with men who are obsessive in their dedication to the street violence and obscene alcohol consumption associated with 'the English disease'. Buford throws himself right into the cages, and emerges to argue that the dense physicality of the football terrace is a truly unique experience. 'This, I thought, is the way animals behave,' Buford wrote: 'herd animals . . . sheep behave this way. Cattle, horses.' But it is a diagnostic mistake to see people forced to huddle together like animals, and conclude that they therefore warrant comparison to animals.

Buford spends time with members of the neo-Nazi National Front, who were recruiting at football grounds at this point, their members overlapping with key figures in football hooligan firms, as they are known. He details the powerful personalities of the firm leaders, and how they inspire a particular devotion as well as providing leadership in how to respond when 'it goes off'. What is missing here is a necessary distinction between 'the firm' and 'the crowd' – the former is more like a criminal gang, with a stratified hierarchy, as well as rituals ensuring loyalty and deference. Being small, these groups demand deeper and much more intense social bonds, derived from a willingness to engage in – indeed, the apparent joy of engaging in – serious violence and criminality. 'Casuals' (hooligans, or ultras) have long sought to mark themselves out from their fellow fans, the general crowd of 'scarfers', with their choice of clothes – a hooligan would never do anything so tacky (and revealing to cops and rivals) as wearing his own team's colours.

The ostensibly baffling thing is that a lot of this historic football firm violence was often perfectly rational. The participants wanted to commit it, they planned to commit it (often going so far as to coordinate out-of-sight, out-of-town meeting points for a scrap with their opposite numbers, away from the police), and they evidently enjoyed it immensely – enough to do it again next time. No one was being 'swept up' in a 'moment of madness' by the 'contagious violence' or 'hysteria' of the crowd, or by sinister agitators with dark motives. The number of people involved in football violence tended to number in two or three figures, not four or five – 'a small minority of troublemakers', as the news would sometimes concede: really, a *tiny* minority, which is distinct from the crowd at large, and nonetheless frequently associated with it.

In his quest to discover the appeal of deranging levels of booze and violence to a small demographic of young British men, what

Buford describes is fascinating. But 1980s hooligan culture appears most of all like a series of social 'fight clubs', tacked on to a football team and a locality. Again, to blame the stomach-churning violence catalogued in *Amongst the Thugs* on 'the crowd', not on the small number of conscious individuals who were habitually and joyfully meting it out, is not just an obvious category error, it is also to let people called things like Bonehead, Steamin' Sammy and Paraffin Pete off the hook.

The word 'hooligan' and the associated moral panic have largely faded from the front pages over time, but only because the football crowd has been reconstituted and reassembled from above. The same Rupert Murdoch media empire that had derided a 'slum sport' and its 'slum people' in 1985 was, barely a few years later, cashing in on it, and using the game to rescue the ailing new satellite station Sky TV. In a landmark deal, Murdoch's newly created merger BSkyB won the rights to show games from the newly formed Premier League in 1992. It heralded a wholesale gentrification of the sport, as money flooded in which would transform it forever. Prior to the BSkyB deal, in 1986 ITV had paid £6.3 million for a two-year exclusive to show top-flight English games. The first Murdoch deal, in 1992, paid the Premier League £304 million for five years of coverage. Jump ahead to today, and the most recent Premier League TV rights deal signed was worth £6.7 billion, for four years.

Concealed within these obscene numbers, and at the heart of this extraordinary transformation, is a tragedy: the avoidable deaths of ninety-seven Liverpool fans at or following the match between Liverpool and Nottingham Forest at Hillsborough, on 15 April 1989. The story of those deaths, and the travesties of justice and cover-ups that followed, may be well known to some readers, and is documented in due detail elsewhere. What I would like to show is how a Le Bonian contempt for the English football crowd led to those deaths, and provided the ideological grounding for the establishment's injurious defamations afterwards, as the traumatised survivors and victims' families sought justice.

The architecture of Sheffield Wednesday's Hillsborough ground illustrates the point in itself. The Leppings Lane terrace, where scores were killed and hundreds injured, was fronted with three-metre-high, reinforced, overhanging mesh fencing, designed to keep fans caged in. The easiest safety valve in the event of a crowd emergency at any sports stadium is the most obvious one: the pitch itself. But football fans could not be trusted, so they were kept locked in their cage. Even as the Liverpool fans in the Leppings Lane terrace were screaming for their lives, police refused to open the few small gates in the fence – and initially pushed back some fans trying to escape by climbing over the top. There was no fence-cutter onsite, and the metal fencing had to be painstakingly twisted and forced open by hand – by which time it was too late. The structural engineer John Cutlack, appearing as an expert witness at the second Hillsborough inquest, said that the official Leppings Lane capacity of 10,100 was 'substantially' excessive for the space available, and that the correct safe figure should have been 7,247 people. It was, he concluded, 'a remarkable failure'.[6]

The tragedy was entirely foreseeable and entirely preventable. Basic safety checks to the Leppings Lane end and its entrances and exits would have been failed, had they been carried out – and Sheffield Wednesday would have been compelled to make immediate improvements. The narrow bottleneck which was supposed to feed 10,100 fans into the Leppings Lane end through just seven decrepit turnstiles – one of several obvious safety flaws – frequently registered dangerous levels of density. Clear warning signs from crushes at previous matches at Hillsborough had not sharpened the police or football authorities' attention. Ian Lavery MP told Parliament in 2012 about a very similar experience he had had in the Leppings Lane end in 1985, of dangerous and potentially fatal density, with no way of escaping. 'The police approach at that time', he told the House, 'was to treat supporters like animals.'

The rot spread from the very top. The officer in charge on that day in April 1989, Superintendent David Duckenfield, had never overseen a game at Hillsborough before. He eventually admitted he had not carried out any of the usual preparations required for the task; he did not read vital safety documents, and did not even visit the ground before signing off the police's operational plan for the day. It was Duckenfield who made, among numerous other avoidable errors, the fatal decision to open an *exit* gate to the Leppings Lane end just before kick-off, allowing 2,000 extra fans who had been stuck outside to surge into the already unsafe pens. This second group had no idea of the dangerous levels of density down in the terraces, and the fans at the front of the terraces had no idea more people were piling in behind them. Obvious though it ought to be, crowd members do not have access to 'helicopter views' of their situation.

Shortly after 3 p.m., as the game continued on the pitch while many of the ninety-seven were already dead or dying, and fans in the upper tier tried to hoist the desperate and wounded to safety, Duckenfield called not for ambulances, but for police dog teams to be sent to the ground. Subsequent investigations found that as many as forty-one of those who died might have been able to survive, had they been given immediate medical attention. But Duckenfield later admitted that his sole focus prior to the match was on preparing to combat fan misbehaviour, rather than on ensuring public safety – as it apparently also was while the horror was unfolding.

The landmark 2012 *Report of the Independent Hillsborough Panel* exposed much of the elite fear and loathing that had created the tragedy, as well as the tissue of lies emitted by the authorities to cover up their own culpability, and blame it all on the crowd. The report found South Yorkshire Police had altered 100 eyewitness statements to remove criticism of their actions. They had also altered 164 of their officers' own statements, replacing descriptions of the fans as 'animals' with the word 'people'.[7] The perspective of rank-and-file police officers present on the day is revealing: one described a 'tide' of fans arriving at 2:45; another wrote, 'when the mob arrived, I have never seen anything like it'.[8] There was even a baseless conspiracy theory active among South Yorkshire Police that a cadre of violent Liverpool fans without tickets had planned an 'invasion' of the ground. Reflecting the prevailing top-down narrative of a drunk, late-arriving, ticketless horde of Liverpool fans laying siege to Hillsborough, that evening David Duckenfield informed the FA's Graham Kelly that Liverpool supporters had 'forced entry through an exit gate', kicking it down – the same gate we now know Duckenfield had himself ordered to be opened. Kelly then repeated this falsehood on the BBC.

The way the tragedy was reported in the hours, days and weeks that followed was one of the greatest establishment stitch-ups in modern British history. The lies about who was to blame, and the condition and behaviour of the Liverpool crowd, began with the police present on the day. At 6 p.m., while the bodies of the dead were still warm, a police photographer was dispatched to take photos of any beer cans he could find outside the ground, to help construct their narrative of a drunken, loutish crowd. It was a narrative readily lapped up across the British media. The *Sheffield Star* described a 'crazed surge' of Liverpool fans forcing entry to the stadium en masse and provoking the tragedy themselves, a version of events echoed in the *Observer*, the *Sunday Mirror*, the *Yorkshire Post*, the *Evening Standard* and others. Three days after the tragedy, on 18 April 1989, *Liverpool Daily Post* writer John Williams blamed 'the gatecrashers [who] wreaked their fatal havoc; their 'uncontrolled fanaticism and mass hysteria . . . literally squeezed the life out of men, women and children'. It was 'yobbism at its most base', as 'Scouse killed Scouse for no better reason than twenty-two men were kicking a ball.' All of it was complete fiction.

The most notorious of these defamations was the *Sun* front page, written and signed off by editor Kelvin MacKenzie on 19 April, four days after the disaster. The *Sun* was Britain's best-selling newspaper, selling more than 3.5 million copies daily at this point. Fresh, outrageous allegations from South Yorkshire Police about crowd behaviour at Hillsborough had come through, making their way onto the infamous front-page splash: 'THE TRUTH. Some fans picked pockets of victims. Some fans urinated on the brave cops. Some fans beat up PC giving kiss of life.' It was, we now know for certain, completely made up. (MacKenzie's preferred headline had actually been 'YOU SCUM', but junior colleagues talked him out of it.⁹) The *Sun*'s lies and defamations about barbarous Liverpool fans attacking police and robbing the dead and dying had come their way via Tory MP Sir Irvine Patnick, a Sheffield Police Federation spokesman, and four South Yorkshire Police officers. In addition to the revolting fabrications on the front page, the *Sun* carried another gross new detail: 'Sheffield MP Irvine Patnick revealed that in one shameful episode a gang of Liverpool fans noticed that the blouse of a girl trampled to death had risen above her breasts. As a policeman struggled in vain to revive her, the mob jeered: "Throw her up here and we will **** her".'

Less well-known than the *Sun* front page, the *Daily Express* carried the same story on its cover that day, with the following headline: 'POLICE ACCUSE DRUNKEN FANS: Officers "saw sick spectacle of pilfering from the dying"'. The *Express* front page carried quotes from a 'senior police officer' who repeated the Le Bonian fictions: 'It was a sickening spectacle. Some of them were like animals. They were drunk and violent and their actions were vile.'

Irvine Patnick MP played a critical role in the *Express* coverage, too, lending legitimacy to the South Yorkshire Police lies by giving quotes in support of them, saying he had seen the bruising on the cops' bodies. He personally took Prime Minister Margaret Thatcher around the ground, the day after the disaster, and 'told her of the mayhem caused by drunks'. Thatcher's press secretary Bernard Ingham was also there that day, and later wrote what he had learned: 'There would have been no Hillsborough if a mob, who were clearly tanked up, had not tried to force their way into the ground.' Patnick was knighted in 1994, and after his role in defaming the dead and bereaved of Hillsborough was revealed in 2012, there were calls for his knighthood to be revoked; David Cameron, as prime minister, refused. In another highly revealing response at the time, Gustave Le Bon's fellow Frenchman and president of UEFA, Jacques George, Europe's senior football official, blamed the tragedy on 'people's frenzy to enter the stadium come what may . . . One had the impression they were beasts who wanted to charge into an arena.'

The network of senior cops, senior politicians, senior football officials and newspaper editors that conspired to cover up the truth, and replace it with horror stories invented from whole cloth, perfectly illustrates how the establishment collaborates to creatively demonise the crowd, and deflect attention from their own fatal negligence.

Eventually, when the 2012 Hillsborough Inquiry finally revealed the truth, Patnick and MacKenzie would issue mealy-mouthed apologies, after decades doggedly sticking to their lies – accompanied by risible professions of having been 'misled'. After numerous inquests, inquiries and trials, not a single officer has been convicted, including David Duckenfield, found not guilty of manslaughter, and several other officers who altered witness statements, and escaped justice on legal technicalities.[10] In the long, tortuous years in which Liverpool fans and their families had campaigned for justice, the gross defamation of the crowd that day, and by extension of football fans and working-class Liverpudlians in general, suited the British establishment's pre-existing agenda. A month before the tragedy, Conservative hereditary peer Lord Onslow had vowed that the government was 'determined to get to grips with the members of the yob class'.[11] A whole class composed of yobs? Slum people? Animals? Louts? Mindless depravity, hysteria and frenzy?

A dark conspiracy to cause violence? A century on from the publication of *The Crowd*, this was Le Bon's work in its entirety, retooled for the age of Thatcher and the Murdoch press.

Despite this failure of accountability, everything changed after Hillsborough – much of it at the institutional and legislative level. The Football Spectators Act 1989 was followed by the seismic Taylor Report 1990, which introduced compulsory all-seater stadiums, and then the creation of the Premier League with its lucrative TV money in 1992. Football became more expensive, more middle-class, safer and more sedate. It is not just the fans' behaviour that has been on a journey since 1989, but the police's too. In 2005 the government established a dedicated UK Football Policing Unit (UKFPU), which today bears the hallmarks of years of expert lobbying by crowd psychologists who have sought to move the police and football authorities on from the mindset that led to the deaths at Hillsborough.

In a sign of the times, the UKFPU annual report for 2022 does not once mention 'crowd control'. Instead, it speaks a great deal about 'engagement' with supporters, 'involving' the vast majority of fans who are not considered a trouble risk, and 'influencing' anyone who might be liable to act up, should the circumstances be aggravating. New police roles of dedicated football officer (DFO) and operational football officer (OFO) are tasked with building 'experience and knowledge of the supporter community' and instructed to 'develop their football community knowledge', deploying at home and away fixtures in all of the top five leagues, plus the FA and EFL cups. Essentially, their job is to enter the crowd and be part of it – a version of the blue-tabard-wearing police liaison officers (PLOs) who mingle in protest crowds, but with a working knowledge of the offside system and their club's new defensive midfielder.

At the forefront of this work, as he has been for decades now, is Clifford Stott. For Stott, the critical factor in whether amped-up crowd members clash with police is the perception of legitimacy and fairness in the police's actions – when cops are aggressive, steam in heavy-handedly, or engage in collective punishment, fans are more likely to react. The goal, he told me, should be to encourage crowd members towards 'self-regulation and consent, and encourage the police to reduce their reliance on coercion. Where the police have these capacities for dialogue and communication, there's less disorder. It's as simple as that.'

Working with the football governing bodies and police forces across Europe and beyond, Stott and his colleagues have had some success using empirically grounded, modern crowd psychology to campaign for a more enlightened approach. In the policing of the fractious Glasgow 'Old Firm' derby, for example, in the 2006–7 season, Strathclyde Police were persuaded to experiment with implementing cutting-edge academic advice based on a better understanding of crowd behaviour and dynamics.

In practice, this meant advance consultations with fan groups and, on the day, riot police hanging back and regular, less threatening beat officers allowing Rangers and Celtic supporters to jeer at each other a bit, from a safe distance, because they know that's part of the ritual – a key part of the appeal of the Old Firm, even. Serious intervention and riot squads were always on standby, in case things did get violent, but for once the police focus was on de-escalating tensions, friendly engagement with fans, and – though it went against all their instincts – trusting the crowd to self-regulate any outlier behaviour from individuals. The result was less animosity towards the police and reduced incidences of violence between groups of fans. It is still a work in progress, though. A 2019 *Independent Review of Football Policing in Scotland* found a clear and consistent view among supporters that policing 'was "being done to them" and not "with them"'.

Another notable experiment in football crowd policing took place at Bradford City's August 2017 season opener, at home to Blackpool. Ahead of time it was deemed a 'medium risk' game, with some chance of disorder between fans of two historic

Lancashire and Yorkshire clubs, and a near-capacity crowd of 20,000 expected, of which 900 would be supporters travelling from Blackpool. With fifty 'yellow-jacketed' public order police officers out of sight and on standby, Chief Superintendent Owen West – a vocal advocate of engagement-led policing and now a university lecturer – deployed just eight police liaison officers for the game. Taking a 'meet and greet role', they 'actively engaged, chatted, and welcomed fans to the city'. The gamble seemed in danger of collapsing into a pile of smashed pint glasses, when, prior to the game, a group of 'high risk' Bradford fans entered a designated 'away pub' full of Blackpool fans. The senior cops, weighing their options from a control room, immediately tensed up and considered scrambling their fifty regular officers into action.

'But we weren't in the moment, the conversation, banter and engagement with the fans; we commanders couldn't "feel" it,' West wrote later.[12]

> But our PLTs [Police Liaison Teams] were right 'in the mix'. The liaison officers assured me it was OK, that they were on top of the situation – and they were right. Consequently, there was no inter-vention by public order cops, no escalation on our part, because the assessment of risk was dynamic and detailed. So there were 'risk fans' from both teams present but our PLTs were in the pub, they were managing the interactions and preventing what was ultimately an unnecessary tactical escalation on the part of the police. They were not just policing the fans but also 'policing the police', if you will. We let it run. It was a risk worth taking.

In an extraordinary moment, one of the police liaison officers even led a 'singsong' between the two sets of fans in the pub. With a mood of jocular conviviality established between the fans, thanks to sparse, low-key engagement from inside the heart of the crowd, and no provocation or escalation from suited-up squads of public order cops, West felt comfortable enough to stand down half of his fifty officers before the match even began, and the other half before the game was over. The Blackpool fans reported that they were delighted to be treated like adults for once, rather than marshalled and bullied, and had a great day out in Bradford.

This kind of policing, drawing on the persistent work of a handful of British crowd psychologists, is pushing against a tide of historic myths and assumptions, and decades of ideologically determined training. The handful of senior officers who are willing to take it on do so in the teeth of considerable institutional resistance – within the police, but also within centres of political and media power, and the football authorities. There will, Owen West warned, be no shortage of people inside and outside the police ready to say 'I told you so' the minute an experiment like this fails. 'We've come a considerable distance, but the history of police reform is littered with disaster,' Stott told me. 'The difficulty is that in a policing environment, change doesn't come easily. In a sense, you can consider football fans a marginalised community, in that there is a lot of coercion going on – there's a lot of people getting arrested. The traditional public order response is to try and police the problem through coercion, through force and displays of force. Whereas our work on crowds has shown that if you take a different approach, where people are more likely to see the policing as legitimate, then you can create an environment where football fans start to self-regulate more, and there is a drop in the levels of criminality.'

Getting British police forces to adopt this expert guidance has proven more difficult. In a 2020 ethnographic study of five matches in England and Scotland, Stott and his colleagues concluded that football policing had fallen behind on some of the reforms they had helped implement in the policing of political demonstrations, designed to reduce conflict, despite being covered by the same statutory guidance.[13] One overarching theme they discovered was a 'problematic relationship between football intelligence and operational planning'. Rather than liaising with fan groups ahead of time, and verbally engaging with supporters on the day in a friendly manner, the police remained firmly outside the crowd and uncommunicative, relying on exaggerated or sketchy intelligence that assumed a worst-case scenario. Senior commanders were too quick to ramp up the 'threat' and 'risk' level, often on flimsy evidence, and so batons were being drawn at the first hints of trouble – inevitably generating and escalating tensions, and leading them to devote more resources to old-school 'crowd control'. Ultimately, the report found that the police were wasting a great deal of public money on being over-prepared for trouble that wasn't at all likely to happen.

Stott and his colleagues also found possible human rights violations incurred by the police's restriction of freedom of expression (Article 10 of the European Convention of Human Rights) and freedom of assembly and association (Article 11). Even in an age where fans are sold gourmet nachos and craft beer, rather than hot dogs and Bovril, some police chiefs seem unwilling to move on.

The government continues to keep a very close eye on trouble at football matches – which, usefully, means there are plenty of dedicated statistics to consider. Football-related arrests dropped every year but one in the eight seasons before the pandemic, falling by more than half, from 3,089 arrests in the 2010–11 season to 1,381 in the 2018–19 season. They then rose again in the first proper season after Covid, 2021–22, to 2,198, prompting sensationalist warnings about resurgent hooliganism, and lurid speculation that people had 'forgotten how to behave' during the pandemic.

Of those 2,198 arrests – still substantially lower than the numbers a decade earlier – by far the greatest number were for possession of pyrotechnics, accounting for a third of all arrests, and a largely new phenomenon. Most of those flares were never set off – they will have been intercepted during a door search, and their owners arrested. As football journalist Jamie Greer has pointed out, cocaine and pyrotechnic use may well have increased at games in recent years, but it has also done so at music festivals, and in society at large; is football again being singled out?[14] When you consider that the aggregate attendance for the 2021–22 English football season easily exceeded 30 million, the figure of 2,198 arrests across the year makes the football crowd look like an extraordinarily wholesome bunch.[15]

The all-seater stadiums mandated by the Taylor Report has changed the experience of attending a football match immeasurably. It has completely removed the physicality and tactility of the crowd experience, and with it, of course, almost all the physical danger. For better and worse, terraces cannot be mosh-pits anymore, succumbing to surges, waves and compression. Crowds are subdivided, monitored and measured to within an inch of their lives. Each person has a numbered seat, an autonomous space that is theirs, demarcated from the rest, easily identified via CCTV; there is a guaranteed level of atomisation, the obstructive plastic seats making even jostling your immediate neighbour in the event of a goal slightly tricky. The modern stadium is a modern theatre, essentially, and like in a modern theatre, egress when the curtain goes down is painfully (i.e., safely) slow: filtering out row by row, you have no choice but to perform the inch-by-inch slow shuffle of churchgoers solemnly leaving their pews.

One common view about football post–Taylor Report is that the energy and volume of the crowd atmosphere has been destroyed by all-seater stadiums and the general embourgeoisement of the game, that passionate working-class fans have been replaced by indifferent, monied middle-class consumers, or fly-by-night visitors with none of the chauvinistic localism which used to define a club. 'You're just a bunch of tourists' was one chant the AFC Wimbledon fans aimed at the Chelsea crowd in that League Cup game – a stinging blow in a climate where authenticity is everything. Football culture demands a long career of suffering in order to establish your credentials as a legitimate crowd member.

It is true that international football tourism has become a big part of top-flight football. In the same way as people might coordinate a foreign holiday around a music festival, New Year's Eve or some other spectacular attraction, they now do so around a visit to Anfield or Old Trafford. The lament of those who declare themselves 'Against Modern Football' (AMF) is that casual contemporary fans weaken the atmosphere and the crowd's internal bonds, rendering it more of a generic entertainment audience, like people who happen to assemble at the cinema on a Saturday night. When Manchester City hosted Liverpool in November 2023, it ought to have been a ferocious contest – two giants of the sport, who had won all of the previous six Premier League titles between them. And yet City manager Pep Guardiola was seen on several occasions leaving his dugout and turning to face the home crowd, evidently frustrated at their silence, and encouraging them to sing up. Responses from rival supporters on social media mocked City's 'plastic fans', gloating that the best team in the world, worth $4.99 billion to its Emirati royal ownership, were missing 'the one thing money can't buy': the passion of an authentic crowd. A few weeks later, Liverpool manager Jurgen Klopp made an identical complaint about his club's home atmosphere. 'Give your ticket to somebody else' if you're not going to make a decent racket, he urged the fans.

There is one concrete policy idea that seeks to restore some of football's lost atmosphere, one for which fan groups have campaigned for years, and which is now finally coming to fruition. This is 'safe standing', or 'railed standing', where crowd members are each allocated a flip-down plastic seat as usual, but are officially permitted to stand up throughout: there are rails in each row at chest height, to lean on, and to prevent any surges or collapses should the excitement get too much. It is such a calm, reasonable solution to a long-running problem. As AFC Wimbledon journeyed through the amateur lower leagues, we had both old-school standing terraces (without perimeter fencing, which was banned after Hillsborough) and then 'safe standing' in our new ground – all excellent, enjoyable, and entirely safe, making for a warmer (literally warmer, which is appreciated when you are playing in England on a January evening) and more convivial atmosphere.

And yet, where there are police and politicians, there is the ghost of Gustave Le Bon. In January 2022, after endless safety checks, consultations and preparations, the 'safe standing' pilot began. It was the first time in three decades that fans at any top-flight English match had been officially permitted to stand. To mark the occasion, Chief Constable Mark Roberts, the National Policing Lead on football – the most senior football cop in the country – gave an interview to the BBC.[16] What he said revealed just how the reactionary view of the crowd is hardwired into the minds of people with power over it:

'If crowds are stood up,' Roberts declared, 'it's easier to throw missiles, engage in hate chanting, racism, sneak alcohol in, take cocaine . . .'

Even by the standards of intellectual reasoning we have become used to from the British police, attributing racism and drug use to *standing up* was quite the surprise. His warnings, offering no evidence but widely and uncritically reported, have now been proven completely unfounded. In July 2023, after eighteen months of safe standing pilots at nine top English and Welsh grounds, the Sports Ground Safety Authority (SGSA), the organisation responsible for inspecting and licensing the ninety-two football league grounds (and Wembley), produced its findings: improved safety, clear aisles, reduced risk of falling, a more positive relationship between stewards and fans, and happier fans in general.[17] Once again, absurd, doom-laden forecasts about crowd behaviour proved to be nonsense when placed under the slightest scrutiny.

Ken Scott is head of inspectorate at the SGSA, and I spoke to him a month after the report came out. 'I know Mark [Roberts], I respect Mark, I disagree entirely with Mark's comments,' Scott said drolly. 'The introduction of the rail is completely neutral to the problems that he identified. So putting a rail in front of someone doesn't all of a sudden make them an aggressive supporter, nor does it turn them into a racist.' Feedback from police officers who supervised the new railed seating was extremely positive. 'They are the people who are there day in, day out and match in, match out, and they're coming back and saying that it's absolutely brilliant. I hope it's going to be sobering for Mark to realise he's wrong, and we can move on. It's even better that it's coming from his own police officers. We're not saying it's made all previously badly behaved fans into saints, but it's done nothing in the other direction – the rail doesn't change behaviour. Fans like [Celtic's] Green Brigade are going to stand, sing [banned] sectarian chants and so on either way – now they're at least doing it more safely.'

A former chartered surveyor, Scott was first drafted in by the SGSA in 2013 to help write the organisation's Green Guide to stadium safety. 'I felt that the biggest Achilles heel of the organisation, and of football generally, was this risk that wasn't being mitigated: people standing in areas that aren't designed for them to stand in.' They commissioned independent research that showed how a return to crowds standing on the terraces could be achieved safely, and the challenge was then to persuade the government to change the post-Hillsborough legislation to allow it, with the campaigning from fans around the country 'a constant drumbeat in the background'.

The year 2024 marks the thirty-fifth anniversary of the Hillsborough disaster, and for Scott it seems to be a relief, more than anything, that the battle for safe standing has been won at last. A key moment along the way was gaining the endorsement of the Hillsborough Family Support Group and other Liverpool fans. Around 14,000 people were persistently standing up on the world-famous Kop at Anfield anyway, and without rails, this risked another tragedy; the club has now been issued with a safe standing licence, with substantial parts of the ground newly equipped with railed seating. 'For me, it's a legacy to the people who lost their lives that day,' Scott said. 'It took so many years of battling to prove their innocence. No one should have to go through anything like that ever again. We won't tolerate the idea that anyone gets seriously injured, or worse, at a football match, because of a risk that we all know is out there.'

The SGSA was formed directly after and directly because of Hillsborough.[18] Up to and including that event, there was a tendency to see crowds of football fans as a homogeneous mass of people, with a predisposition towards making trouble. It turns out that football fans, like all crowds, have a diverse array of desires, needs and behaviours. Some of them might want to be a bit more exuberant, to bounce up and down, sing and swear throughout the ninety minutes, while others may have mobility issues and need better exit routes; there are parents with kids who are going to get bored and distracted, or need the toilet or an emergency hamburger; there are older fans who just want to watch the game in peace, with an unobstructed view. Understanding the complexity and variety of crowd behaviour has completely changed the accepted truisms of events safety planning, Scott said.

'I think one of the things that we don't often get credit for is how much we've learned since 1989,' he concluded. 'Prior to that, if you read all of the inquiries [following] the disasters, whether it be Ibrox, whether it be Hysel, whether it be Bradford, it was always a case of a horrible missed opportunity. The intention back then was always to control the crowd, rather than manage it. After Hillsborough, and the Taylor Report, things really did change – and I'm not just talking about the SGSA, I'm talking about all of the organisations involved in crowd safety. Finally the style of policing has moved away from controlling crowds, to asking, "How can we work with psychologists to understand them better?"'

While surveilled modern sports crowds try to rediscover some of their lost vigour, the authorities will always be on the lookout for things 'going off'. As distant as it may now be, the spectre of

1980s hooliganism still haunts the game – a ghost summoned when it is most convenient. The British media love warning of a 'return to the dark days of the 1980s' – to the point that it has become a cliché – the minute anything goes wrong. Is this fair? It is certainly true that in the last few years bottles and coins have been thrown at players, and racist abuse has been seen at every level of English football. It's not great – but it's also miles away from the churn of cheap lager, piss, Sieg-Heiling and gleeful ultra-violence Bill Buford documented in *Among the Thugs*.

Even now, you are treated with little-to-no trust that you might plausibly be a responsible adult. Collective punishments in response to individual transgressions are still the norm. Even in lowly League Two, where I've barely ever seen any trouble, I've recently seen fans sternly told off for *vaping*, outdoors, in the area behind a stand; and I've seen a quiet, sober fan aggressively wrestled and kicked out of the ground by thuggish security guards for wearing a red scarf, because the away team was wearing red that day (it was just a plain red scarf, unaffiliated with the away team). In the 2023–24 season, my club banned the entire fan base from bringing plastic bottles into the ground, including water, at the beginning of August, because one fan had thrown a full bottle of Coca-Cola onto the pitch, once. This is how stern teachers treat infant-school children.

But people keep coming back, myself included – not least because things are gradually getting better. For Ken Scott, the treatment of British football fans should be entering its 'mature phase', at last.

'It's worth looking at the development of stewarding as a model,' Scott reflected. 'The professional steward is something that wasn't around in the late '80s. If you distil it, football matches are essentially private events, being carried out by private individuals, so why should the police be there? Stewards often have better interpersonal skills, they are well-known to the fans, they can calm situations – you can remove the need for police, so that police are only there as the last resort. That, for me, is a huge step forward in the way that we do things in the UK, and long may it continue.'

Despite all the matches I go to, it hadn't really occurred to me, but he's right – in the partisan world of football, there's always a sudden frisson in the air on the occasions that police officers appear in the stadium, as sometimes happens midway through an ill-tempered second half. It's like your house party has just been raided, and the crowd visibly, audibly prickles at the sight. But these occasions are becoming rarer.

In the 2022–23 season, over 50 per cent of professional football matches played in England and Wales did not have a police presence at all.[19] And what better sign of progress could you ask for – indeed, what better tribute to those who died at Hillsborough – than that?

5

The World Turned Upside Down:
Carnival Crowds

For those who love it, Notting Hill Carnival is the best weekend of the year. Indeed, for the aficionado, even the build-up in the early weeks of August contains a latent energy. As the London summer wears on, the capital's residential streets lie quieter and more idle than usual: those who can afford it are on foreign holidays in sunnier climes, while the desk-bound martyrs left behind still drudge into work. But something is simmering, there are scattered clues of the crowd-in-waiting – billboard posters in Jamaican green, gold and black announcing Carnival after-parties, or a passing car blaring dancehall or Afrobeats out of its open windows – like bugles announcing the coming procession that is just over the hill, a fleeting sound that is fat with promise. And what is it heralding? On each of Carnival's two days, a congregation of 1 million people, a parade of 100-plus sound system trucks, forty towering static sound systems, some sixty bands and 300 food and drink stalls, crammed into a 3.5-square-kilometre site, a space where just 47,000 people normally live.[1]

One of the greatest things about joining any large crowd, whether it is for a carnival, a major concert, a sporting event or a protest, is the growing anticipation of its powers, the horizon of great density and sensory overload which looms ever nearer, and louder. This frisson of nervous excitement can be a physical sensation in itself, a tingle of anxious adrenaline. You know it will be almost overwhelming, you can feel its murmuring swell of collective energy emanating outwards from the centre towards you, even before you hear or see it, in ripples and then in waves.

As you journey from your home towards the crowd, little foretastes of its pleasures arrive in the form of your soon-to-be fellow crowd members: the crowd not yet bonded together, but marked out by their dress, or their behaviour. Like a supermarket employee in uniform on the bus, they are out of place, but their attire tells you where they are headed. On Notting Hill Carnival weekend, the exploded rainbow that is Carnival clothing is unmistakable: the bold colours, mesh vests and hot pants, the eruption of glitter on a girl's cheek, the Trinidadian, Barbadian or Jamaican flag bandana tied around a wrist, the contraband cans of beer in hand, the bottles clinking in blue plastic off-licence bags, the groups talking with the same excitable, gesticulating high energy and high volume as you and your friends board the otherwise still sedate, workaday train, still some forty minutes from your destination.

These are usually quiet and inhibited places by mutual social agreement, but on Carnival weekend, they are liberated. You have the sense of being a small tributary stream, barely a trickle, meeting and joining with another trickling stream, then a slightly larger one, and then, at each stop, gaining more momentum – all bound by the unspoken thrill that together you are about to become an unstoppable force, moving with zeal and momentum towards others going the same way, and that the end result, the thundering river, will be as powerful as it is inevitable.

The climax of this rising feeling of excitement and anxiety is the moment of arrival: the moment you grace the stop of the concrete steps in a football stadium or a concert arena or, for Notting Hill Carnival, the ticket barriers at Westbourne Park tube station – and they give way suddenly to reveal the messy fringes of the crowd. Before you, a web of streets fizzing with concrete heat and human warmth, a sea of bodies already vibrating with movement and laughter. As you meld seamlessly into the maze, the syrupy sweetness of Wizkid and Tems's hit 'Essence' is drifting over the crowd, punctuated by whistles and horns. The bobbing heads lean back to the narrow sky, their flag scarves and open palms are raised up, and they sing as one, '*You don't need no other body / only you fi hold my body*'. It's a love song, a corny, smoochy love song, but its message of intimate coupledom is purely ironic here, sung with the glee of the massed chorus, drowning out the original blaring from the booming speaker stacks. We are here because we need *all* these bodies.

The way that people move through congested areas at Carnival – which is to say, almost all of them – is an acquired skill. You form a snake, bolshiest or tallest person at the front, often holding hands, or caressing the shoulder of the person in front of you to indicate that *I'm with this lot coming through too, please don't close up just yet!* I often find myself protecting our little dance circle (and it is tiny, but big enough for a couple of bedraggled carrier bags of booze to be thrown on the ground) like I'm a central defender at a corner: shoulders back, elbows back, leaning back ever so slightly, using my weight to stop our circle caving in. Sometimes the crowd is so packed you end up dancing literally back-to-back with someone whose eyes you never meet – a level of anonymised intimacy which would be ridiculous in any other context.

When squishing uncomfortably past someone, one of the small joys of Carnival is sharing a brief joke with a passing stranger ('Good luck getting through there mate, ha-ha'). The hand on a shoulder helping them squeeze through the throng. The smile and half-rolled eyes at the craziness of it all, the nod of thanks. The regular snatches of conversations with strangers at Carnival are a delight: *Oh my god I love your shirt where did you get it, what a fucking banger this one is, total madness innit, sorry have you got a lighter, do you want a toke on this, you having a good one yeah, it's rum and coke, sure help yourself no worries, hey excuse me aren't you Kasia's mate.* There is something freeing, and exciting, about knowing that this kind of conviviality does not exist anywhere else, that today all bets are off, that today feels different, that it *is* different.

I mean, of course, it's different: at 10 a.m. on a Sunday morning I am performing my annual ritual, decanting a whole bottle of rum into two larger bottles of ginger beer, and pushing slivers of lime through each bottleneck. It is a discombobulating way to start a Sunday. There follows a substantial but hurried breakfast, a gathering of vital accoutrements – shades, hat, sunblock, waterproof jacket, beer, rum, water, vape – and by 11:30 we are on the first of three trains from south to west London, beers in hand. These are special days which begin differently, and end differently – with your phone dead, head lolling tipsily on the tube home, legs buzzing with warmth and humming with lactic acid after completing 36,000 steps – thirty kilometres, all in Carnival's 3.5-square-kilometre site.

In the heart of the Carnival crowd, in the heat of the mid-afternoon, your five senses seem to blend together like wine. Alcohol, marijuana and jerk barbecue fumes fuse with the distant rumble of soca and dancehall sub-bass from the trucks and sound systems, all of it thickening the late summer air. It is the giddy feeling of being completely and unavoidably submerged in the crowd, and yet powered up by it – diving in headfirst, losing a part of yourself, and your independence, and being glad to do so. In the midst of all this noise and bustle and intensity there is a lightness, a gentle dizziness, as if you could collapse dreamily into your dancing neighbours' arms and be held up by them. Spilled rum and ginger beer caramelises in the heat on your bare forearms, already sticky with sweat. Time slows down, and five hours dancing, laughing and talking nonsense could be five days.

The next days are suffused with the afterglow of crowd joy, but also the poignancy of 'Carnival tabanca' – the ennui and lovesick longing for that overflowing cup of freedom and conviviality: the phantom limbs of a million strangers, denied to you for another fifty-one weeks. Specific memories linger and coalesce in the haze.

I find myself returning to the few fleeting moments where it occurred to me to take a step back and marvel at it all; hopping up onto a small front garden wall for a better view of all those smiling faces, those arms raised aloft in unison, those groups of old and new friends lost in conversation. And then, like stepping through a portal in a cheap science fiction film, you return to street level, and are immediately welcomed back into the mayhem again.

It is a paradox of Carnival that while its outré costuming and musical brilliance thrives on the unabashed expression of *individual* creativity and charisma, its true appeal is the liberation to be found in equalising everything. The essence of Carnival is ego death via the levelling effect of mass assembly and collective joy. 'Each man is as near the other as he is to himself; and an immense feeling of relief ensues,' wrote Elias Canetti in the classic *Crowds and Power* (1960). 'It is for the sake of this blessed moment, when no one is greater or better than another, that people become a crowd.' The Carnival crowd is, like the fiery protest crowd, arguably prefigurative, a form of socialism-in-the-making, a breathing, writhing insight into the kind of self-organised collectivity, cooperation and joy denied to us in everyday life under capitalism, working bullshit jobs to generate profits for other people. *Let's have a look at what you could have won.*

Carnival is not just an event, or even a small chain of events – in Rio de Janeiro, in Port of Spain, in London, in New Orleans, in Venice – but an idea, one that spans not just continents but centuries, with deep roots and a constellation of loaded meanings and motifs. The Cádiz *carnavalero* and songwriter Paco Rosado once said that Carnival is 'a philosophy, an aesthetics of the abnormal . . . above all things, Carnival is freedom, a necessary escape from the everyday.'[2] When the Franco regime accepted that they were losing their battle to abolish the city's pre-Lenten Carnival, they relinquished just enough control to permit what they called '*fiestas típicas*', or traditional festivities. Tellingly, though, that is what they had to be called. The word *carnaval* remained prohibited, even when many of its constituent practices, like the singing and costuming, were permitted to resume. It carries too much weight, too much threat of insubordination – and so it remained unspeakable.

Carnival is the crowd at play, and, perhaps, at its best: acting out a set of rituals which are innate to who we are, a vital and constant presence through the *longue durée* of human experience and evolution. There is, as Johan Huizinga argued in his 1938 study *Homo Ludens*, a 'primordial quality' to human play, in adults as in children. Play is older than culture, he writes, because culture 'presupposes human society, and animals have not waited for man to teach them their playing'. As Barbara Ehrenreich's masterful *Dancing in the Streets* recounts, dancing, singing, music-making, costuming, masquerading and taking intoxicants with others, in a general atmosphere of irreverence, are a vital, ancient part of who we are as social animals; they are the method by which we first shook off the last drips of primordial soup and came together to fix a proper meal. Dancing together, she argues, is a human evolutionary imperative, preceding even speech as a social glue: just look at the profusion of Palaeolithic cave paintings of people dancing in unison.[3]

The theory goes that our ancient ancestors had to assemble in groups larger than just the family unit: initially, anthropologists think, groups of about ten to fifteen people. To help in the formation of social bonds, early human beings learned to dance – moving and drumming in rhythm to scare off predators. In strictly Darwinian terms, and at the risk of blinding you with science: these first crowds of human dancers survived, while the wallflowers got eaten by tigers. After we learned to dance together, we created languages; and as time passed, we started to construct civilisations. We built roads and sanitation systems, created organised religions and governments. Eventually, we invented glow sticks, superclubs and UK garage.

Civilisation has come some way since early humans danced around fires, casting a pattern of coordinated shadows on the cave wall, and had such a good time that they decided to record it for posterity. But are the cave painters of Palaeolithic Borneo or South Africa that different from someone posting a video of last night's gig or dance floor to their Instagram? Not so much has changed since then.

Carnival, like crowd membership in general, is part of who we are as self-organising, social, cultural beings. Its spirit is still discernible, even when it is caged, or camouflaged in sanitised or 'family-friendly' contexts: in the embarrassing tedium of a Mexican Wave during a World Cup game where nothing is happening on the pitch; in an Elton John singalong at Glastonbury; in a damp, musty suburban park on Bonfire Night. All of these moments contain the sublimated desire for the more reckless, anarchic lineage of Carnival, and are not to be dismissed or mocked (apart from the Mexican Wave – you can mock the Mexican Wave). Tamed or not, the impulse to the carnivalesque is ever-present, and irresistible. The repressed will keep on returning and returning – and adapting, just as Carnival itself has done across millennia. Even when the form changes, the fundamentals remain constant: the costuming, hedonism, dancing, music and inversion of everyday social relations – eliding barriers and levelling hierarchies.

In his pioneering 1936 study of medieval Carnival culture, *Rabelais and His World*, Mikhail Bakhtin writes:

> Carnival does not know footlights, in the sense that it does not acknowledge any distinction between actors and spectators. Footlights would destroy a carnival, as the absence of footlights would destroy a theatrical performance. Carnival is not a spectacle seen by the people; they live in it, and everyone participates because its very idea embraces all the people. While carnival lasts, there is no other life outside it. During carnival time life is subject only to its laws, that is, the laws of its own freedom. It has a universal spirit; it is a special condition of the entire world, of the world's revival and renewal, in which all take part.

The true spirit of Carnival should be, as it was in the medieval age, totalising – nothing remained outside it, nobody was spectating, because everyone was participating in it. Within it, there is, theoretically at least, absolute freedom – from social rank, religious codes and behavioural norms. With its total removal of barriers, it is inherently anti-elitist. Medieval Carnival was about the extravagant, humorous celebration and satirising of the usual tensions between 'high' and 'low' status – in order that they might collapse. Bakhtin salutes 'that special marketplace atmosphere in which the exalted and the lowly, the sacred and the profane are levelled and are all drawn into the same dance'.

Nothing could remain static, or serious, or restrained, when the medieval Carnival crowd was at play. This was not just an abstract notion, but physically embodied. The moral codes and behavioural norms of the day are disrupted by giving in to the human body – even when it is profane or grotesque, via caricature, masking, costumes, outlandish behaviour and mockery of the polite, formal and saintly.

Elsewhere in his literary criticism, Bakhtin discusses the carnivalesque in terms of Dostoevsky's 'polyphonic' writing style, whereby a pluralistic range of voices is able to speak and coexist at once, 'unmerged' and independent, apparently free from authorial oversight. As Carnival crowd members, we revel in the fact that nobody above is pulling our strings, or scripting our moves – that we are free to be ourselves. At both the Notting Hill and Cádiz Carnivals in the twenty-first century, the scope for bold, eccentric, individual self-expression remains a huge part of the appeal – even if you're not personally up for wearing day-glo hot pants, or loudly singing about how the mayor is a corrupt bastard.

And yet, just as often, the pleasure in crowd membership comes from moments of choral or physical synchrony, of singing or speaking with one unified voice, dancing or drilling in time: the opposite of polyphony. The paradoxical appeal of crowd membership is that it can offer each person the thrills of polyphony *and* the affirmation and amplification of joining the choir (monophony). Your individual voice is empowered in the crowd, whether you are singing along in time to 'Sunshine on Leith' with 26,000 fellow Hibernian fans, all of you sporting the same green-and-white team colours, *or* expressing your unique personality by, say, wearing a tuxedo and doing a waltz to dub reggae in the middle of Notting Hill Carnival. Both are valid forms of participation, and both will be celebrated by the rest of the crowd.

For as long as hierarchical authority has existed, those at the top have lived in fear and suspicion of expressions of collective joy that are defined on the crowd's terms – in fear of the carnivalesque, wherever it appeared. In *The Civilising Process*, Norbert Elias describes the rise of 'good conduct' or etiquette as a means of social control in the early modern period, steered by moralising authority figures who wanted to turn back the medieval tide of bodily fluids and casual insubordination. The evolution and growth of the bourgeoisie meant the spread of bourgeois values: the new rules and censorious codes of behaviour required as markers of social status, in imitation of the aristocratic courtly sensibilities the bourgeois aspired to. But the wealthy and powerful did not deploy these distinguishing social codes only to themselves, as a way of sharpening the boundaries of their own class, but also outwards, in an attempt to police working-class behaviour that aroused fear, envy and embarrassment in them.

As people from different social classes began to live in closer proximity to one another, the behaviour of others came into closer focus. Rules of civility, courtesy and etiquette were cudgels used to beat back festive practices, conviviality and customs that were deemed unbecoming or profane. Rising social tensions and inequality placed the carnivalesque under even greater scrutiny from priests and politicians. In early seventeenth-century England, when class, religious and regional conflicts were intensifying rapidly, and the English Civil War was on the near horizon, folk festivities and political violence frequently overlapped. Morris dances, football and stoolball matches, skittles, bowls and bull-baiting, skimmingtons, church ales, mops, wakes and revels often descended into drunkenness, debauchery and rioting.[4] ''Tis no festival unless there be some fightings', ran a popular Civil War–era expression.[5]

Even with puritanism on the rise, commoners in villages across Europe poured a great deal of enthusiasm into their hyperlocal rituals and festivals – and did so in the face of growing suppression from above. High days and holy days like May Day, Whitsun, Shrove Tuesday and Christmas drew particularly broad and exuberant levels of participation. And once they had celebrated, drunk and sung seditious songs around bonfires and maypoles, proceedings sometimes escalated into riots and assaults on the aristocrats who would ban their fun. One particularly spirited pre-Lenten Carnival in Udine in Italy culminated in the sacking and looting of twenty palaces and the murder of fifty members of the local nobility and their aides.[6] It certainly makes Pancake Day seem a little tame.

At this point, most acts of suppression of the carnivalesque crowd took place at a local level, via magistrates, priests and nobles – but with tensions intensifying, central government got involved. In 1642, as the English Civil War began, Parliament ordered the closure of all London theatres, as dangerous fonts of 'lascivious Mirth and Levity'. And while Christmas was not 'banned by Cromwell' in the period, as is widely believed, the puritans' policing of collective joy in the name of piety did bring Christmas rituals under fire. In 1643, an ordinance was passed by Parliament exhorting the public to abandon folkloric Yuletide celebrations which were 'giving liberty to carnal and sensual delights'. It was followed in 1647 by An Ordinance for Abolishing of Festivals, which sought to strike out not just Christmas but Easter, Whitsun and other feast days – with mixed success. A popular broadside ballad, 'The World Turned Upside Down', was circulated in the 1640s in protest at these gross infringements of the usual saturnalian winter revels: 'The wine pot shall clinke, we will feast and drinke / And then strange motions will abound / Yet let's be content, and the times lament, you see the world turn'd upside down.'

Theatres were perhaps the primary fulcrum of public, popular culture in the early modern period, attracting government interventions and prohibitions even after puritanism had peaked. Eighteenth-century licensing legislation gave the Lord Chamberlain exclusive powers to vet and veto all new plays, without oversight, before the Theatres Act 1843 refined this to allow him to ban any plays where it was necessary to do so 'for the preservation of good manners, decorum, or the public peace'. The threading together of these three nouns is instructive. It brings us back to Norbert Elias's analysis of behavioural codes as a form of social control: the establishment sees bad manners and grassroots festivity as a slippery, dangerously steep slope towards unrest and riot.

The Industrial Revolution only intensified the European establishment's long struggle to disperse the Carnival crowd. The growing urban bourgeoisie wanted raucous mass celebrations banned from the nicer parts of town, while mill and factory bosses demanded a disciplined, ideally teetotal workforce. Ehrenreich suggests that pews were introduced to churches in the eighteenth century because the congregations' ecstatic singing and dancing was getting out of hand and becoming a threat. After all, the practice of worship should be dictated by the priest, who actually speaks to God, not these uncouth commoners down below.[7]

Throughout the early modern period, many of Europe's most famous and popular carnivals and county fairs were banned altogether, or co-opted and tamed, or restricted to more remote parts of town, and hence to smaller crowds. In some cases it was deemed enough to fragment the totalising life of Carnival into discrete parts, such that 'feasting became separated from performance, spectacle from procession'.[8] Some fairs and festivals were banned over and over again, re-emerging in slightly different forms only to arouse the same fear and loathing in the upper classes, and get banned again.

Legislating against the carnivalesque has been a relentless process, and is usually effective, in the short and medium term at least. Just two days after Gustave Le Bon watched the Tuileries

Palace go up in flames, across the English Channel the House of Commons was passing the Fairs Act 1871, a piece of legislation designed solely to enable magistrates and the government to abolish such drunken and immoral local festivities, without discussion or debate. It was immediately implemented, and in the decade that followed, over 700 such fairs were banned – a grey curtain of reaction smothering grassroots popular culture.[9] The concerns and contempt of the establishment are written explicitly into the opening words of the legislation, which is still on the parliamentary statute book today:

> Whereas certain of the fairs held in England and Wales are unnecessary, are the cause of grievous immorality, and are very injurious to the inhabitants of the towns in which such fairs are held, and it is therefore expedient to make provision to facilitate the abolition of such fairs.

The gradual formation of more regimented, organised and centrally determined social relations during the Industrial Revolution coincided with the evolution of crowd politics – from the politics of the food riot to petitions, mass meetings and rallies, and eventually towards trade unions, universal suffrage, and more representative and bureaucratic political parties. 'Public order', which is to say, police and state authority over the general population, was a notion that had to be invented, codified and written into law. Public order was created so that it could be defended, as a shield for those in power, protecting them not just from direct political challenge from the crowd, but also from the spirit of Carnival. The establishment does not want the world turned upside down, thank you very much, even if it is in the name of revelry rather than revolution – they prefer the way it is already.

The roots of Carnival in London go back to the Caribbean, and the roots of Carnival in the Caribbean go back to the era of transatlantic slavery. Colonial plantation masters would host masquerade balls as a last blowout before the abstinence of Lent, celebrations from which the Africans they had enslaved were banned. The attempted eradication of African cultural practices and social life, as a denial of the humanity of enslaved people, was a key part of the process. But the enslaved communities created their own festivities nonetheless, based on their own dance traditions, mocking their plantation masters through masquerade (or 'mas') and satirical calypso songs.

Notting Hill Carnival sits directly in this lineage, and likewise arose – as did Pride in New York – out of a very specific and marginalised political struggle.[10] Following the arrival of more than 300,000 Caribbean people in Britain, beginning when the flagship *Empire Windrush* docked in the Thames in 1948, many Caribbean Britons settled in Notting Hill. Though the imperial motherland had called upon them to come, to rebuild a country devastated by war, they were not made welcome. They encountered regular discrimination and racist violence, from the organised far right, the Metropolitan police and the general population.

In May 1958, a young Antiguan called Kelso Cochrane was murdered by six alleged members of the White Defence League in Notting Hill. There were no arrests. Rioting and further violent attacks from neo-Nazis followed in August of that year. Racial discrimination was still legal in Britain, meaning a 'colour bar' in pubs and cultural spaces was often in place, at the whim of white venue owners and landlords. On 30 January 1959, the Trinidad-born Marxist journalist and activist Claudia Jones organised the first 'Caribbean Carnival' in St Pancras Town Hall, a show of community solidarity, strength and joy in the face of persistent oppression and violence. The steel pans and other bands, the processions and costuming and bass-heavy DIY sound systems steadily developed from there. It became an annual event, growing in size each year.

In the souvenir programme for London's first Caribbean Carnival in 1959, Claudia Jones addressed the need for pan-Caribbean

unity in the face of racist violence, indeed murder, and paid tribute to 'the role of the arts in bringing people together for common
aims'.[11] The idea that political unity and even resistance can be
achieved through conviviality and crowd joy did not begin in St
Pancras Town Hall that January, but something else important
did. In Jones's words, Carnival is the 'spirit of a people that
cannot be contained, that which therefore contains the genesis of
their own (self-articulated) freedom'.[12] The political power of the
carnivalesque crowd was inscribed on it from the start. And when
there is so much liberatory strength to be found in gathering
together to dance, sing and raise a glass, no wonder those in
power always want to break up the party.

Although the event is increasingly attended by enthusiasts of
every ethnic heritage, Matthew Phillip, CEO of the Notting
Hill Carnival Trust, is keenly aware of the event's specifically
Caribbean roots. Above his desk in west London hangs a nineteenth-century drawing, 'Carnival in Port of Spain, Trinidad', by
a visiting British artist called Melton Prior. The gleeful Black
dancers in the centre of the drawing are dressed as devils, aristocrats and harlequins, their legs and arms alive with motion,
while a supercilious white vicar looks on from the side of the road.
Trinidad's plantation-owning European colonial elites had
banned Black people from their Mardi Gras balls, banned them
from celebrations in the streets, and later in the nineteenth century, when they formed their own carnivals in response, banned
them from drumming. The great significance of the drawing,
Phillip says, is that the crowd of Black carnivalgoers occupies the
middle of the street, at long last – holding a mirror up to their
devilish masters, the people who would deny them this essential
right, and rite.

'Carnival is about the people reclaiming the streets for a
couple of days of the year to express themselves,' Phillip tells me.
For someone who is effectively the most senior Carnival bureau-
crat, he seems relaxed about how official everything needs to
be. 'Residents selling homemade food on their doorsteps, or a

random guy going around selling snow cones, who is, you know, not quite legit – all these little ingredients add to the event. You might get one or two drummers that plot up somewhere on the street and just start playing.' As long as everyone's safe and happy, he says, this is how it should be. 'Carnival belongs to the people – we're merely custodians, trying to make it happen in a safe way and protect its culture. But it belongs to the people, and the people will always ensure that it remains on the streets. The essence of Carnival is that celebration of freedom, and participation. I like to say it's a participation sport, rather than a spectator sport.'

Phillip has been part of Carnival his entire life – his father was a co-founder of the Mangrove Steelband, and he's always played steel pans, or drums, or worn a costume. He has a calm demeanour, which helps when dealing with the vortex of organisational stresses and issues on Carnival weekend itself. Running Carnival has always seemed like a phenomenally difficult job, a thankless task loaded with risk, with large parts of the white British establishment (the right-wing press, Tory politicians, wealthy local residents) desperate to see you fail. Of course, managing such a production could never be just one person's job, or responsibility. It is an extremely complex, indeed crowd-like negotiation, between an endless array of institutional bodies and community stakeholders, sound-system providers, bands, grassroots organisations, food stalls – and the 2 million carnival-goers themselves.

Springing to life early in the morning on the first day of Carnival, a central operations room in a local school oversees everything. Representatives of the ambulance services, the Met, the Fire Brigade, TFL and the British Transport Police, the two local authorities (Westminster and Kensington & Chelsea), the licensing team, the Greater London Authority, the communications team, the health and safety team, and St John's Ambulance come together for regular updates, questions, concerns, fire-fighting and monitoring, via endless banks of cameras and on-the-ground reports. There are a lot of moving parts even before the crowd raises its first plastic cup of rum, or pot of glitter. The paperwork alone has the potential to suffocate this mass joy, and it would be quite easy for this to become a carnival of bureaucracy: permits, licences, bills, invoices, contracts, all fluttering down from the west London sky like grim confetti. When his organisation took over the official running of Carnival in 2018, Phillip had other ideas about how to keep the crowd both safe and happy.

'The first thing we did, and the most significant thing we did, was to remove as many barriers as we possibly could,' he said. Those waist-high metal barriers – known as 'Met barriers', after the police force who are so fond of them – were everywhere, causing unexpected and unpleasant surprises in dense crowds, impeding people's freedom of movement. 'As an event organiser, I think the worst thing you can do is place barriers that are not there on a normal day. If you're in the Carnival crowd, walking through narrow streets like Notting Hill, you can look up, and use the buildings to guide you, to give you an idea of where there's a road, and where there might be space. But it won't tell you if somebody's placed a barrier across the road you're walking down – your sight is limited.' Even parts of the year-round street furniture are removed for the duration of Carnival, to facilitate fluid movement around the site: there are places where *removable* traffic islands have been installed, so they can be lifted out for the weekend.

Matthew Phillip's office in the Tabernacle in Notting Hill – a grandiose nineteenth-century church turned into a bustling community hub, decorated with Carnival photos and mementos – means he is embedded in these streets all year round. Which is fortunate, as it's a year-round job. Next to his desk a large paper map is displayed, with a red line for the parade route and a series of colour-coded blocks for the different bands, sound systems, stages and other major attractions – orange for the masquerade bands, yellow for the Brazilian bands, green for the steel pans.

The NHC Trust have worked with numerous sophisticated computer-modelling companies, consultancies and other cutting-edge crowd technologists. They have used heat-mapping tools to track crowd density, watched countless videos from inside and above the crowd to refine mobility around the site, and even deployed a police helicopter for a dynamic aerial view. But to manage this many moving parts, sometimes nothing beats the 'board game pieces on a giant paper map' approach beloved of eighteenth-century naval captains.

Phillip and his team spend a lot of time thinking about crowds, and how they move. 'My favourite personal theory about crowds is that they're like water,' he says. They can flow into unexpected places, seep through gaps invisible to the naked eye, and 'find space to go into even if it looks far too tight. Some people are comfortable in tight crowds. If there's a need, they'll find the space.'

What is unique about the power of Carnival is that it offers its participants the thrill of freedom and conviviality, rather than hedonism per se; after all, there is no shortage of music, dancing, flirtation, drinking and drugs available in a city like London during the rest of the year. This is a distinction, and an appeal, which is clear to anyone who has attended. To outsiders, to the establishment, things look very different, and the way Carnival crowds are discussed by the media is rich with Le Bonian disdain and fear. 'Mobs' are frequently invoked, and if there is any kind of confrontation between the police and members of the crowd, even if the police started it, the word 'riot' will surely appear too. 'INTO BATTLE! Riot Shields out as the Police Storm Carnival Mob', read a *Sun* headline in 1977, attributing the trouble to 'a rioting mob of black youths' in its opening paragraph.[13]

Headlines across Carnival's entire fifty-five years have sought to make its continuation feel untenable: a violent, alien incursion into polite, white, British life. 'Rampage at the Carnival' (*Daily Express*, 1976); 'Trapped in the Crossfire: Family Tell of Terror in Riot Battle' (*Daily Mirror*, 1977); 'Riot at the Carnival' (*Daily*

Mail, 1978); 'Carnival Mob Stone Police' (*Daily Express*, 1989); 'The Carnival MUST Be Over' (*Sun*, 1989); 'Notting Hill Carnival CARNAGE' (*Daily Express*, 2016), and this verbose 2023 *Daily Mail* headline: 'Thugs Rampaging with Zombie Knives. Eight Stabbings, 75 Police Officers Hurt. Open Drug Use. And Revellers Urinating in Gardens. To Call This a Celebration of Black Culture Is an Insult.' The pun 'Notting HELL Carnival' crops up repeatedly across the decades.

The 1989 Carnival was so heavily policed that it occasioned a dedicated grassroots report in response, produced by the Association for a People's Carnival (APC). The report, *Police Carnival 1989*, provides numerous detailed accounts of police aggression, cops in riot gear bearing shields and beating revellers, and the appearance of 'sterile roads' where only police were allowed, along with 'arbitrary barricades' to prevent free movement around the site. It was a level of crowd control that had never been seen before. 'The whole thing was clean, efficient and brutal,' reflected Trevor Carter, who had been at St Pancras Town Hall with Claudia Jones back in 1959: 'It would seem that somewhere from on high the decision has been taken that this festival is going to be destroyed.'

Analysis in the *Guardian* in the aftermath of the 1989 'police carnival' attributed this to the 'Newman strategy', the approach bequeathed by former Met commissioner Sir Kenneth Newman. He had stepped down two years earlier, but his ideas had become orthodoxy in police training. Newman was considered a specialist in public order policing, which he learned in the colonies – beginning his service in the Palestine Police Force, and later taking senior roles in the Royal Ulster Constabulary during the height of the conflict in the 1970s. As Met commissioner he spoke of 'the gloomy prospect of being constantly at war with a section of the community', with 'hostile crowds' causing problems in 'multi-ethnic areas', and tensions raised by 'political extremists', rather than by their own policing.[14] Regarding the Black community and Black culture as an 'enemy within' leads naturally to this kind of militarised thinking and approach: one in which the police stay firmly outside the crowd, hemming it in, riot gear on and shields raised.

The continuities between this kind of policing in 1980s London with British colonial policing of Carnival celebrations in the nineteenth-century Caribbean are unsurprising, as they are underpinned by the same racialised, Le Bonian view of the Black crowd. Along with its repeated efforts to restrict or ban aspects of Trinidad's Carnival, British colonial police intervention often led to clashes with the local Black population during the event. The exact location in which a carnival takes place is another subject of great significance and long-standing dispute. *Battlefront*, the newspaper of the UK's Black Parents Movement, reflected on this continuity in August 1987:

> The [colonial] authorities tried to confine the carnival to the savannah (a big open grassy space) and take it off the streets. In the 1970s and early 1980s in London when the Home Secretary and the police tried to get carnival off the streets and into a park such as Hyde Park or Battersea Park, all these memories were revived.

It is an argument that continues into the present, with regular demands by Notting Hill Carnival's critics that it be relocated to Hyde Park. These demands are usually framed as a simple, logical solution which 'still lets everyone have their fun' – a disingenuous argument that ignores the significance of where the crowd is permitted to assemble. It is intrinsic to Carnival's *raison d'être* that it should be in the streets where people live – where, originally, a host of working-class Caribbean migrants lived, before many were priced out – and that it does not become just another drab corporate festival in a park, *brought to you in association with Barclaycard and BAE Systems* or the like. The whole point is that the city be transformed and the streets be taken over by the crowd, in all its costumed extravagance. The familiar and quotidian become unrecognisable, like on a 'snow day'.

To Phillip, the Hyde Park proposal is absurd, offensive to the spirit and history of Carnival – and furthermore, it wouldn't even work. The capacity for live events in the park is 65,000, less than a tenth of the daily Carnival crowd. And where there are high fences and a contained space for the crowd, ticketing and reduced accessibility are sure to follow. 'Introducing an economic barrier to entry would alter the diversity of the crowd,' Phillip said. 'But I think they know that.'

Sure enough, the presence of venture-capital-funded corporate music platform Boiler Room and energy drink super-brand Red Bull at Notting Hill Carnival in recent years has raised hackles among some attendees: Red Bull have hosted their own stage, with big-name Caribbean and British acts performing in a fenced-off arena near the Carnival site, for a well-connected, ticketed audience. It is the antithesis of the entire point of Carnival. Acts of enclosure of the Carnival crowd – of any festive crowd – perform the same function as enclosure of the common lands.

The former Harrow Council leader and 2024 Conservative mayoral candidate Susan Hall calls for Carnival to be moved to Hyde Park every year, whatever the weather: a dance she performs for the right-wing press, who applaud with gusto. She has called the event 'vandalism' and 'dangerous', has alleged that it puts residents 'through hell' and argued it should be moved to Hyde Park 'for the safety of the police, the innocent that attend and the poor residents that live in the area'.[15] The cavalier fashion in which she carries out this annual ritual suggests Hall knows it won't happen, but it provides her and the press with a mutually beneficial piece of dog-whistle racism and culture-war agitation every August. Performatively lashing out at Carnival, and by implication at Black culture and its predominantly Black crowd, will always win plaudits in some quarters.

Aside from the Conservatives, wealthy west London residents and the right-wing press, the most vocal critics of Notting Hill Carnival are still the police. In 2017, the Met Police Federation, the rank-and-file officers' union, called for Carnival to be banned outright, calling it a 'disgrace' and alleging that 'a huge number of officers are getting attacked every year at this event.' There had been thirty-one attacks on officers that year, they said, and 313 arrests were made across the weekend. Carnival is the only event, Phillip tells me, where the Met automatically and immediately release the crime stats to the media, without waiting for anyone from the press to ask. It is a consistent part of their narrative: to do their utmost to associate Black culture and public assembly with criminality, still waging the same war that helped kick the whole thing off in 1958.

Crowds will always receive differential treatment depending on who they are composed of. In 2019, the *Huffington Post* looked into arrest figures for several major events across a three-year period, and found the number of arrests at Notting Hill Carnival – about three or four per 10,000 people – were almost identical to the arrest numbers at Glastonbury, which never receives dystopian headlines or op-ed handwringing about wanton criminality.[16] To take another example, an excess of drunkenness and antisocial behaviour – requiring an increased police presence – at the Henley Royal Regatta in 2016 was reported across the British press in a tone of light-hearted indulgence, the headlines referencing 'posh revellers' and 'rowdy drunken toffs'. Not one paper evokes a mob or a riot or implies any danger to the public. When London Mayor Sadiq Khan was asked whether arrests at Carnival meant it should be moved to Hyde Park, he pointed out that there were more arrests per capita at the Euro 2020 final; yet nobody is talking about banning England from playing at Wembley and moving their matches to Hackney Marshes.

But the alarmism and exaggeration of certain crowds' worst behaviours is a constant. In 2022, the Met Police Federation announced that seventy-four officers had been injured in the line of duty at that year's Notting Hill Carnival, and issued the following statement: 'These are people's sons and daughters. These are children's mothers and fathers. This happens every year. It's an utter disgrace.' It is certainly a shocking statistic, if you take it at face value – seventy-four police officers injured? What on earth had induced the Carnival mob to attack them like that? A subsequent FOI request revealed the real data. Firstly, seventy-four was simply wrong, and that number should have been sixty. Of those sixty police injuries, thirteen were from 'lifting and handling', three were 'slips, trips, or falls', one officer got a swollen foot, and another hurt their back 'from carrying or wearing officer safety equipment'.[17] A full 90 per cent of the injuries incurred by officers during Carnival were categorised by the Met themselves as 'minor non-reportable'.

Just like Carnival, the overwhelming majority of music festivals pass by with almost no incidents or trouble of any kind. And as with football matches, the really notable thing is how *little* crime and animosity, violence and injuries there are in these festive, often inebriated crowds. There were 600 music festivals in the UK alone in 2019.[18] Fifteen different UK music festivals drew crowds of 60,000 or more in 2022, with Glastonbury at the top of that list with 210,000 attendees. An astonishing 6.5 million people attended UK festivals altogether that year, as Britain emerged from the pandemic.[19] Not one of those hundreds of festivals 'descended into anarchy', or anything close to it.

On the rare occasions when things do go substantially, abnormally wrong at a festival, you are guaranteed to hear about it, and it is guaranteed that the crowd will be the first and last people blamed. The documentary *Trainwreck: Woodstock '99*, about the revival of America's world-famous hippie festival for the era of nu metal, presents a perfect example. Over three days in 1999, the much-hyped celebration of 'the spirit of '69' descended into an entirely avoidable, melodramatic catastrophe, until some of the 250,000 pissed-off young rock fans were pulling down fences and setting massive structures on fire. The film amounts to three hours of trash, rioting, arson, looting, toxic masculinity and Korn.

The two middle-aged money men running Woodstock '99, John Scher and Michael Lang, here appear to be motivated entirely by profit, with no discernible concern even for the bad publicity generated by the fiasco they have created. The organisers treat their crowd with total contempt, failing to provide clean drinking water, or shade in 100-degree temperatures, or hygienic toilet and washing facilities, or affordable food, or appropriate levels of first aid, stewarding, information and security. You can sense the Woodstock riots brewing throughout the film, as Lang and Scher barefacedly lie to the press in their daily briefings, letting things rapidly deteriorate, confident they will be able to blame 'an unruly mob' of 'anarchists' – a 'lunatic fringe' who are 'both entitled and fearful of growing up', along with nu metal bands like Limp Bizkit and Korn – for propagating a culture of neanderthal behaviour. Even two decades later, they seem unrepentant. It is a textbook deflection away from their own negligence and profiteering and onto the crowd.

As irate young festivalgoers scream out an a cappella version of Rage Against the Machine's 'Killing in the Name' – 'Fuck you, I won't do what you tell me' – they pull down the fences and build ever bigger bonfires, culminating in a row of huge trucks exploding one by one, like something from a cheap action film. At this point, the local state troopers are finally dispatched in full riot gear to start bashing heads. In the midst of all this chaos, we get a vox pop interview with one especially thick-necked frat boy type, in a white t-shirt and bandana. 'They're all about making money off us, and we're pissed,' he says, his friends gurning in the darkness behind him.[20]

It's a useful case study of rioting and the 'mindlessness' of crowds. These lads could well be the worst people in the world, and you might well find their conduct reprehensible; I probably wouldn't choose to hang out with them. But they are undeniably individuals in possession of their senses, choosing their own path, in control of their own behaviour, and acting like rational human beings. Why did they *fuck shit up*, to use the delicate nu metal phrase of the time? Because they were angry about how they'd been treated by the organisers. They had every right to be angry, they wanted revenge, and in the void of stewarding and security left by Scher and Lang, they were given every opportunity to take it. It might be many things, but it's not mindless.

In a coda to the fiery fiasco that Woodstock '99 became, one of the crowd members who has been reminiscing throughout the documentary, recounting the carnage he witnessed decades earlier, takes a step back to reflect. We've just seen the entire festival, not to mention its pie-eyed PR narrative about peace and love, collapse into historic ignominy and disaster. The festival, the documentary and the twentieth century itself seem to have come to a close with a Molotov cocktail of cynical profiteering, bad hair, macho headbanging and corroded idealism. It is a truly grim scene. And yet, a cheeky grin creeps across the goatee of our now-forty-something talking head: 'It's still probably the best time I've ever had.' This is supposed to be a big laugh line in the documentary – *surely not*, you the viewer are supposed to exclaim – but actually it makes perfect sense.

One of the virtues of the Social Identity Model of crowd behaviour is that, a century or so after the birth of crowd theory, the discipline has finally found a way to move beyond questions of violence, totalitarianism, contagion and deindividuation, and ask why people seek and find joy and comfort in a crowd of like-minded souls to begin with. Most of the new generation of crowd psychologists I've spoken to seem to understand the benefits of a little bit of firsthand empiricism – to try and get to the heart of the psychological and emotional pleasures of crowd membership, rather than just stand outside it with a clipboard, tutting. For Anne Templeton at the University of Edinburgh, it is 'the pure euphoria' of a music festival crowd that has her heart. 'It can be complete strangers you're smooshed up against, but you're jumping up and down, singing, sharing drinks – I love that feeling. The validation and collectivity of singing something together that is important not just to you, but everyone around you. That collective synchrony is absolutely beautiful.'

It is notable that Templeton mentioned sharing drinks as a crowd perk – this is a talking point which crowd psychologists are fond of. Recent studies have found that people will much more readily cross a threshold of disgust, or their usual hygiene norms, and engage in 'risky behaviours' when they are suffused with a warming, in-group feeling of security, trust and comradeship. They do so to a fault, in fact. It is something that applies to people on the Hajj, the pilgrimage to Mecca, where there is a ritual of head-shaving: pilgrims will happily share razors with other crowd members there, even if there is blood, because of that in-group bond and trust.

It is a familiar experience to me from the first crowd events I attended towards the end of the pandemic, after a period in which anxiety about viral transmission had become a constant presence. And yet, as soon as I found myself in the hedonistic atmosphere of a club with friends and like-minded souls – this was a reunion for the famous dubstep night FWD>>, a long-standing, tightly bound community of people, not merely a random club night – all that caution melted into the sticky Printworks floor. We were passing our drinks around, taking vapes out of each other's mouths to steal a puff, hugging, kissing each other on the cheek, doing all the things we had so assiduously avoided doing for the preceding two years, out of health anxiety and social obligation. And yes, admittedly, two of our party caught Covid that night. So it's true that social identification with a trusted crowd can encourage certain risky behaviours – but this is not the same as the Le Bon version, where you suddenly go mad and lose your sense of self in the crowd. Rather, your inhibitions are lowered because you feel more comfortably *yourself*. If we behaved irrationally that day, it was because we were having a bloody lovely time, surrounded by a crowd we trusted.

The University of St Andrews academic Fergus Neville has shown that feelings of enjoyment and heightened emotions in crowds stem from a sense of 'relatedness'.[21] The more you feel related to other people in the crowd, the stronger the in-group bonds, the shared beliefs and interests and identification, the more likely you are to have a positive experience. Put simply, crowds of like-minded people make us feel good. Neville points to what the American civil rights activist John Lewis described as a 'freedom high – almost an altered state of jubilation, a sense of being swept beyond yourself by the righteous zeal of the moment, whether it was a march or a sit-in or an arrest . . . a feeling of intimacy'. The crowd's paradox is that it offers a feeling of intimacy with people you don't know and, even having joined the crowd, may yet never speak to, share eye contact with, or touch. In that sense it is an easy form of intimacy, won without the cost of hard work we are all required to put into more long-lasting relationships with our actual friends, partners and family. Crowd membership offers us a form of unconditional love.

There is one particular moment in modern British history where the masses found a new medium for the ancient, ecstatic rites of Carnival, and it terrified the establishment so much that they were forced to legislate it out of existence. The explosion of rave or acid house culture in warehouses and fields in late 1980s Britain gave her generation 'dancefloor friendships played out without words' and 'an unshakeable feeling of being part of something huge and beautiful', former raver Frankie Mullin wrote in VICE.[22] For the novelist Hari Kunzru, reflecting on his youth, approaching the site of a rave and feeling 'the bass pulsing up ahead, the excitement was almost unbearable. A mass of dancers lifting up like a single body . . . [an] ecstatic fantasy of community, a zone where we were networked with each other, rather than with the office switchboard.'

Rave emerged in the same period that the furore over football hooliganism was reaching its tragic climax, and it was likewise met with a response which could have been scripted by Gustave Le Bon himself. The Thatcher-into-Major-era junta of the tabloid press, police, landowners and the Conservative Party made it their business to smother rave's congregation of squatters,

dropouts, drug-takers, hippies, hunt saboteurs, anti-road protesters and travellers. As Ed Gillett's book *Party Lines* lays out, the
war on rave culture, approximately 1987–94, was inextricably
linked to the moralistic and draconian policing of so many other
1980s crowds: the striking coal miners, the Black carnivalgoers,
the traveller communities, the urban rioters, the peace and poll
tax protesters, the gay clubbers during the HIV/AIDS crisis.
Crowds of people who are already marginalised from power are
treated with a casual kind of brutality by the state, and the same
dehumanising language and disproportionate policing tactics
crop up in each case.

No stone was left unturned to defame and disperse these
crowds. The police raid on the Love Decade party in a warehouse
in Blackburn in July 1990 is thought to be the largest mass
detention in British history, with 836 arrests. Echoing the use of
the tactic of 'punishment by arrest' against peaceful, law-abiding
protesters, only eight of those 836 were ever charged, while many
others successfully sued for damages after being assaulted by
the police. Greater Manchester Police went to the absurd lengths
of invoking an 1882 bylaw against 'licentious dancing' to shut
down gay clubs; their chief constable, James Anderton, made
his feelings clear when he said that gay people with HIV/AIDS
were 'swirling around in a human cesspit of their own making'.[23]
Using similarly unabashed, fascistic, Le Bonian language, a 1992
Daily Telegraph headline branded travellers as 'hordes of
marauding locusts'.

The climax and indeed final straw for the rave era was the
epochal Castlemorton Common Festival, a days-long outdoor
free party across a glorious spring bank holiday weekend in
Worcestershire in 1992. The free festival escalated rapidly in size,
thanks first to word of mouth and then – a good lesson in the law
of unintended consequences – the added amplification of media
hysteria, peaking at around 30,000 ravers. Writing about Castlemorton in the *Evening Standard*, Anthony Burgess summed up
the establishment mood as he railed against 'the megacrowd,

reducing the individual intelligence to that of an amoeba' and its 'dehumanisation purchased in the name of freedom'. To be sure, for many revellers participation in the rave scene flowed from a motive of pure hedonism, while for a small handful it was, as conservative critics breathlessly argued, a bountiful opportunity for drug dealing and other forms of untaxed profit. But discernible in that moment is also a clear, utopian desire to reclaim the commons, and the egalitarian festivities that went with them. Castlemorton Common was and remains the largest piece of unenclosed public land left in England – commoners can and do still graze their cattle there – so what better ground on which to revive the repressed saturnalian spirit in us all?[24] The 'free' in 'free party' meant freedom in a number of ways, beyond the fact that nobody had to pay to get in.

With the police outnumbered and outwitted, and the establishment both embarrassed and horrified by the sheer scale of Castlemorton, legislative suppression quickly took over. The festival amounted to nothing less than an 'invasion' of his constituency, Conservative MP Michael Spicer declaimed in Parliament the following month: 'New Age travellers, ravers and drugs racketeers arrived at a strength of two motorised army divisions, complete with several massed bands and, above all, a highly sophisticated command and signals system. However, they failed to bring latrines. The numbers, speed and efficiency with which they arrived . . . combined to terrorise the local community to the extent that some residents had to undergo psychiatric treatment in the days that followed.'

Spicer went on to reflect that with so many revellers in one place, only the army would be able to clear such a gathering in future, and concluded – as so many people in his position have done throughout history – that 'the problem of mass gatherings must be dealt with before they take place.' And so, press attacks and police crackdowns on the rave crowd were finally escalated to what would turn out to be a historic and deeply draconian legislative clampdown. Among its myriad targets, the Conservatives'

Criminal Justice and Public Order Bill 1994 (CJB) became notorious for criminalising the rave scene with targeted specificity, outlawing any self-assembled public congregation around dance music with more than twenty people present. 'For this purpose,' the legislation famously declared, '"music" includes sounds wholly or predominantly characterised by the emission of a succession of repetitive beats.' What began as a transcendent collective celebration had become a question of the right to free assembly. The title of one classic rave track from the period, 'Dance Before the Police Come!', by Shut Up and Dance, speaks to tensions that were of that moment, but also feel as old as human civilisation. The experience of freedom offered by Carnival is always likely to be punctuated this way.

The CJB did not pass into law without a fight. A series of climactic 'Kill the Bill' protest parties were organised throughout 1994, drawing tens of thousands of people – ravers, hippies, Trotskyists, anarchists, civil liberties organisations – and culminating in bare-chested, dreadlocked protesters shaking the gates of Downing Street to a soundtrack of whistles, cheers and repetitive beats. In a video of one Kill the Bill protest, a protester clambers to the top of the Downing Street gates and nonchalantly smokes a fag, while comically underdressed cops in short-sleeved shirts look on in dismay. At this point, Downing Street had only been gated off from the public for five years. It is a telling time capsule, because it is hard to imagine any crowd of protesters expressing their disapproval this close to Number 10 ever again.

For the final protest in October 1994, the police were not so under-dressed, or so laid-back. While there had been a few skirmishes with police during the march, by late afternoon, as the protest concluded in Hyde Park, the scene was calm enough. Some protesters were happily dancing to mobile sound systems, while others watched the speeches, or sat down on the grass for a well-earned rest. Things were winding down and people were heading home when mounted police appeared out of the blue, executing cavalry charges inside the park, followed by lines of riot cops steaming in, batons raised, to assault the festive crowd. Reporter Danny Penman, covering the protest for the *Independent*, was meandering through the park, away from the main crowd, when he was suddenly hit from behind by police truncheons. 'They just battered everybody,' he recalled.[25] At one point crowd members were forced up against the Hyde Park railings by riot police with shields and truncheons, and when they tried to escape and climb out of the park to freedom, were beaten back by officers on the other side. In an atmosphere of police brutality under-scored by chaotic incompetence (at times, different groups of officers were in open conflict with one another), the Met even swooped a helicopter down low over the crowd, seemingly to intimidate them.

It was an appropriately militaristic and messy climax to what Ed Gillett identifies as a wider conservative 'war on deviance and disorder' in the early 1990s, a war on any group who wanted to gather together but fell 'outside a narrow, archaic and morally conservative sense of propriety and British identity' – effectively, any marginalised community, any one of the many overlapping 'enemies within'. It is perhaps no coincidence that John Major's newly elected Conservative government focused its stated priori-ties on decency, decorum and good behaviour, via the Victorian cosplay of Major's 'back to basics' campaign – recalling the his-toric sermonising Norbert Elias identified in a much earlier era. As in previous centuries, the moralistic, purportedly Christian policing of conduct was a handy way to deflect attention, in this case from the social consequences of Thatcher's long war on working-class collectivity – and the ensuing economic devasta-tion – and to shore up the establishment against the perceived dangers of the self-assembled subaltern crowd.

In *Crowds and Power*, Elias Canetti sought to categorise the many types of crowd and their behaviours, and one particular distinction is helpful when thinking about large festive crowds. 'The open crowd is the true crowd,' he wrote, 'the crowd abandoning itself freely to its natural urge for growth.' (The Sermon on the Mount, he noted, was delivered to an open crowd.) The open versus the closed crowd is a useful binary for subdividing types of music crowds, since unlike Canetti's open crowd, the closed crowd is invited, defined and tamed by institutions or private corporations, is finite in shape and size, and is ticketed, gated, fenced and surveilled. On this basis, the rise and rise of stage-based, ticketed music festivals amounts to an attempt to enclose, regulate and ultimately domesticate the open crowds of Carnival or the free party and rave scenes. You could go further, be a purist and argue that Reading, Leeds or Bestival constitute a betrayal and co-option of the ancient spirit of Carnival. They are not 'participation sports' in the same way, and they certainly have plentiful footlights. But the innate longing for Carnival is still there, and these fenced-off, domesticated iterations of Carnival still offer most of the same feelings of freedom and collective joy; it would be churlish to deny it.

Of course, almost all live music events are structured around a clearly defined hierarchy between performer and audience – only one party has their name up in lights, gracing the gigantic stage, the altar – which is why it is such a thrill when that hierarchy is briefly subverted. The moment when a singer, high up on a festival stage, offers their microphone to the crowd, just before the chorus, is always a joyful one. It feels only fair, and is always greeted with great enthusiasm, as if to say, yes, it is our turn, actually – because you wouldn't be here without us. Even theatrical spectacles are incomplete without their crowds.

The most historic Glastonbury headline performances (say, Orbital in 1994, Pulp in 1995, Beyoncé in 2011, Stormzy in 2019) are generally agreed to be those where the perfect band or singer for that cultural moment is met with the rapturous, era-defining crowd response they deserve. It could never be *solely* the songs, and their delivery, and the stage presence and charisma of the artist or band, that define a historic performance – they must meet their mass audience halfway, and have their greatness authenticated by the crowd in real time. Radiohead's Thom Yorke, who is not exactly known for his warmth, was responsible for a moment of charming human poignancy in their 1997 head-line set when, thirty minutes in, he asked for the lights to be turned onto the hitherto darkened Glastonbury crowd, 'so that we can see the people, because we haven't seen them yet'. What followed was a moment of mutual awe and delight, better remembered than any of their songs that night: the dramatic revelation of many tens of thousands of people.

There is a case for saying that we have become too docile and well-behaved in the way we enjoy music and other cultural crowd experiences: that there is a little too much spectating, and not enough participating. Barbara Ehrenreich argues that the twentieth century – and specifically the rock and pop revolution of the 1950s and '60s – witnessed the successful conclusion of centuries of establishment efforts to contain and tame audiences.[26] A truly participatory, popular, cultural and festive life was transformed into pure rock'n'roll spectacle. It bears repeating that Shakespeare's (standing) theatre audiences used to mill around while the play was on. They ate, drank, sat on the stage and interrupted the actors with their own comments. By contrast, modern theatre and concert audiences have 'learned to hold themselves in a state of frozen attention', seated in absolute silence and shushing the slightest rustling or murmur. Ehrenreich suggests that it requires an act of significant physical restraint to hear music you love and *not* move some part of your body, tapping your foot or nodding your head in time with the rhythm. 'The silent, internal work of muscular inhibition' is a win for social conservatives and the powerful, and a denial of crowd joy to the rest of us.

But not everyone engages in a depressing act of physical inhibition when they join others to enjoy music – even when they are in seated, ticketed theatres. The screaming, arms-flailing teenage fans of Elvis Presley, the Beatles and others were so rowdy that they generated their own moral panics – and accompanying police overreach. At one of many chaotic screenings of the Bill Haley film *Rock around the Clock*, at a cinema in Lewisham in 1956, a teenage teddy boy told a journalist: 'You should have seen this place last night. Jiving on the stage they were, till the cops came.'[27] Another screening in London that year, in which teddy boys ripped out the seats of the Trocadero cinema, mirrored the 1913 debut in Paris of Stravinsky's shockingly modernist ballet, *The Rite of Spring*, which also ended in a riot.

More recently, there is one particular form of crowd behaviour at gigs and festivals which illustrates the value of the Social Identity Model more robustly than any other: moshing. To the majority of people, even to many punks, metallers and rap fans, joining a moshpit ranks as a truly incomprehensible way to have a good time. Why on earth would you put yourself through *that*? The moshpit is the answer to the question, 'What if you decided to head-bang along to this high-energy music, but with your whole body, while scores of strangers hurtle into you doing the same?' It is effectively a mass brawl masquerading as dancing, taking the form of pogoing, slam-dancing, windmilling, high kicks – in short, thrashing around like a loon. (Indeed, if you're really in the weeds of underground hardcore scenes, there is also headwalking, floor-stomping, penny pick-up, the axehandle, spin kicks, crab-walking and the wild lawnmower; although at a certain point you do wonder if some of the hardcore punk music bloggers cataloguing these moves might be having us on.[28])

Moshpits have warranted serious scientific attention. The physicist and metaller Jesse Silverberg coauthored a 2013 paper, 'Collective Motion of Moshers at Heavy Metal Concerts', which used computer modelling to re-create a moshpit in all its algebraic complexity.[29] Silverberg and his colleagues found that far from being pure chaos, the movements are largely predictable, and follow recognisable patterns of collective behaviour. Even particular types of moshpit – the frequently banned 'wall of death', in which two halves of a crowd are instructed to bisect down the middle and then, at the agreed moment, run headlong into each other, or the vortex-like 'circle pit' – seem to follow a predictable pattern.[30]

In among all that physicality and consensual violence, there is care, and exemplary crowd self-policing. The first thing every punk, metaller, rap kid or other mosher learns is that the instant it looks like someone in 'the pit' is having a bad time, might be hurt, or, God forbid, slips and falls, everything and everyone must cease moving until that person is lifted up and set right, and smiling – or, if they are hurt, the crowd is immediately (and if need be, forcefully) parted and they are escorted to safety and first aid.

From a crowd psychology point of view, moshing is an expression of fidelity to and faith in your fellow crowd members, as well as a source of individual pleasure. 'It's normative behaviour,' says Anne Templeton. 'The more sweaty and messed-up you get in the moshpit, the more you're a good in-group member, the more enjoyable the experience is for you – it's what you're expecting to happen, and it's central to what it means to be part of that group. We tend to move in closer proximity to our fellow in-group members.'

I remember the first moshpit I ever experienced: seeing Hole play at Brixton Academy in 1995, with their captivating frontwoman, Courtney Love, in a state of furious semi-meltdown. Even after watching videos of heavy rock gigs on TV, I really hadn't known what to expect, and even as a tall thirteen-year-old, the experience was overwhelming, terrifying, violent, and brilliant. Emerging into the cold Brixton night with my t-shirt soaked through with sweat, my very 1990s centre-parted curtains plastered to my forehead, is one of my fondest, most visceral and physical teenage memories. The first experience of a moshpit feels like playing in the ocean as a child, trying to bodysurf on the waves, getting it wrong and being swallowed by the wave and flipped upside down, salt water in your nose and all – an experience of total disorientation and sudden panic as you lose control and have your feet swept from under you, such that you emerge unclear which way is up. You come out dazed and confused, and plausibly bruised, but also beaming, buzzing with adrenaline – and desperate to go back in and do it again.

It is not that moshing gives you a unique physical high, the kind that leaves you vibrating with catharsis and endorphins, because you could get a similar high, much less enjoyably, by running 10 kilometres in the rain on your own. It is more than that, because that catharsis and those endorphins are acquired collectively, and can only be acquired collectively, in the company of people you trust. A moshpit of one is not a moshpit at all, it's a piece of performance art. And moshpits, like carnivals, do not respect footlights. The crowd transcends its role as a passive audience, fulfils its innate potential, and becomes its own entertainment.

6

The Invention of Modern Life: Urban Crowds

I could see, quite clearly, the swirling, living motion of five hundred people walking, two and three abreast, from and toward the fourteen entrances and exits of the concourse . . . no one was bumping into anyone else – every time I thought I myself might be about to bump into people near me, both I and they were already accelerating slightly, or decelerating, or making a little side step, so that nobody ever collided.

– Tony Hiss, 'The Experience of Place', describing Grand
Central Terminal's commuter ballet,
the harmony 'that makes a city possible'[1]

Consider the ways the density of the modern city is depicted. The neon tension headaches of Times Square in New York or the Shibuya Crossing in Tokyo. The cold comfort and monotony of a row of grey tower blocks. The slow drill of men in suits pouring over London Bridge to work in the City. Edouard Manet's portrayal of the easy conviviality of a new urban leisure life, *Music in the Tuileries Gardens* (painted nine years before the Commune). Madonna's much-imitated time-lapse music video for 'Ray of Light', where teeming humanity becomes an indistinct, sped-up blur of bodies: streaming en masse over zebra crossings and through subway stations, shirtsleeves flying on the trading floor, and two vast, glitchy rivers of red and white headlights zipping along the dark freeway. Or the awe-inspiring Grand Central Terminal in New York, one of the most recognisable and well-used film locations in cinema history, with its towering, cathedral-like windows casting beatific light across the gargantuan space, the celestial mural painted across its ceiling suggesting the possibility of transcending the rush-hour commute and arriving at a destination in a constellation far away.

These grandiose railway concourses are a site of great significance for the crowd in the modern age. When stations like Grand Central were completed they were a perfect bubble of early-twentieth-century modernity, encapsulating the electric, futuristic and freeing thrills of mass transit and mass living. But they also exemplified the anxieties of modern city life, not least to the constant stream of new arrivals from the provinces, for whom the concourse was usually their first-ever experience of a crowd, and their first experience of a city.

'One was now in the urban danger zone where visitors from the country were thrown to the wolves,' the Swedish academic Orvar Löfgren wrote of the *fin-de-siècle* train traveller:

> Clutching their suitcases, people embarked from the relative safety of the train into this jungle, populated (as they had been reminded back home) by all kinds of shady characters, con-men and tricksters, or as the Danish term runs: *bondefanger,* from the German *bauernfänger*, literally meaning 'people making a living of trapping peasants'. To newcomers, the station atmosphere signalled a need to be on the lookout, monitoring the sea of strangers surrounding you. Was this a threatening or reassuring atmosphere?[2]

Even a century later, these scenes are common avatars for all that is wrong with city living. The bustle! The stress! The *people*! I often think about a mildly terse conversation I had with a school friend who had moved to a town in New Zealand, returning to visit London from one of the most sparsely populated and scenic countries on earth. He was relating to me, with a mixture of disgust and bewilderment, his first encounter in many years with

Victoria Station, in the middle of rush hour. It was just *awful*, he said. So chaotic. So much clamour, and movement, and density, and noise. And above all, there was an impersonal meanness to it all – he seemed to feel it was a deeply inhumane experience, as well as a stressful one. And isn't it all the sadder to feel so alienated among so many human beings? He was articulating the archetypal urban malaise: to feel alone, and lonely, in a crowd.

And I understood his lament – on the face of it, at least. Victoria Station at rush hour *is* awful; of course it is. But I also took offence, on the city's behalf, at the implication that this is what London life is like, spiritually, typically and regularly, because it's just not the quintessential city living experience. None of us would ever choose to spend any time in Victoria Station at rush hour, if we could avoid it, and most Londoners can and do avoid it. But it's a useful go-to image to conjure, one I've heard before, particularly from other city refuseniks trying to explain why it's all too much to bear: too stressful, too frantic, too crowded, too impersonal, too unfriendly.

Cities are sites of excess, and for sceptics of urban living, that excess is characterised by the unwelcoming crowd that lives in their head. The two are intertwined because the crowd is an urban phenomenon, so that a city without crowds is a disaster movie, or a war zone, or some other dread-filled dystopian vision (a pandemic, say) – a sign that something has gone very wrong. And yet to some observers, it is not empty cities but full ones which represent all that is unnatural: a society that has failed to properly contain its excesses. For twenty-first-century Malthusians, the idea of a city full of people, *full of strangers*, still carries the same alienating undertones as the 'urban danger zones' of those *fin-de-siècle* train concourses.

The UN forecasts that the world's population will grow from 7.9 billion today to 9.8 billion by 2050, an extraordinary rise in such a short space of time. The spectre of overwhelming urban population density, as a fearsome and imminent reality, has a long history, going back to the Industrial Revolution and beyond.

The current era of reactionary urban crowd-bashing takes nine-teenth-century fear of the urban masses – the great unwashed, decadent, immoral and stupid, having too many children and 'burdening' overstretched public services – and gives it a twist for the era of modern migration-phobia, culture wars and climate crises. Today, 56 per cent of the world's population live in cities; the World Bank forecasts that by 2050 that proportion will rise to nearly seven out of ten. The urban crowd is growing much larger, and is doing so with astonishing speed.

Japanese cities are often made to play the part of the global future-city that awaits us all. The great exemplar is the Tokyo Metropolitan Area, a mega-sprawl incorporating Tokyo and its neighbour Yokohama, together hosting a population of some 40 million people. Squeeze into your coffin-like pod in a capsule hotel. Dare to navigate the Shibuya Crossing without being overwhelmed, knocked over and flattened into the tarmac. Board a subway train so dangerously packed that the station employs professional crowd-pushers who stand on the platform, shoving you in with white-gloved hands. Parts of Tokyo certainly do suffer from extremely high density, and urban overcrowding has myriad neg-ative outcomes for our health and well-being, even in wealthy societies – but the way these stories and images are shared in the West are as a kind of warning: the ghosts of cities yet to come.

Is there safety in numbers? Does the urban crowd provide cover for criminal or antisocial behaviour, or do a thousand pairs of eyes actually make these much less likely? Which is scarier, and which suggests more danger: the overcrowded city scene, or the deserted one? The packed train station concourse at rush hour, or the eerily empty back street at night? Wanted men, crim-inals, gangsters and terrorists are frequently depicted in film and TV melting into the urban crowd and disappearing – while the frantic, darting eyes of the cop or hero rake in vain across a sea of bobbing heads, unwittingly going about their business, chat-ting, laughing, all alarmingly ignorant of the grave danger in their midst.

Edgar Allen Poe's sinister short story 'The Man of the Crowd' is surely the Urtext of these TV and film scenes. Poe's narrator engages in the very modern practice of urban people-watching, gazing out idly through a coffee-house window in fascination at the movements of merchants, clerks, labourers, hawkers, pickpockets, thimble-riggers and drunks, before becoming fixated on the man of the title. Struck by the figure's inscrutable demeanour, the narrator dashes out to follow this perplexing, semi-fiendish, decrepit older man, trailing him for many hours through the crowded streets of London, pawing his way through the rainy night and its 'species of infamy', gin palaces and filthy slums, and into the bleak morning light.

It is, as Poe's epigraph has it, *such a great misfortune, not to be able to be alone.* His story gives a chilling account of the fears aroused by the sheer unknowability of the new urban crowd – of what, and whom, may lie within it; what nefarious motives all these strangers may have, and how easily those motives can be concealed. The narrator's obsession spirals outwards from the fact that he cannot read his subject – he cannot easily place him in a category. The old man is an avatar for what was felt to be the new urban crowd's implicit strangeness and untrustworthiness. The intimacy and familiarity of the old ways, of rural life, of sparse, bucolic landscapes in unchanging communities where everybody knew each other, and their place, was being scrambled by the phenomenal upheaval of modernity. In the new metropolises, the people *are* the landscape. And, for the first time, you could disappear into them completely.

Urban anonymity – to be 'in solitude on account of the very denseness of the company around', as Poe put it – was felt as a curse by many nineteenth-century bourgeois commentators. Friedrich Engels, hardly an enemy of the new urban proletariat, lamented that the 'very bustle of the streets' contained 'something that is abhorrent to human nature itself'.[3] This is the Edward Hopper version of big-city living, rather than the thrilling riot of movement depicted by Monet, George Grosz or the

Italian futurists. But what if, far from being an existentially alienating experience, becoming lost in (and perhaps to) the crowd
was one that helped you to feel more truly yourself than ever
before? What if embracing such 'anonymity' and diving headfirst
into the unknowable street scene was actually a route to greater
self-knowledge? For those with the privilege to feel, and be, safe
moving among the urban crowd, plus the gift of idle time in
which to do so, wilful submersion in the throng of city streets can
be a surprisingly soothing pleasure.

Developing the idea of the *flâneur* from Charles Baudelaire,
Walter Benjamin saw these new urban wanderers merging with
the crowd, finding pleasure and refuge in it and its potential for
spontaneity. They represented a new kind of urban subject, with
a new kind of urban gaze: men of means and leisure, wandering
without purpose or urgency through the city and its crowds. 'The
crowd is the veil through which the familiar city beckons to the
flâneur as phantasmagoria', Benjamin wrote. The newly popu-
lous city created new subjects, new citizens: people who sought
to understand and appreciate the dreamlike modern city through
its crowds – because the two were codependent, and arrived
together, inseparably, and drove each other forwards. The sensory bombardment of all that jostling human movement, the
sights, smells and sounds generated by the explosion in urban
populations, the turbocharged social forces accelerating through
massified city living: for those who could free themselves from
the misanthropy and fear articulated by Le Bon, or Poe, or
Engels, the shock of the new could be one of liberation.

For the situationists of the '60s, the *flâneur*'s practice of the
dérive (drift) offered opportunities to subvert the capitalist city's
transactional paths and imperatives, to walk against the general
commercial flow of the city and, in doing so, to reimagine and
remake it. Perhaps this aspect is one worth rescuing from the
movement's now rather unfashionable, self-important adherents,
especially if we embrace the idea that the *flâneur*'s female equiv-
alent, the *flâneuse*, will have something to say about the city and

its people too.[4] To be so unconcerned by the strictures of working life under capitalism – not to mention any caring or other responsibilities – as to experience the urban crowd this way, is a position of privilege. It is not for nothing that a friend once drolly labelled the practice of the psychogeographic *dérive* as 'white men walking'. If working-class women had long moved alone through the city crowds, the twentieth century finally offered middle-class women previously sheltered in drawing rooms – like Woolf's Mrs Dalloway – the opportunity to do the same.

But the problems of 'walking while female', 'walking while Black' or 'walking while Muslim' in the contemporary Western city impose a 'complex and often oppressive negotiation', as the Jamaican-born essayist Garnette Cadogan wrote, recording his shock at the constant threats of violence he received from police and white citizens alike in 1990s New Orleans and New York.[5] 'Jamaican police could be pretty brutal, but they didn't notice me the way American police did,' Cadogan continued. 'I could be invisible in Jamaica in a way I can't be invisible in the United States.' To be out in public, ambling through crowds of strangers without the privilege of the white *flâneur*, requires a constant navigation of the limits on freedom of movement created by the threat of racism and patriarchy, manifested in disproportionate and prejudicial policing, suspicion and outright violence.

Tragically, the urban crowd does sometimes provide convenient cover for monstrous behaviour. The dismaying frequency with which women are molested on crammed city trains has led to the establishment of separate women-only carriages at rush hour, in cities in Japan, India, Mexico, Malaysia, Egypt and beyond. It is a grim truth, and only one of many ways in which cities are harder to navigate safely for some people than for others. The easy mobility with which any individual is able to slip in and out of urban crowds – or to be decadent and idle in the city without arousing undue attention or suspicion – is always contingent on the wider society's openness and tolerance, which does not always extend to people marginalised from power. The freedom to not be noticed is an integral part of the freedom of crowd membership, and it is not afforded to everyone.

The late-nineteenth-century explosion in urban population meant cities were suddenly teeming with crowds that were larger and more socially diverse than ever before. For the first time, city-dwellers were not just moving around together on mass transit, but enjoying a mass civic, cultural, and leisure life together. One new initiative helped catalyse this change like no other in the late nineteenth century: the creation of international expositions, exhibitions and world's fairs. Successively staged in London, Paris, Chicago, Vienna, Philadelphia, Barcelona and New York, they were like nothing that had ever been seen or experienced before: huge sites of congregation and play which inadvertently acted as momentous social engines and laboratories. Infrequent though they were, by necessity, world expos helped forge a modern citizenry and more cohesive civic identities, as well as pioneering the notion of events-related tourism and the twentieth-century evolution of city- and nation-branding. And they were by no means guaranteed to succeed. Such was their novelty and scale, neither the ministers, mayors and capitalists who convened these grand spectacles – requiring the hefty financial support of the state – nor the public at large could quite believe that tens of thousands of people from different social classes could be gathered together, brushing past each other, standing in queues or gazing at exhibits together, without some kind of violent catastrophe.

At what is generally considered to be the first world expo, the Great Exhibition of 1851 in Hyde Park, London, there were dire warnings of riots, and troops were placed on standby nearby. Hyde Park itself was a notoriously dangerous part of London at the time, where the risk of robbery was so great that people had taken to only crossing it in convoy.[6] But in spite of bourgeois fears of what all these proles, pickpockets and other members of the criminal classes might do when they were gathered en masse, and allowed easy access to their betters under cover of the throng, there were only twenty-five arrests made out of 6 million visitors, across the five-and-a-half months' duration of the fair – an extraordinary figure, and testament to the idea that crowds generally make cities safer places to be. It was a roaring success, famous for its impossibly vast glass structure, the Crystal Palace. At one point on its busiest day, 7 October, 92,000 people were in the building at the same time: the largest number of people to ever be indoors in a single location.[7]

These events heralded the era of mass urban encounters and collective pleasure-seeking – the world most of us live in today. Hyde Park was just the beginning. The Exposition Universelle in Paris in 1889 drew more than 32 million visitors over its six months – at its peak, a staggering 397,000 people on a single day. Four years later, the World's Columbian Exposition of 1893, better known as the Chicago World's Fair, elevated these achievements to fresh heights. Over $700 million in modern terms was spent on building what became known as the White City, a dazzling temporary playground of gleaming white palaces, fountains, rides and exhibits, seven miles from downtown Chicago, on a reclaimed, mosquito-infested swamp on the shores of Lake Michigan.

For its cheerleaders, the Chicago World's Fair marked 'the beginning of the twentieth century', the Rubicon moment where the United States signalled its transition from agrarian frontier-ism to a civilisation of great modern cities and consumer capitalist abundance.[8] It was a carnival of boosterism and extravagance, featuring vast classical colonnades, fountains of red wine and perfume, a thirty-five-foot tower made of 13,000 oranges, a giant chocolate Christopher Columbus and a silver-encrusted toilet; exhibits of iron ore, copper and petroleum; artillery, animals, aquariums and fine art; heavy industry and delicate lace, ice bobsleds and hot air balloons, the first zipper and the original Ferris Wheel – every industry imaginable was represented. Everything about the fair celebrated grandeur (the biggest!), novelty (the first!), or both: here was the largest

building in the world, the Manufactures and Liberal Arts Building, which could seat 300,000 people in its main hall, and the
largest choir in the world, with 2,500 singers. The fair was big
enough to warrant its own dedicated railway line and its own
newspaper, the *Daily Columbian*.

But the greatest innovation of all was not in any display case,
or any overblown structure. It was the living, breathing assembly
moving among them that was truly historic. Here was the invention of modern urban conviviality, 'the surging sea of humanity',
as the opening day was described: the transgressing of class and
other boundaries and a future where citizens were permitted
access to a more universal leisure life.[9] 'Oh, the great, hurrying,
well-dressed, self-possessed and self-respecting crowd', wrote a
visitor from Kansas, a Mrs Stearns, in a letter to her local newspaper the *Linn County Clarion*. 'Which is the greater, the fair,
or the representation of our great country?' These were events
without precedent that helped stitch together an albeit contingent
and restive new social coalition, threading together new unified
civic identities, as well as providing valuable practical experiences
in how to navigate a large urban crowd.

Not everyone enjoyed these challenging novelties. Under the
headline 'Crowds Seek the City', a report in the *Chicago Record*
complained that walking through downtown Chicago had
become like running the gauntlet, 'walking zig-zag' to dodge jabs
from umbrellas, bangs and thumps from 'well-intentioned
strangers' and their bags and accoutrements.[10] 'We are liable to
be physically wrecked,' it concludes melodramatically. 'It is
impossible to avoid collisions . . . A walk downtown is one unmit-
igated nightmare of horror.'

The Scottish-American immigrant and industrialist Andrew
Carnegie had an altogether more upbeat impression of the vast
crowds' convivial behaviour and self-regulation, and hailed this
success – as many admirers did – in patriotic terms. 'The impression made by the people en masse was highly complimentary to
the American,' he reflected:

I never heard a foreigner give his impression who failed to extol the remarkable behaviour of the crowd, its good manners, temperance, kindliness, and the total absence of rude, selfish pushing for advantage which is usual in corresponding gatherings abroad. The self-governing capacity of the people shone forth resplendently. The foreigner's verdict is that without official direction or supervision every individual governed himself and behaved like a gentleman.[11]

While these expos were of great significance for the creation of local civic identities – with people from the slums and the big houses mingling together for the first time – their intrinsic internationalism was a big part of the appeal to visitors. At the Chicago World's Fair there were pavilions provided and paid for by forty-six foreign nations, showcasing culture and produce from Europe and beyond; Norway even sent a Viking longship across the Atlantic. At its best, this was a paragon of cultural exchange and universalism, shot through with hope for the electrifying thrills of new technology and a peaceful twentieth century. But it also featured 'ethnic villages' showing what were effectively live human exhibits of Samoan islanders, Dahomeyans, Egyptians, and Inuit, recruited for a scant fee and put on display performing humdrum activities for the gawping visitors.[12] These were very far from being convivial spaces for all, let alone utopian ones – any more than were the Western nations they were designed to enrich and glorify. But the grim racism and Orientalism at the heart of the 'international' aspect of the international expositions was also wrapped up in a wider truth: that the new urban metropolis would precipitate encounters with new cultures and new possibilities in the crowd.

Unsurprisingly, Marx and Engels were not fans of these festivals of colonial capitalism and commodity fetishism. But they understood their significance, writing of the 1851 Great Exhibition:

This exhibition is a striking proof of the concentrated power with which modern large-scale industry is everywhere demolishing national barriers and increasingly blurring local peculiarities of production, society and national character among all peoples . . . With this exhibition, the bourgeoisie of the world has erected in the modern Rome its Pantheon, where, with self-satisfied pride, it exhibits the gods which it has made for itself.[13]

The bourgeoisie, it is reasonable to assume, would have happily agreed with that assessment themselves – and in Chicago they were even more self-satisfied when the fair defied expectations and turned a profit, in spite of its exorbitant outlay.

After a long summer, in its penultimate week, on 9 October 1893, the fair celebrated Chicago Day, the anniversary of the city's devastating fire, and set a world record for outdoor event attendance, drawing 751,026 people in a single day. It was the 'grandest spectacle in modern times', indeed so grand that the attractions were almost impossible to see that day, such was the sheer size of the crowd. But the exhibits were beside the point. Barely a few decades earlier, Chicago's entire population was only a tenth of the size of the crowd present on that one day.

The story of the modern world is the story of our learning to live together, to be social animals, but on a mass scale. These extravagant late-nineteenth-century expos marked a second social leap forward, to follow the first, in the Palaeolithic era, when we left the family cave and joined together to form the first non-familial social bonds. The year after the Chicago World's Fair, the International Olympic Committee was founded in Paris, and the first modern Olympic Games were held two years later, in Athens. The age of mass urban social life had begun.

If it is the cooperation, conviviality and self-policing of crowds of strangers which 'make the city possible', that does not mean that the contemporary city treats them with a great deal of hospitality. There is a pessimistic case for saying that the archetypal twenty-first-century citizen is the complete opposite of the idealised *flâneur* or *flâneuse*. An isolated, lonely, overworked individual, denied the idle pleasures of aimless wandering and the delights of chance encounters in the crowd; unfamiliar with any local community because they have to keep moving from one insecure rental property to another; over-policed and over-surveilled, time-poor and chained to their car. In this private box, blinkers on, they tunnel straight ahead, on the same path every day, from their small, overpriced flat, to their largely empty hybrid-working office, to their private gym, and back to their flat. It is a miserable caricature, but not without basis in reality. The loneliness crisis is real, and there's more than a grain of truth in it for too many inhabitants of modern Western cities.

To be sure, there are many contributory factors to this atomised lifestyle, not least the nature of modern work and housing in gentrifying cities. But whether through government cuts or concessions to the expansive ambitions of private enterprise, a key reason we have all become a bit more crowd-shy in recent decades is the prolonged, top-down assault on public space and the wider public realm – what are sometimes called the urban commons. From properly funded libraries to pleasant, open parks and squares, free or affordable sports and leisure facilities, safe, accessible and cheap public transport, comfortable street furniture and free public toilets, and a vibrant, varied, uncommodified social and cultural life – all the best things about city life fall under the heading of the public realm, and all of them facilitate and support happy crowds rather than sad, alienated, stay-at-home loners. All are under threat in the twenty-first-century city, thanks to the considerable effort that has been put into 'designing out', or pricing out, free and open crowds.

The time has come when elites can no longer claim plausible deniability about the realities of crowd behaviour and psychology. Ministers, civil servants and police chiefs are being told directly by social scientists that crowds bring us happiness and security, that there is no deranged, drooling, bloodthirsty 'mob', that human beings don't 'stampede', and that if the state is serious about avoiding crowd tragedies and violent disorder, they ought to read some of these academic studies and act on their advice. And yet, even as Gustave Le Bon's crowd theories become ever more discredited, a new kind of threat is being posed to free assembly in the privatised plazas of the modern city.

When a crowd of citizens gathers, the 'town square' is usually its first port of call: the appropriate stage for its demands and denunciations. The conducting of democratic discussions in public space, at the geographical heart of a city, goes back to the agoras of ancient Greece. Most contemporary cities likewise have one famous location which is a byword for democratic participation, inhabited by the ghosts of protests and political rallies in years gone by, and open to more in the future. Activists and protesters have gathered in these iconic open spaces, set up camps, held meetings and heard speeches, and transformed those places into more than just convenient meeting points to make demands for change. When occupied by a crowd, these squares become a symbolic embodiment of grassroots democratic power.

The connection of a singular place to sprawling political movements became so strong during the uprisings of the early 2010s that shortened place names like Syntagma, Gezi, Tahrir, Maidan and Zucotti became synonymous with their upheavals and, thanks to excitable, round-the-clock media coverage, instantly recognisable to people who have never visited them, or their host cities. It is the crowd uprising represented by a single site and, in the digital age, also as a hashtag: #Gezi. The downside is the very reductiveness that this entails: if you understand the crowd's complex, dynamic and multifaceted cries for freedom only through that one iconic site, you are missing many other stories, demands and geographies – the years of worker agitation in factories beyond Cairo's Tahrir Square, for example.

Each piece of urban space provides its own distinct architectural dynamics for the crowd that assembles there. In *The Roundabout Revolutions*, Eyal Weizman drew inspiration from a photograph of the 1980 Gwangju Uprising in South Korea, where 'the roundabout organised the protest in concentric circles, a geometric order that exposed the crowd to itself, helping a political collective in becoming.' This is very different from the geometry of a hierarchical or Leninist political organisation, or any traditional political rally. Here the leaders are on a raised platform, or 'top table', and the crowd faces the front in rows, listening attentively and taking their ideas and orders from above. A key feature of some of 2011's 'revolutions of the squares' was that the crowd or protest camp arranged itself, and did so 'horizontally', without orders from above – distributing itself in network fashion, rhizomatically, around the public square. In one part of the square you might find a working group of volunteers discussing media strategy; in another, a group working on community outreach to the city beyond; in another, a creche; in another, a kitchen. These nodes talk to each other, and overlap, and swap members, interlacing crowd members' individual creativity and skills.

Faced with this broad shift from the factory floor to the town square as a site of struggle – as documented in David Harvey's *Rebel Cities* – politicians have learned to recognise when a focal piece of urban space has become a 'crowd problem'. In 2014, three years after the transformative *indignados* movement was born in Plaza de la Puerta del Sol in the centre of Madrid, and following another mass demonstration which brought it to a standstill, the city's right-wing mayor, Ana Botella, reached the end of her tether. She petitioned the national government for permission to ban all future protests from the streets and squares of the city centre. 'The Spanish capital cannot tolerate for everyone's public space to be systematically occupied by those who have made Madrid the target of their protests', she explained, calling for political gatherings to be banned from all 'historical-artistic settings, areas with significant tourism presence and strategic transportation routes'. In other words: all the places where people are most likely to protest – the symbolic square, the famous arterial road, the bustling transport hub, the high-profile spots where political demands will be seen and heard.

Botella's request was turned down flat by a government led by her own party – apart from anything else, she was told, it would be impossible to enforce. Her only mistake, perhaps, was to articulate full-throatedly what politicians across the world have for centuries sought to do more subtly, and by degrees: to subdue the democratic potential of all urban public spaces – through policing, through legislation, through surveillance, and through urban design.

Yasser Elsheshtawy, a professor at Columbia University and the author of *Planning Middle Eastern Cities*, has spent his career studying the way people behave in the urban environment, particularly in his native Egypt. The awe-inspiring spectacle of Cairo's huge Tahrir Square protests in 2011 encouraged revolutionary sentiments and crowds to self-perpetuate and multiply, reaching an unstoppable crescendo. When I spoke to Elsheshtawy a few years after the revolution, he told me that the square has long had such associations: 'Since the military takeover or revolution in 1952, Tahrir has always been a site of demonstrations and speeches, so it carries a lot of historical weight. In terms of practical design, it's abutting downtown, it meets the Nile, it can be accessed from many different roads, its sheer size lends itself to spectacle. Even the way the buildings around the perimeter form a wall helps the crowds feel and look more intense – it's almost like a stage, in fact.'

For Eyal Weizman, Tahrir's suitability was critically determined by its relationship with the city's general population, and how it fed crowds in and out. As with the other 'roundabout revolutions' of 2011, these sites are never static. 'Urban roundabouts are the intersection points of large axes, which also puts them at the start or end of processions,' Weizman wrote:

Occupying a roundabout demonstrates the power of tactical acupuncture: it blocks off all routes going in and out. Congestion moves outward like a wave, flowing down avenues and streets through large parts of the city. By pressuring a single pivotal point within a networked infrastructure, an entire city can be put under siege.

When the enemies of the crowd – the enemies of democracy – got themselves organised, Tahrir Square would soon become 'just a traffic circle again', as a *Washington Post* headline put it.

Egyptian elites were so spooked by the power of Cairo's crowds that in the aftermath of the military coup of July 2013, the security services killed at least 817 supporters of the Muslim Brotherhood, in a horrific 'dispersal' of two protest camps elsewhere in the capital; the death toll was likely more than 1,000. According to Human Rights Watch, it was one of the greatest massacres of demonstrators in a single day in modern history.[14] What the Egyptian government did next was telling: it removed Tahrir Square from the equation altogether, blocking entrances, posting heavy security all around the perimeter, even tanks, to prevent people entering – to prevent any further uprisings. The revolutionary crowd's famous site of congregation was itself such a threat that it had effectively to be shut down.

'There are a couple of places in Cairo which used to be gathering points for Islamists,' Elsheshtawy told me, 'where just by landscaping and installing street furniture, you break things up, so instead of having a huge space, you have broken up, disjointed little spaces – and the crowd will be more manageable.' He cited the Mostafa Mahmoud Mosque, and the area in front of the Abdeen Palace in downtown Cairo: large, open pieces of public space, where the outdoor prayers at the end of Ramadan would normally give Islamists an opportunity to gather – inviting another government intervention in urban planning. 'At Mostafa Mahmoud Mosque, they created this huge, landscaped roundabout with a fountain right in the middle of that space, and they diverted traffic around it, so that even though people go and pray there, it's not as massive as it used to be.'

In the Bahraini capital Manama, the government did the opposite, but with the same goal. Anti-government protests in

Bahrain focused on the Pearl Roundabout, named after the Pearl Monument at its centre, a 300-foot-high sculpture built in 1982 representing six dhow 'sails' supporting the pearl at its centre. In 2011, inspired by the uprisings in Tunisia and Egypt, a protest encampment sprang up at the Pearl Roundabout, much like those that acted as nerve centres and nodes for the sprawling crowds of Tahrir Square, Puerta del Sol and Gezi Park. After this site was brutally cleared by riot police, the Bahraini government removed any possibility of a repeat performance by destroying not just the Pearl Monument, but the entire roundabout. State-run Bahrain Television announced that the 'vile' anti-government protests had 'desecrated' the monument and it had to be 'cleansed'.[15] It is hard to flock to the town square to speak truth to power when those in power have just demolished the town square.

The possibility of designing out angry crowds from cities – using town planning as a tool to shore up elite power – is not a new one. The most well-known example is probably Baron von Haussmann's transformative renovations of Paris in the 1850s and 1860s, intended to stymie the still-unfinished revolutions of 1789 and 1848. Features that now seem essential parts of the French capital's landscape, in particular the very broad, straight, tree-lined boulevards, were designed, in Walter Benjamin's memorable words, for 'the securing of the city against civil war'. The idea was that such wide boulevards would undermine one of the Parisian working class's main strategic weapons, the barricade; it would simply be too difficult and time-consuming to construct them effectively, thus impeding further revolutionary outbreaks. The Champs-Elysées is seventy metres wide, accommodating an absurd eight car lanes. In addition, the boulevards would offer military vehicles and other troops the easiest of routes from the barracks to the poorer, more rebellious districts of Paris.

Just like modern Paris, modern London contains many seemingly innocuous, seemingly welcoming, often famous parts of the public realm that have been specifically tailored to limit the power of crowds and undermine free assembly. Trafalgar Square is famous not just for Nelson's Column, or its lions, but for its two fountains, each sitting in a large raised pool of standing water. The fountains were constructed in 1845 (only five years after the square itself was completed), specifically to limit the size of public gatherings, such were elite fears about the growing urban throng; at that moment, the worry was about Chartist gatherings so near to Westminster. The fountains are generally understood today as a bit of fun, an enterprise in public art and jollity. In fact, they were designed to take up almost half of Trafalgar Square's standing room so as to reduce the size of any crowd that assembled there by the same amount. The war against the crowd is always being waged by other means, built into the bricks and mortar of the city around us.

The post-revolutionary Egyptian government has taken this cynical approach to urban design to another level entirely. Following the military coup he led in 2013, deposing Egypt's first democratically elected leader, Mohamed Morsi, President Abdel Fattah al-Sisi's highly repressive authoritarian regime has not just shut the crowds out from Tahrir, but commenced a mammoth and megalomaniacal project to lift politics out of the capital and away from the Egyptian masses altogether. Announced in 2015, Sisi's plan is to build a brand-new city in the desert twenty-eight miles south-east of Cairo, relocating government agencies and ministries, Egypt's parliament, foreign embassies, and a substantial presidential compound. It sounds like a medieval fable about the hubris of a crazed despot – which is effectively what it is, if you subtract the word 'medieval'.

The new city is currently referred to only as the New Administrative Capital, an appropriately colourless name for such a dystopian project. Its vast expense is being covered in part by the Egyptian military – who stand to reap huge financial benefits if it finally comes together – along with the private sector. Its political function is not merely the further entwinement of the military in civic life, or the aggrandisement of a would-be dictator, but spatial, in the most cynical fashion. Sisi's project amounts to a turbocharged version of Baron von Haussmann's changes to nineteenth-century Paris. The single surefire way to disarm the people, the electorate whose sovereignty you crushed with the barrel of a gun? Design the crowd out from the beginning. Build a new centre of power altogether, devoid of public squares, populated by wealthier Egyptians living in gated communities, with state-of-the-art surveillance systems and military positions strategically embedded across the city.

'On February 11, 2011, the people of Egypt walked from Tahrir Square to Mubarak's presidential palace to force him to resign,' reflects Mustafa Menshawy in his book *Leaving the Muslim Brotherhood*. 'Once the president moves to the New Administrative Capital, such a demonstration of public will is not going to be possible again.' What better way to secure the city – and your own increasingly terroristic premiership – against any backlash from the people?

If Sisi's fantastical twenty-first-century despotism represents an extreme attempt to design out the unruly urban masses completely, and the Trafalgar Square fountains and Haussman's broad boulevards represented the spatial logic of the revanchist, authoritarian nineteenth-century city, we can also see more subtly pernicious anti-crowd practices reflected in the glass and steel totems of cities like London and New York today. In most contemporary Western cities, even something as ostensibly mundane as street furniture is now usually calculated to mitigate against gatherings, against the grave sin of idle sociality in public, and against free, open and uncommodified leisure.

Peppered with 'hostile architecture' to prevent loitering and public conviviality, our streets and squares are being redesigned to funnel us directly towards work or the shops – they are spaces built for 'homo economicus', that is, human beings interacting purely transactionally, rather than as social citizens. Indeed, many parts of our cities are not really built with human beings in mind at all, but as 'growth engines' for capital. The modern neoliberal city needs efficient shoppers and workers, not *flâneurs* and dawdlers. What look like potential meeting grounds for crowds in the modern city are frequently apparitions: shiny, expensive, privatised city-centre regeneration zones, where genuine public spaces have been replaced with privately owned public spaces (POPS). These new urban plazas are built by private construction firms and maintained by their corporate owners, usually as a legal requirement attached to their lucrative new rent-accumulating office or commercial buildings: to 'put a bit back' into the city from which they are extracting extravagant amounts of profit.

These spaces are often mute: they do not scream their anti-publicness with barbed wire and huge red signs. Instead they are intrinsically, quietly hostile to the *civitas*: to the urban crowd, and to democracy. POPS are patrolled by private security guards and subject to the rules and whims of the private companies that own them. These owners are entitled to ban any kind of gathering, however peaceful, and move along whoever they care to, with no reason, explanation, or democratic oversight. It is their very masquerade, the fact that they appear to be public – and are under no legal responsibility to point out to passers-by that they are privately owned – that is at the heart of the problem.

New York City, according to the city administration's own recent estimate, is home to more than 590 privately owned public spaces, the majority packed into Manhattan, threaded between the skyscrapers. As in many other Western cities, these plazas were the developers' trade-off, a tawdry and cynical gift to the public that would allow them to build higher, or to waive responsibilities such as affordable housing requirements. POPS are what the urban crowd receives as a concession in exchange for even fatter profits for private property. Many of New York's private plazas are designed to remain empty, unadorned, and unwelcoming, driving people into the surrounding bars and shops owned by the same companies. 'On a recent weekday during evening rush hour, there were more pigeons than people in the almost

7,500-square-foot through-block arcade at 7 Hanover Square' in downtown Manhattan, noted Audrey Wachs in a recent survey of the city's POPS.[16]

They are, all told, a quite phenomenal swindle against the public, and public assembly. A 2017 audit by the New York City comptroller's office found that more than half of the 333 POPS sites they surveyed had failed to install the public amenities stipulated by law – not providing seating, for example, or a water fountain – or that they restricted entry to the public completely. This is even before you get to the rules which the landowners are *allowed* to enforce, with the help of comprehensive surveillance technology and private security guards – usually dressed up to look disarmingly like police officers, just to further enhance the theatrical simulation of public life.

These rules usually comprise some or all of the following: no performing, no rallying, no music, no amplified sounds, no pets, no ball games, no skateboarding, no consumption of alcohol, no glass bottles, no taking tops off, no cycling, no barbecues, no sleeping, no filming, no photography. While there are a few specific targets in each set of POPS rules – rough sleepers are almost always a target; young people at play are another – they are overwhelmingly aimed at proscribing the convivial crowd, the political crowd, the cultural crowd; even a crowd which simply wishes to relax after work and enjoy some fresh air together.

The intentions of the political crowd collided with the realities of the twenty-first-century city in 2011, when London's answer to Occupy Wall Street sprang up, and attempted to establish an anti-capitalist protest camp called Occupy London Stock Exchange. The problem was that the seemingly public space outside the Stock Exchange, Paternoster Square, was not public at all. To the crowd's surprise, it turned out that this was in fact private land, owned by the Japanese Mitsubishi Estate Company. At their request, the protesters were swiftly moved on by the police and the company's private security guards, barriers were erected, and the following sign was put up:

Paternoster Square is private land. Any licence to the public to enter or cross this land is revoked forthwith. There is no implied or express permission to enter the premises or any part. Any such entry will constitute a trespass.

It was an apt lesson in the way that neoliberal power translates into physical space, and infringes the crowd's right to free assembly. As the architecture critic Rowan Moore pointed out, the duplicity was especially heinous since 'every architectural statement, planning application, and press release, in the protracted redevelopment of Paternoster Square, described this "private land" as "public space".'[17] These are mirages, where an oasis of public life should be.

Our freedom to gather in the public square with others is further compromised by the surveillance revolution, another insidious constraint on free assembly and social spontaneity in the city – a restriction of the ease with which open crowds might establish themselves and grow. It is still unclear just how often police forces in the UK, US and beyond have used 'Stingray' or 'IMSI catcher' devices, which mimic mobile phone masts to gather information from mobile phones in the vicinity in real time, even eavesdropping on phone conversations – but we know from a variety of leaked and declassified documents that numerous police forces on both sides of the Atlantic have access to them. And we know that the US Department of Homeland Security used Stingrays at least 2,351 times between 2013 and 2019; but in the absence of transparency, this is almost certainly an underestimation.[18]

Drones, too, have been extensively deployed to monitor protests from the air, and are already being used as a form of evidence gathering to facilitate prosecutions. In the case of Lore Blumenthal, given a two-and-a-half year prison sentence for arson at a 2020 Black Lives Matter protest in Philadelphia, the police tracked her down using aerial surveillance in combination with an online breadcrumb trail, including photos they found of her on Instagram, and even details from Blumenthal's Etsy and LinkedIn accounts.

In the UK, developments in surveillance technology, the war on terror, and a New Labour government determined to appear tough on anti-social behaviour, combined to make London the most-surveilled city in the world in the 2000s. A report commissioned by the Information Commissioner's Office found that, during the 1990s, 78 per cent of the entire Home Office crime prevention budget was spent on implementing CCTV – and that a further £500 million of public money was spent on it between 2000 and 2006.[19] While London has been overtaken since then, the capital remains the tenth most-surveilled city in the world – with the caveat that China's figures are hard to gauge, beyond the fact that its vast surveillance apparatus has expanded at a phenomenal rate – now numbering 127,423 cameras, or thirteen cameras per 1,000 people.[20]

The famous Riot Act of 1714 could be read by a magistrate to twelve or more persons who were 'unlawfully, riotously, and tumultuously assemble[d] together'. The crowd would then have one hour to disperse before arrests began. Jump forward to the twenty-first century, and we find both New Labour and Conservative governments inventing new judicial instruments that can be used to disperse suspicious urban crowds, including ASBOs, curfews, dispersal orders and public space protection orders (PSPOs). Under the Anti-Social Behaviour Act 2003, local councils could designate 'dispersal zones' for up to six months at a time, which then allowed the police to force groups of two or more people to leave the area for at least twenty-four hours, if they were of the opinion that antisocial behaviour was either happening, or likely to happen (adding a sinister note of 'pre-crime' to an already arbitrary process). The Tories refined this tool with the Anti-Social Behaviour, Crime and Policing Act 2014, allowing officers to disperse people from public space for up to forty-eight hours if they had 'reasonable grounds' to suspect that their removal would reduce 'the likelihood of members of the public in the locality being harassed, alarmed or distressed'. The only legal or bureau-cratic oversight these dispersal orders have is that they must be in writing, and signed by the officer in question – effectively, an official note saying: 'Go on, sod off.'

It is worth reflecting that before the rise of the private car, our city streets were relatively accessible and well-shared public spaces, affording the possibility for just the social spontaneity, crowd formation and play that are now so rare. The car is the emblem of the twentieth-century privatisation of our lives, and the privileging of the needs of the wealthy over public well-being and happiness at large. The way cars have been allowed to dom-inate the urban fabric has had a hugely deleterious effect on cities as democratic and social spaces, not to mention on our health.

Urban historian Myles Zhang writes that New York's streets before the car were 'for everyone: horse-drawn carriages, trolleys, omnibuses, and pedestrians. With residents in dense tenement areas unable to access public parks and playgrounds, the street doubled as recreational space and as an extension of the side-walk.' The age of automobile supremacy introduced hard borders, squeezed pedestrians into narrow pavement-channels and made public life not just miserable, but often near-impossible. Zhang estimates that Manhattan avenues are approximately 100 feet wide, with a full seventy feet given over to cars; and yet, only 22 per cent of Manhattan residents own cars.[21] At the nadir of this process in the 1950s and 60s, some of the loveliest central public squares in major European cities were used as car parks – some-thing that now seems horrifying, as you move freely around Piazza Maggiore in Bologna, or Gammeltorv and Nytorv in Copenhagen.

Not only are cars literally poisoning us and the world around us, while killing hundreds of pedestrians every year, they are also a spectacularly inefficient and antisocial form of transport, both when clogging up the roads and in the myriad parking spaces they require that pockmark our cities like chronic acne.[22] At its most dysfunctional, the neoliberal city is one choked with solitary drivers, stuck in traffic jams, spewing out toxic fumes, growing steadily more irate as they sit in their heavily fortified metal box, glaring out at the public from behind glass, swearing at each other and the roadworks needed to make the city function for the population at large. It sounds rather histrionic, perhaps even dystopian, but it's something I see as I'm walking around London every day.

'We are the only animals that build habitats that harm us,' observes Eloi Juvillà, director of Building and Logistics for Barcelona.[23] According to several studies, air pollution causes 3,500 premature deaths a year in that city's metropolitan area.[24] And it really doesn't have to be this way. Visiting Barcelona under the progressive leadership of Ada Colau, the mayor from 2015 to 2023, I had the revelatory experience of moseying through the famous boulevards of the Eixample district one Sunday afternoon, to discover that all parked cars had been removed, the droning noise and poisonous fumes of motor traffic had been shut out, and the broad, tree-lined Carrer de Sants was filled with the convivial buzz of human life instead. Kids were doing cartwheels and riding bikes, whole families were taking a post-prandial stroll together (the *paseo*, like the Italian *passeggiata*), musicians sat on the kerb and strummed their guitars, and groups of older folks were sitting with coffees and glasses of wine at outdoor tables planted defiantly in the middle of the street.

This was the Obrim Carrers (Let's open the streets) initiative, introduced in 2016 on a few key arterial roads every weekend between 9 a.m. and 8 p.m. Obrim Carrers is independent of the more famous Superilles (Superblocks) scheme, another of Colau's radical policy instruments, where all the inner streets in each three-by-three square of nine blocks are closed to through-traffic, and the streets are returned to the people who live there. (Residents are allowed to drive through at a maximum of 10 km/h, and all previously kerbside parking must be redirected underground.) This programme has successfully turned multiple toxic city streets into green, pedestrianised spaces, installing picnic benches, trees and plants, colourful children's play areas, toy and book libraries, drastically reducing deadly nitrogen oxide and particle pollution levels, and making the city's open spaces public and welcoming once again. People hold birthday parties and potlatch meals, workshops, games, lectures, music performances and dances, and kids' entertainments, and mingle with neighbours and strangers alike.

These are effectively pro-crowd policies, supportive of exactly the spontaneity, conviviality and uncommodified cultural and social lives that the neoliberal city has denied to us – and they are finally getting the advocates they need in city halls around the world. Barcelona's Superblock model has already been adapted and applied in Berlin, Vienna, Rotterdam, Bogotá and Los Angeles, with hundreds more cities expressing interest, while other cities have developed similar programmes such as the Strade Aperte (open streets) in Milan, the Low-Traffic Neighbourhoods in London, and Paris Respire (Paris breathes); Paris mayor Anne Hidalgo has also proclaimed 'the reconquest of the Seine', with over 3 km of riverside highway reclaimed for the public.

In September 2020, with social life tentatively revived in London, I went to a bar near where I live in Peckham with a few friends. It was a warm evening, Covid-19 was still about, and we sat outside with our pints. The area's main thoroughfare, Rye Lane, is also its commercial hub and high street: a typical class- and race-straddling mixture of businesses in a gradually gentrifying part of London, comprising the usual chain super-markets, fast-food outlets, banks, student-friendly bars, pound shops, a small record store, old-school butchers and fishmongers, several West African and East Asian groceries, and a number of independent restaurants and takeaways.

Two months earlier, the local authority had closed this main street to all traffic bar bicycles, to enable safer social distancing on the slender and usually packed pavements. It had been a small consolation that summer, in a period of profound social estrangement, to arrive there to do my shopping as usual, and see mostly older locals sitting out on plastic chairs, chatting away in the middle of what was normally a chaotic high street. As my friends and I emerged onto Rye Lane that night to head home, at around 11 p.m., we were greeted with an extraordinary sight: an impromptu cricket game going on in the middle of the street. About forty or fifty people had stopped to watch, and play at being (very) casual fielders, and we did the same, and anyone who wanted could try bowling – my friend Luke, who plays amateur cricket, had a go and was disappointed to send one floating down the leg side.

The night air was buzzing with a very particular kind of chatter and laughter: the rare and giddy atmosphere of urban spontaneity – the glee of seeing something genuinely new, and a familiar landscape transformed. It turned out that the workers from Holdron's Arcade (a collection of tiny micro-businesses) and their colleagues next door in Khan's Bargains (a vast local institution that seems to stock everything, from everywhere in the world) had made it into a lockdown tradition, after closing up for the night – and welcomed anyone who wished to join in. One night they'd switched from cricket and held a mass volleyball match across the width of the road instead. None of that conviviality would have been possible, or even conceivable, without the space for the open crowd to form.

Nevertheless, even with these positive policy solutions pushing back against creeping acts of privatisation and cynical urban design, many of the opportunities for crowds to gather in the modern city come with a significant price tag attached. The actions of progressive mayors and city halls around the world are to be lauded – and hopefully expanded – but much of what constitutes urban social and cultural life in the neoliberal city falls under the heading of the heavily gated, securitised and surveilled, commodified, urban 'events economy'. Perhaps the biggest threat to the freedom of the twenty-first-century crowd – to assemble, to associate, to flow at its own leisure – is the phenomenal success modern capitalism has found in monetising it and, in doing so, bringing it to heel.

Tracking the evolution of the postwar counterculture, Jeremy Gilbert makes the point that the emergence of stadium rock and pop concerts effectively absorbed the wild energies of, and ultimately replaced, major hippie 'free' festivals such as Hyde Park in 1968–71, Woodstock in 1969 and the Isle of Wight in 1970.[25] 'It became conventional wisdom in the live entertainment industry that a music festival was simply too big and chaotic for it to be possible really to make money from it, predictably, and to be able to organise and police the crowds,' Gilbert said. 'That's the context in which the stadium concert becomes the alternative format, because a stadium is built to contain and regulate the physical disposition of huge crowds. In Foucaldian terms, it's a space of surveillance, a space in which everyone can be surveilled, as well as one in which everyone can see the performers all at one time.'[26]

While some parts of the contemporary establishment are still clinging to Le Bon's analysis, as a foundation from which to pathologise, disperse and brutalise crowds – the mythology of the mob is tenacious – others have recognised the innate human desire for collective joy and, rather than seek to repress that desire completely, have instead seized upon it as a money-making opportunity. There is no greater evidence of the attenuated and domesticated nature of the twenty-first-century crowd than the phenomenal rise of the urban events industry. It has become an integral part of the running of the contemporary city, and the reimagining of citizens as income-generating instruments.

There have always been cultural events – seventeenth-century maypole dances and Whitsun ales were *events* – but never before have they constituted an 'events industry' on such a scale: heavily sponsored, gated, securitised, stewarded, surveilled, expensively ticketed, and carrying a range of media and corporate partners. City administrations love these kinds of events: they are the perfect fodder for 'place-branding' in the post-industrial age. It doesn't hurt that their crowd members now generate extra free publicity for the host city via social media, or that such events attract both domestic and international tourists, meaning hotel and other supplementary spending, on top of hefty fees accrued from the profit-driven companies who organise them. Crowd members have become so used to the growing list of restrictions that are a condition of entry – no bags bigger than A4 size, no water bottles, no outside food, present your passport, look into this camera so we can add you to the database – that they rarely complain about how much they are monitored, herded and ordered about, from one queue to another, in the name of security and profit.

A report I conducted for the *Guardian* in 2019, based on FOI requests to all of London's thirty-two local councils, found that the city's world-renowned public parks were being blighted throughout the summer by a dramatic rise in for-profit, fenced-off and ticketed music festivals.[27] Council budgets had been stripped to the bone by nine years of Conservative austerity, and in their desperation, councils seemed to be saying yes to every festival bid they received. A report by MPs in 2017 found that a staggering 92 per cent of parks budgets had been cut since 2010–11. Numerous London councils now annually surrender their parks to paid-for festivals for weeks at a time, at the height of the summer – the one period everyone wants access to them. One festival might only last two or three days, over a weekend, but the amount of time required to construct and then 'demount' miles worth of twelve-foot-high steel perimeter fencing, stages, tents, power supply, cabling and so on, means that large swathes of these theoretically peaceful, accessible open spaces are being enclosed and effectively part-privatised for whole chunks of July and August. As a result, they become off-limits to citizens who just want to play, walk and relax, without having to pay £70 or more to enter a giant securitised zone – or having to listen to Mumford & Sons once they have done so.

London & Partners, the public-private partnership set up by Mayor Boris Johnson in 2011 to promote the capital, estimated that event leisure tourism contributed £2.8 billion to the city's economy in 2015 alone, £644 million of which was from overseas 'events tourists'.[28] Increasingly, tourists are visiting cities not for the destination per se, but for the events occurring there. Chief among these are sporting events, which generate more than 70 per cent of major events-related spending in London – music is actually some way behind on this score. Amid huge fanfare in the past few years, a growing number of major overseas sporting events have been specially staged in London, effectively 'on tour' from their US leagues, as the NBA, NFL and MLB (basketball, American football and baseball) seek to expand their commercial reach in Europe. According to London & Partners, 250,000 people attended 'NFL on Regent Street' in 2017, which wasn't even an American football match, just a promotional event for the NFL at large.

Where there are crowds, there are potential consumers, and in the absence of state support, commercial sponsorship (now euphemistically called 'partnership') is integral to the events industry's every move. In 2024, the capital played host to the *Tata Consultancy Services* London Marathon, the *Ford* Ride-London, the *Guinness* Six Nations, the *Gemini* Boat Race, the *Emirates* FA Cup Final and the *EFG* London Jazz Festival. Meanwhile, Pride in London somehow managed to rack up forty-two 'partners' in 2023, from 'headline sponsors' United Airlines to Tesco, Coca-Cola, Netflix, WeWork, IKEA and UPS, amid persistent criticisms that the politics has been drained out of an event originally started as a grassroots rebellion against homophobia and transphobia, in favour of a tide of corporate pinkwashing. There is still live music in Hyde Park every summer, just like there was in the late 1960s – but in the place of Jimi Hendrix, Pink Floyd or Fleetwood Mac performing for free, we find *American Express presents* BST Hyde Park. In 2024, standing tickets for Andrea Bocelli in Hyde Park started at £101.15 (£89.95 plus £11.20 fees), rising to £324.95 (£299.95 plus £25 fees) for a 'Gold VIP HydeAway' seated ticket.

The problem for critics of this new reality is that much of the events industry is sincerely focused on making the crowd safer and happier. It is hard to refute the argument that the more carefully planned and managed a large event is, the safer it proves for those attending, and the more the crowd will enjoy it. Not only do you minimise the risk of death, injury or potential trouble, but everyone – not least the most vulnerable members of the crowd – benefits when you have the right number of toilets, the right number of exits, the right transport access, accessibility for people with mobility issues, good sight-lines, food and water and childcare facilities.

These are all good things; a catastrophe like Woodstock '99, where all these events industry provisions were absent, is not a preferable alternative. And a reasonable argument is often made by organisers of free cultural festivals that corporate sponsors can pay for these provisions, and pay for events such as Notting Hill Carnival, Pride and Mela to stay free and unticketed, and accessible to all. But it's hard not to suspect that something is being lost along the way, in an era when venture capital–backed music video platform Boiler Room receives Arts Council funding to broker Notting Hill Carnival sponsorship deals, and livestream its intimate hedonism to the world, or long-standing free community festivals, such as south London's beloved Lambeth Country Show, suddenly have high fencing and a heavy security presence, prompting outrage and boycotts.[29]

It is notable, given that the whole point of a city is population density, living cheek-by-jowl, having someone to converse with who isn't related to you, just how hostile city elites have always been to the gathering of people. Or, to be precise, how hostile to particular types of people: 'the masses', the subaltern – the crowd without power. It is a paradox that lies right at the heart of the modern city. We need people here, en masse, to do the jobs that are here – because if people leave the city in substantial numbers, as they do sporadically, things can get a little bit 'Detroit'. But once the urban crowd has clocked off, their tendency to assemble usually becomes a problem, particularly if they are doing so on their own terms and without spending enough money. And so a great deal of effort has been put into designing out free and open urban crowds, or enclosing the urban commons via gating, walling, monetary barriers, increased surveillance and policing, or in some cases via the subterfuge of privately owned public spaces.

But the desire to gather in the most famous parts of our city centres, turning them into a modern-day agora or carnival, is still one of society's most vital and most ancient instincts. The association between the traditional geographical location of crowd joy, and the crowd joy itself, is beautifully articulated in a Finnish expression, *Torilla tavataan!* which literally means 'To the town square!' or 'To the market square!' – because that's where you go when your ice hockey team wins, or it's New Year's Eve, or you just had a particularly cracking harvest. It has become a catch-all expression in Finnish, broadly: 'Let's celebrate!' What is perhaps heartening, in light of the litany of restrictions outlined above, is that when this natural instinct is frustrated, when the town square suddenly has a massive fence around it and some corporation is charging a fortune to enter what should be urban space held in common and accessible to all, the crowd does not simply accept its fate.

On New Year's Eve 2022 in central London, hundreds of thousands of people had gathered as usual for the annual midnight fireworks display, organised by the mayor of London's office. For years this was a free and open event, attracting crowds of up to 500,000 people. This changed in 2014, when Boris Johnson introduced the novelties of ticketing, fencing, an entrance fee and a capacity of 100,000. What were the other four-fifths of the New Year's crowd supposed to do? Johnson told everyone else to stay at home and watch the fireworks on TV instead. At the time, speaking as shadow minister for London, Sadiq Khan criticised his Tory rival's decision as 'unfair and ineffective . . . driven by cuts, not safety'. He then proceeded to keep it a ticketed, fenced-off affair when he became mayor eighteen months later.

On 31 December 2022, London's New Year's Eve fireworks were once again, as has now become the norm, ticketed, fenced off, securitised and completely sold out. The 100,000 ticketholders were inside the cordon, gathered around the *lastminute.com* London Eye (previously the *Coca-Cola* London Eye), having bought £15 tickets to watch the twelve-minute display. As the £1.3 million generated by these ticket sales did not come close to covering the event's costs, however, a further £3 million was spent by City Hall out of its own (*our* own) public revenues, in order to put on what was now essentially a private event.

London's excluded New Year's Eve crowd weren't having any of this, and irate groups of revellers set about forcing their way past the hoardings, fencing, security and police. Scuffles broke out, and there were some minor injuries. It was not a decorous scene; no doubt the people forcing their way into the cordon were drunk and obnoxious and made life needlessly hard for the low-paid stewards. But what else do you expect, on New Year's Eve of all nights, if you try and keep the crowd from the town square to which they belong, and which belongs to the crowd?

7

Myths and Scapegoats: Fatal Crowds

Amid the gathering storms of the 2020s, with signs of ecological collapse all around us, it is telling that the world's most obscenely rich men are seeking an ever more hermetic isolation from the crowd. 'The billionaires and their bunkers' have become an apocalyptic talking point in recent years. Forward-thinking disaster capitalists are building high-security underground shelters in remote areas, equipped with bowling lanes and swimming pools. Elon Musk wants to escape to Mars. Peter Thiel keeps trying to build a vast, secluded compound in a remote part of New Zealand. It is hard not to read these stories as indications that the world's tiny handful of super-elites understand very well where the world they own so much of is headed, and are using their ill-gotten gains to get the hell out of Dodge – and away from the rest of us.

The solutions might be comically loopy, and are certainly tinged with megalomaniacal paranoia, but the looming problems underlying them are very real. In the coming decades, interlinked and self-propelling food and water security crises, extreme weather, wars and famines, as well as more global health disasters, will drive greater mass migration, ever more rapid urbanisation, and ever greater urban density. More than 50 per cent of forcibly displaced people already live in cities; further climate crisis displacement will only lead to more of this rural-to-urban migration. As discussed in the preceding chapter, city populations will have exploded in size by 2050.

The high-density crowds of the twenty-first century have already been victim to some truly horrifying, deadly disasters. The Hajj pilgrimage in Mina, Saudi Arabia, in 2015, in which at least 2,400 people died. The Halloween celebrations in Seoul in 2022, in which 159 people died. The football match in Indonesia in 2022, in which 125 people died. It is awful to reduce each of these individual lives lost to a number, not to mention that doing so omits the enduring grief of those they left behind and the trauma of those who survived, often with life-changing injuries – and yet these are only a small selection of recent crowd tragedies. Since the start of 2020 – four calendar years at the time of writing – there have already been twenty such crowd tragedies where more than ten people have died. There have been hundreds globally since 2000. All of these crowd tragedies were preventable, because all crowd tragedies are preventable.

Closest to home for me, spiritually and literally, is one that occurred as recently as January 2023. The famous concert venue Brixton Academy in south-west London – where I have been throwing myself around in moshpits without parental oversight since I was thirteen – was the scene of a harrowing incident when, amid extensive chaos and confusion, two women were killed in the crush as fans tried to get into a concert by the Afrobeats star Asake. This time, media reports in the critical hours afterwards blamed people turning up to the venue without tickets, hoping to force their way in – a vogueish crowd bogeyman, the chancers who have committed the sin of not participating in respectable society by paying to access it.

It is an allegation usually layered with a low note of classism and racism. The subaltern crowd (in this case, mostly young Black music fans) does not play fair, does not adhere to the same social norms as you do. You'd buy a ticket, wouldn't you? Like most forms of crowd demonisation, the 'ticketless mob' is a creation of hearsay and rumour. For how could we possibly verify that people turned up at Brixton Academy without tickets in significant numbers? The evidence as stated in press reports was, basically, that it seemed busy inside and outside the venue, and a few fans said they *heard* that's what some people were doing. Who knows, maybe it was a contributory factor – but the bar needs to be a little higher than that, evidentially speaking. Even a BBC Radio 4 documentary promising to uncover the 'real truth' behind the tragedy, focusing on corrupt security staff taking bribes to admit people without tickets, failed to address several other strange and alarming bits of evidence: 1) video footage of police throwing a crowd member down a flight of stairs; 2) a police dog running loose through the venue, and 3) what appears to be a member of security staff in high-vis, kicking the crap out of a fan lying on the floor.[1] There are still far too many unanswered questions to be clear about what happened that night.

In the aftermath of the 2021 Astroworld disaster in Houston, Texas, most of the blame targeted the festival headliner and host, the rapper Travis Scott, for inciting the 50,000-strong crowd, and continuing to perform while fatal crushes unfolded in the dark beneath him. The show went on for a full forty-two minutes after police first reported that a number of people had fallen under the weight of a crowd collapse, such was the density. Harrowing footage from within the crowd shows fans in tears, chanting 'stop the show' and crying for help. Eight people lost their lives that night, and two more died as a result of their injuries. Eventually, though Travis Scott was found not to be criminally liable, he still faced barrages of criticism and multiple civil lawsuits from attendees and families of the deceased, some of which have been settled out of court.

In Le Bonian terms, here was the sinister agitator and demagogue who had whipped the madding crowd into a hysterical frenzy, before it callously and violently devoured its own; in its derangement, the crowd kept partying while some members wailed and fell unconscious in its midst. There was zero evidence for this reading, but it fitted a certain type of misanthropic narrative. 'At Least 8 People Dead after Crowd Panics at Travis Scott

Concert', read the *Entertainment Weekly* headline. The chain of events and implied causality here is a Le Bon legacy too: the story being told is that the crowd panicked, and *therefore* at least eight of them died in the ensuing melee. It is simply not how these things work.

These red herrings were accompanied by preposterous conspiracy theories, which ran riot on social media and were then covered in the mainstream press: that Astroworld was not in fact a music festival at all, but a Satanic cult ritual, and the dead were sacrifices. 'The music industry is demonic and collects souls', read one TikTok comment that received 34,000 likes. This was absurd, macabre theatre, taking up column inches which could have been devoted to meaningful analysis.

My conjecture would be that very few of those TikTok users actually believed Astroworld was an elaborate Satanic ritual – but it made for better headlines and a more appealingly lurid discourse, perhaps even an escapist way of processing the real-life horror that had unfolded. Either way, it was preferable to sifting through reams of risk assessments, safety protocols, egress diagrams and site design permits.

In the aftermath, far too little media and public attention was directed towards the promoters Live Nation, the Harris County Sports and Convention Corporation, who manage the venue, the Houston and Harris County authorities who granted the permits, or the Houston Police and Fire Department, who were present in large numbers and also had the power to stop the gig. 'Normally, if it was something drastic,' Scott quite reasonably told the police in the ensuing investigation, 'someone would have to come hit the button or pull the plug.' The rap legend and polymath Chuck D, of Public Enemy, was even more damning on this point, publishing an open letter that began:

> I cannot believe we're at the point where I gotta say this out loud: Travis Scott is a performer, an act, not a concert promoter. He doesn't run the sound or venues or festivals or their staff. He

doesn't build stages or coordinate logistics, he's not an expert in crowd control or security or emergency medical services. But he does trust Live Nation and all the other concert promoters who are supposed to do all of this. And yet here we are, 10 deaths and counting. 10 broken families. The world is mourning. I'm tired of these corporations shucking their most crucial responsibility. These folks simply say Rest in Peace and move on. This negligence can't continue. Folks want answers. I'm not buying the Young Black Man did it. He's being blamed for a crime while the old white men running the corps that Travis and his fans trusted with their lives stay quiet in the shadows, counting their money and watching their stock prices go up and up.

The discourse that followed each of these crowd tragedies will be more than familiar by this point. Whenever something goes wrong in a crowd, the headlines and the public conversation in general still fixate on the same, moralising, unevidenced tropes: bad crowd behaviour, drunkenness, drug-taking, delinquency, violence, hysteria, mindlessness, sinister agitators, and a callous lack of concern for fellow crowd members in trouble. All of which reveals the moral turpitude of the crowd in question – leaving an open goal for some racism or Orientalism, which is often implicit to the conversation: *these animals left their peers to die, trampling over their helpless bodies.* Alternatively, if you're feeling more universally nihilistic, it reveals the moral turpitude of humanity in general. *Why are people like this? Why would the crowd do this to itself?*

Above all, the suggestion is always there, whether in black and white on the tabloid front page, or circulating in the public conversation more insidiously, that the people inside these fatal crowds had agency over the disasters that befell them. If they had only behaved differently. If only they weren't so selfish. If only they weren't so drunk. If only they weren't so irresponsible. If only they weren't so pathetically in thrall to . . . their rap god, or their heavy metal subculture, or their political leader, or their football team. If only they hadn't all lost their heads. It's tragic, of course, but the crowd itself could have – and therefore should have – stopped this from happening.

Those who have studied these crowd disasters in all their traumatic detail will tell you that the myth of the madding crowd is not just insulting to the dead and the grieving, but actively harmful to ensuring crowd safety in future. Deflecting blame onto the imagined behaviour of the mob leaves little room for serious analysis of what went wrong in a fatal crush, and distracts us from the practical reforms that would stop them going wrong again. The academics, forensic teams and crowd safety professionals who have watched all of the harrowing CCTV and smartphone footage, read the post-mortems, collated the eyewitness reports, analysed the diagrams and tabulated the data want the people involved in designing and hosting mass events to learn what could be life-saving lessons.

Professor Keith Still is a man often called upon for inquests, investigations, public explanations and criminal trials in the aftermath of a crowd tragedy – though naturally he prefers the less saddening or gory side of his work, the preventative side. Still has run training courses, consultations and workshops for thirty-five years, helping to improve event safety design and procedures everywhere, from the Beijing Olympics to Aberdeen's Hogmanay, from the Hong Kong Jockey Club to the Jamarat Bridge in Saudi Arabia used by millions in the Hajj. When we speak via video chat, he is unable to share specific thoughts on the causes of the tragic crowd crush at Astroworld, because he is legally bound to silence while advising on the ensuing investigations and lawsuits. His official motto is taken from Cicero: 'Let the safety of the people be the highest law.' If he had an unofficial motto, it would be what he reminds the media every time he is invited on TV following a crowd disaster: 'People don't die because they're panicking, they panic because they are dying.'

When people die in a crowd, it is almost always from 'compression asphyxia' – a crushing of their lungs through excessive density, which makes it impossible to breathe. They don't die because they are scared, or behaving hysterically, or irrationally. They don't 'stampede' – horses stampede, wildebeest stampede; people do not – and yet that word is ubiquitous in discussions of crowd deaths. People are rarely ever trampled on, even unwittingly or unavoidably, even when crowds collapse. In one of Professor Still's data tables categorising twenty-first-century crowd tragedies, under the heading 'Failure elements', one cause of safety failure crops up more often than any other: 'Design (Capacity, Crowd Flow)'. The vast majority of crowd crushes can be traced back to the planning stage, where any potential pinch points, bottlenecks and other density risks should have been identified and designed out. 'They inevitably tend to point the finger at the crowd for being at fault,' Still says, 'rather than asking, what were the underlying fundamentals? What was the underlying causality?'

When he is called in to investigate a crowd disaster, the first two documents he asks to see are the risk assessment and the crowd management plan. 'The characteristics, the DNA of these accidents, are always the same,' Still reflects: 'insufficient preparation, lack of staff training, lack of wayfinding, poor signage, and allowing the volume of people-flow to exceed capacity, or throughput.' He is surprised by how naive some event organisers are. 'I didn't realise that that could happen here!' he mimics, sarcastically. 'We've got this huge space, how could people possibly get crushed in it?' The venue for Astroworld, NRG Park, was significantly *under* its maximum capacity when ten people were crushed to death – but those people had no way out of an area enclosed by barriers on three sides, while a long list of safeguards, monitoring and emergency mechanisms seem to have been absent.

Another problem, Still says, is that, wary of litigation and reputational damage, event organisers and venues rarely admit publicly to a near-miss on a crowd tragedy. 'They don't capture that information, they don't share it, they don't learn from it, because it opens them up to all sorts of potential liabilities.' This culture needs to change too.

The only way to ensure greater crowd safety across the events industry, Still says firmly, is widespread, standardised, higher-quality education and training. Still and his colleagues have developed a range of tools that allow people in the industry to visualise crowd density risks in the dynamic way they unfold, using graphs and diagrams and computer animations, colour-coding the crowd as green, amber and red as density builds up. On the non-technological level, 'the language, the vocabulary around crowds is often so poor,' he says. Words like 'hysteria' and 'stampede' are fallacies, 'panic' is wilfully misunderstood, and even describing a place as 'packed' or 'like Piccadilly Circus' is entirely unhelpful.

Instead, Still and his team teach event professionals to understand and discuss density in precise statistical terms: one, two, three, four or five people per square metre – five is the upper limit for standing spaces.[2] Above that, things get dangerous: people lose control of their movement, the crowd is susceptible to waves of motion, and crushing and collapse become serious risks.

Another obvious measure would be to invest more in training on-the-ground stewarding staff, and to improve their working conditions – even if this is a secondary concern to the overall de-risking of the event environment via design. One former event steward, who had worked at Brixton Academy and the Lovebox Festival, told Will Pritchard in an article for *DJ Mag*, '[It was] possibly one of the most unsafe work environments I've experienced: an army of teenagers meant to crowd-manage tens of thousands of people, working fourteen-hour shifts with hardly any breaks'.[3] Training, Pritchard concluded, was 'minimal, and largely unmemorable but for a few details'. There is no legal requirement for event stewards to hold a particular qualification in the UK, and most are paid the minimum wage or little more.

More importantly, there is no nationally mandated, minimum standard of crowd safety qualification for the people at the top – the suits pulling the strings, scoping out the site design and signing off the emergency protocols. What those individuals do have a keen eye on, though, all the more so in a competitive events marketplace, is their own profit margin. 'With economic pressures and austerity affecting major events,' Still reflects, 'larger numbers of venues are saying: "Can we get more people in here? Can we sell more tickets? Can we sell differential tickets, i.e. can we sell more expensive tickets if we give them preferential treatment, front of stage areas and so on?" There's all manner of ways of making sure that an event is economically more viable, but you never compromise on safety: there's always a consequence for that.'

It has become commonplace, in the years since the pandemic, to observe that people have 'forgotten how to behave' in the wake of Covid lockdowns and social distancing – how to behave appropriately in public, in crowds, and in general. Why, asked the *Guardian* in 2022, are British audiences so out of control? Everything from rowdy heckling at comedy gigs to violence at football matches and even (daftest of all) theatregoers eating crisps too loudly, has been bundled together as evidence of a historic collective degeneration, and regression to a primeval crowd state.[4] The pandemic, so the theory goes, drove everybody mad, perhaps feral – we were caged and then unleashed, forgetting we were supposed to be civilised social animals.

Notwithstanding the fact that the myriad psychological consequences of the pandemic – of the lockdowns, the missed schooldays, births, weddings and funerals, the masking, the arrested development, the vast numbers of avoidable deaths – have barely been researched at the time of writing, I would like to formally call bullshit on this entirely unevidenced observation. It is not as if stag parties at Jongleurs comedy clubs or England football fans all comported themselves like finishing-school pupils until March 2020. And the cooperative social muscles the human race spent millennia developing together – outside their caves, having a bloody good dance – did not suddenly and irreparably atrophy after ten or twelve weeks spent mostly indoors, as stifling as that period may have been.

Fulfilling the 'educate' part of its public service remit, just prior to Notting Hill Carnival in August 2023, BBC News produced a four-minute video called 'How to Stay Safe in a Crowd'. It focused on footage of a worrying level of crowd density at the 2022 Carnival – a bottleneck on Ladbroke Grove, a major artery, where too many people were attempting to move in different directions at once. It certainly looked unpleasantly congested – and it's understandable that people want to know what they should do if they find themselves in a high-density crowd like that. Unfortunately, the answer usually is: by that point, very little.

The video warned of 'just how dangerous out-of-control crowds can become'. It's worth unpicking the language: *dangerous out-of-control crowds*. Ostensibly, it makes sense. Yes, it is a potentially dangerous scene, and no, they are not in control. But the association of uncontrolled crowds with danger suggests the crowd possesses a will to danger, and a will to anarchy, which just isn't borne out by evidence. No one in a dangerously dense crowd is at fault for its density and danger. No one sees the dangerous level of density ahead of them, because how could they, unless they were descending a steep hill? Some of the crowd may be *in danger*, but they do not possess danger, or the ability to stop that danger – these are misconceptions that a smart, evidence-based understanding of crowd dynamics and people-flow can and should negate.

In the same BBC News video, the chair of the UK Crowd Management Association (UKCMA), Eric Stuart, gave viewers one top line reason for all this danger: 'People's behaviour has changed. Security guards and stewards are having far more difficulties.' In fact, every bit of BBC advice on 'how to stay safe in a crowd' is credited to the UKCMA, the organisation that represents event security firms – who are not experts in crowd behaviour or event design, but a quite specific security industry body. The video then moves on to the BBC intoning, in its best patrician finger-wagging style, that the police urge everyone 'not to attend ticketed venues without a booking'. Once again the onus is on you, the individual crowd member, to ensure the safety of a vast, complex mass event through your good behaviour – rather than on the organisers to ensure safe site design, clear wayfinding, plentiful egress routes, well-trained staff, clear communication and robust emergency protocols.

The largely hypothetical ticketless horde, that latest incarnation of the crowd-as-scapegoat, rebounds to the same planning fundamentals Keith Still insists on. Say there *were* hundreds of fans intending to turn up to your mass event without tickets – well, you should have a contingency plan for that, and the capacity to deal with it safely. The one recent occasion where we do have evidence of this happening was England's appearance in the Euro 2020 final at Wembley, when up to 2,000 fans forced entry without tickets – throwing bottles, intimidating other fans, some of them disabled children, and physically attacking the underpaid, under-trained stewards as they went. It was a truly awful scene, and pure luck that no one was seriously hurt or killed.

The Baroness Casey Review condemned the exceptional antisocial behaviour and aggression of the England fans in question, and rightly so – the responsibility for that violence lies entirely with those individuals. But the report also found that 'the arrival of large numbers of ticketless fans at Wembley on the day of the final was predictable,' and not properly addressed. Brent Council had flagged concerns about exactly this ahead of the match and were ignored.[5] The lack of alternative large gathering spaces elsewhere in London to watch such a rare and historic match – aka fan zones – was also cited. 'There was an absence of risk assessment for the occasion that Euro Sunday represented,' the Casey Review concluded. 'This amounted to a collective failure by partners involved.'

It is sad that once again some England football fans made themselves exceptions to the rule, because for the most part, joining a crowd improves our social skills, empathy and kindness towards strangers. The new generation of academic crowd experts have found that, far from callously partying while people panic or die around them, the social bonds and identification that thrive in crowds actually raise people's pre-existing levels of care and concern. There is a growing body of evidence suggesting that crowd members will do remarkable things to help out people who are ostensibly strangers. 'Crowds have an amazing ability to police themselves, self-regulate, and actually display a lot of pro-social behaviour,' Edinburgh University's Anne Templeton told me. 'People want to support others in their group and will go out of their way to do so.'

Templeton mentioned the 'bystander effect', the theory that the more witnesses there are to a crime or an act of violence, the less likely they are to intervene. It is effectively a misanthrope's Urtext masquerading as science, with an extremely shaky evidence base.[6] The totemic event that prompted Bibb Latané and John Darley's 1970 book *The Unresponsive Bystander* was the 1964 rape and murder of Kitty Genovese outside her home in New York. It was a horrific crime, committed in public, and all the more grotesque for being witnessed by thirty-eight bystanders who did nothing to help. This quickly blew up into a much wider moral panic, and became a story of social breakdown, prompting years of head-clutching about *what had become of us as a society.*

But the bystander parable was not all it was cracked up to be. Subsequent investigations discovered that there were nowhere near thirty-eight witnesses; that some of those who *were* in the vicinity did not see the murder being committed; and that several of those who did, called the police immediately. 'In fact,' Templeton said, 'people provide an amazing amount of help in emergencies to people they don't even know, especially when they're part of an in-group. In emergencies, crowds want to help each other.'

She pointed to her research into the 2017 Manchester Arena terrorist attack, in which CCTV footage showed how members of the crowd had endangered their own lives to perform first aid on the wounded before emergency services arrived, remaining in the room where the bomb went off, when for all they knew attackers were still at large.[7] As soon as news spread of the attack,

Mancunians outside the venue rushed to provide food, shelter, transport and emotional support for the victims. Civilians are so keen to help out in emergencies, in fact, that there is a danger they will get in the way of the professionals, Templeton told me. 'A lot of the guidance we're trying to give to first responders and events teams is "work *with* the crowd" – to see them as a resource for good, and understand how to work with them.'

Conclusion: There to Be a Crowd

Crowds came to form a shield against their own dying. To become a crowd is to keep out death. To break off from the crowd is to risk death as an individual, to face dying alone. Crowds came for this reason above all others. They were there to be a crowd.

                                            – Don DeLillo, *White Noise*

This book exists because of the dogged persistence of the ideas of one eccentric French conservative, who watched the Tuileries Palace spewing black smoke into the Paris sky in 1871 and decided he had seen enough of the crowd. It is hard to think of another intellectual discipline where the foundational text, read and cited around the world across decades, is so completely detached from reality, indeed from empirical evidence, and has been so completely debunked. Yet in spite of the progress made in recent years, no amount of diligent work in universities will ever persuade the establishment to accept that mob rule, madding crowds, herd mentality, contagious violence and human stampedes are pure fictions, because it will always be in their interests to keep spinning those yarns.

The Bastille mob is still lurking everywhere, because they still need it to be, just as Gustave Le Bon did. It is a mob composed of shadow puppets, looming ever larger against the wall, MPs, police chiefs and tabloid editors crouching in front of the light, miming its exaggerated features and terrifying movements.

After a decade of battling populists, Russian troll armies and 'online mobs', Western media pundits are equally liable to blame the crowd in their heads for the politics they oppose. Rafael Behr, writing about the nastiness of British political discourse, after Conservative deputy party chairman Lee Anderson told asylum seekers to 'fuck off back to France', invented a fictional mob to help carry the can for the MP. 'It is the face that leers from the crowd, eyes bulging, veins throbbing, fizzing with idiosyncratic fury: the Lee Anderson look.'[1] What depths of Behr's imagination did this blood-curdling crowd come from? And why shouldn't one of the most senior politicians in the country be solely responsible for his own repellent provocations?

The digital age has made it easier for the establishment to invoke fearsome crowds that don't exist: first 'Twitter mobs' and then 'the woke mob' have become bêtes noires for the era of social media. 'We will never, ever surrender to the woke mob,' Florida's Republican governor Ron DeSantis declaimed in his re-election victory speech in 2022, fancying himself Churchill fending off the Wehrmacht. Pundits like Tom Chivers – a liberal science writer, the kind you might expect to have an interest in empirical evidence – take it in turns to deliver sermons with titles like "How the Mob Can Silence You", without ever identifying who the collective subject of that sentence is.[2] One polite critic, or a handful of abusive, anonymous Twitter users, does not a crowd make. Yet the right and the liberal centre have found themselves united in an epochal fight to the death with the mobs in their heads, shadowboxing until they collapse. Le Bon's belligerent ideas never entirely disappear, because they are so useful to those in power; they simply adapt to the *zeitgeist*.

It is rational for those in power to continue to demonise and pathologise crowds, because crowd membership offers us a level of freedom and strength we can never achieve alone. It amplifies the very best in us, empowers us, and makes us happier, more secure people. 'Crowds are one of very few places where we define reality on our own terms,' Professor Stephen Reicher said in 2021.[3] 'Crowds give us agency, crowds mean that we don't live in a world made by others – we make that world, we make history. And that is why crowds are so exhilarating.' Joining an open crowd gifts you the audacity of new possibilities: the unique feeling that in stepping out of your usual routine, and collectively remaking a familiar landscape, you have opened up a new horizon with unknown contours.

The lure of the crowd persists, in spite of the many lies told about it by those who would prefer us to remain shut away at home, pixel-weary and alone. For all the establishment's dystopian fantasies about online mobs, it is a red herring, and should be ignored, because the digital plane is not the terrain we should be fighting on. We live in a material world, and nothing compares to the solidarity and euphoria available to us when a physical crowd is bonded together. We must keep our lives, and our social networks, embodied, occupying physical space. I urge readers not just to think differently about the history, psychology and behaviour of crowds, and to show them the respect they deserve – but to join in too. Follow Matthew Phillip's Carnival advice and participate, rather than merely spectating; we have allowed ourselves to be inhibited by the high priests of decorum for too long. We need to embrace a bit of chaos in life: to let ourselves go with the flow of the crowd, in order to be more truly ourselves.

'We will all go together when we go', sang Tom Lehrer, in his sardonically cheerful account of mutually assured destruction, at the height of the Cold War. *No one will have the endurance / to collect on his insurance / Lloyds of London will be loaded when they go.* There is something coldly comforting, in the face of climate emergency, that there really is no solitary escape, no lifeboat for one, and no future in the bunker, however rich you are. Our fates are only becoming more interlinked. For all that the phrase has been rendered sanctimonious by its regular use in election campaigns, we really *are* all in it together. To defend the self-assembled crowd is to defend democracy. We must find the political in the social again, and fight to create genuinely public, open spaces in our cities, where crowds can gather and move freely.

To defend the crowd is also to defend culture, because culture only exists as a collective social enterprise, as the product of civilisation: the glue that bonds human beings together. A virtuoso solo musician with no audience can satisfy only themselves, and then only for a short while – and learns nothing about the power their music might possess. Don't we all benefit from lives impelled by curiosity and conviviality? By taking risks, overcoming our initial anxiety at the throng in front of us, and being rewarded by the joy and security to be found in common experience? Don't we all long to live in a world that moves to the polyphonic rhythms of something bigger and more dynamic than our own internal monologues?

In August 2020, as most of us emerged blinking into the sunlight again after the enforced privacy of the Covid lockdown, the British tabloids reported that the Tower of London's ravens had become so disquieted, so bored in the absence of the usual tourist clamour and attention, that they were flying off to seek entertainment elsewhere. This, as any schoolchild knows, is a dark portent for the nation; *England shall fall* and all that. Ravenmaster Christopher Skaife repeated the legend: 'If the ravens were to leave, the Tower would crumble to dust.' And then he added an existential twist: 'The Tower is only the Tower when the people are here.' Without the crowds that are drawn to them, our most notable buildings are just bricks and mortar. And without the public that brings warmth to the streets and squares, our cities are just cold and vacant abstractions, film sets with no actors.

Social distancing did not begin with public health guidance during the Covid lockdowns, but long before. Attacks on public assembly and the carnivalesque by those who fear and loathe the crowd have gradually whittled away the opportunities for spontaneous, liberating, physical congregation. It is time to claw those opportunities back, to head out into the public square and close the gaps between ourselves.

One of the greatest mistakes we have made in recent decades is to accept the idea that freedom is a quality that can be found and enjoyed only by the individual acting alone. Freedom lies within the crowd; it is our obligation to dive in and find it – together.

Acknowledgements

This book emerged out of a very specific moment in the spring of 2020 when we were first in Covid lockdown, and I was missing people – and crowds – a great deal, and watching videos of football crowds singing online, in particular Hibs fans singing 'Sunshine on Leith'. But it is also the product of twenty years of work covering crowd events of one kind or another – throughout which these ideas were germinating. One of my first published articles was about flash mobs and urban spontaneity, for the *New Statesman*, in the mid-2000s. This book is the product of the wisdom of crowds: of countless conversations with interesting people – about crowd behaviour and policing, on demos, at Carnival, at football matches, in festivals and nightclubs – too numerous to share or even recall in full. So a broad but no less sincere thank-you to anyone who has ever talked to me about or inside crowds, including the people who told me they hate or fear being in crowds – that was more useful than you could have imagined.

It has been wonderful to be reunited with my editor Leo Hollis. For someone to be so sharp with line edits and so generous with his own considerable expertise has made the writing process a genuine pleasure. This book has also benefited enormously from the precision copy-editing of Lorna Scott Fox, Jeanne Tao's production editing, and the publicity work of Catherine Smiles and Tim Thomas, all of whom I am very grateful to. Likewise, thank you to Verso's John Merrick for encouraging me in the midst of a party crowd in 2022 to stick at this idea.

I want to acknowledge the inspiring work of Barbara Ehrenreich and Mike Davis, who both passed away in the autumn of 2022, when I was stuck, and wondering how to persist with this idea. Their writing – for Verso and elsewhere – made me rethink everything, for the better. As my friends know, I never stop banging on about how much I love Ehrenreich's *Dancing in the Streets*, which will also be clear at several points in this book. If I have summoned half of her intellectual curiosity, humanist enthusiasm and joie de vivre here I will be very pleased. Rest in power.

Thank you also to the Society of Authors and the Authors' Foundation, who provided a vital work-in-progress grant to help me develop the proposal in its early stages; these organisations provide vital support. To Matt Turner, who helped me develop the idea and the proposal at an earlier stage with several rounds of excellent and incisive edits. To Tom Killingbeck, for his generous and insightful publishing advice. To Professor Martyn Amos, who was a great and cheering interlocutor on all things crowds while I was writing. To David Wolf, who commissioned and edited my long read for the *Guardian*, 'The Power of Crowds', during the first lockdown in 2020, and therefore got this whole train of thought moving. And to all my other editors who have encouraged and published my writing about riots, demos, festivals, music, urbanism, policing, public space, history and the rest.

To Katherine Leedale, for being such fine company, both when there were no crowds, and when there were. Thank you for keeping me sane during the pandemic, and for tolerating all those videos of Scottish football fans singing, blaring out from my laptop.

To Hettie O'Brien, for her uplifting enthusiasm for the idea for this book from the outset, and for being the perfect book-writing companion during our respective ups and downs – and for taking emergency phone calls about *flâneurs* and landscape painting while on her lunch-break.

Acknowledgements

To Kasia Tomasiewicz, Dr Kasia Tee, dear friend and *Cursed Objects* co-host, without whose unconditional cheerleading, intellectual sparring and motivational voice-notes I would be truly lost.

To Niamh McIntyre, for her unstinting support, in particular for tolerating my monomania during the final months of writing in the bleak midwinter, and her indulgence of my mad series of checklists and diagrams.

To my family: to my parents, Helen and Rod, my cousin Sara and my sister Sally, as well as Mokube, Enzo and Skye, for providing some much-needed fun and games and light relief in the weeks that I was finishing the book.

To all my friends, not least for listening to me wittering on about crowds incessantly for the last few years: I can assure you I haven't finished. To the group chats – which I won't name, for OPSEC – cheers to you all. The title of this book was only finalised after extensive consultations with the aforementioned. It takes a village to raise a crowd, or something like that. Thanks, everyone.

Notes

Introduction

1. For more details on Form 696 and the Metropolitan Police's war on grime music, see Dan Hancox, *Inner City Pressure: The Story of Grime*, William Collins, 2018, pp. 170–83.
2. Shruti Tewari et al., 'Participation in Mass Gatherings Can Benefit Well-Being: Longitudinal and Control Data from a North Indian Hindu Pilgrimage Event', *PLOS ONE* 7, no. 10, 2012.
3. Lt Col Stuart Crawford, 'Mob Rule Must Not Win, Remembrance Day MUST Be a Line in the Sand', express.co.uk, 6 November 2023.
4. Barbara Ehrenreich, *Dancing in the Streets: A History of Collective Joy*, Granta, 2007, pp. 23–4.

1 Paris Is Burning

1. Prosper-Olivier Lissagaray, *The History of the Paris Commune of 1871*, Verso, 2012, p. 231.
2. Ibid.
3. Ibid., p. 267.
4. Gustav Le Bon, *The Crowd: A Study of the Popular Mind*, T. Fisher Unwin, 1903, p. 87.
5. Lissagaray, *History of the Paris Commune*, pp. 277–8.
6. Gustav Le Bon, *The Psychology of Socialism*, Macmillan, 1899, p. viii.
7. Gustav Le Bon, *The Psychology of Revolution*, G. P. Putnam's Sons, 1913, p. 70.

8. Alice Widener, *Gustave Le Bon: The Man and His Works*, Liberty Press, 1979, p. 27.

9. Susanna Barrows, *Distorting Mirrors: Visions of the Crowd in Late Nineteenth-Century France*, Yale University Press, 1981, p. 162.

10. Le Bon, *The Crowd*, p. 65.

11. Ibid., p. 36.

12. Ibid., p. 28.

13. Ibid., p. 77.

14. Ibid., pp. 34–5, 36.

15. Ibid., p. 36.

16. Ibid., p. 33.

17. Ibid., p. 45.

18. Mareike Ohlberg, 'The Era of Crowds: Gustave Le Bon, Crowd Psychology, and Conceptualizations of Mass-Elite Relations in China', in Antje Flüchter and Jivanta Schöttli (eds), *The Dynamics of Transculturality*, Springer Cham, 2014; Joseph Bendersky, '"Panic": The Impact of Le Bon's Crowd Psychology on U.S. Military Thought', *Journal of the History of the Behavioral Sciences* 43, no. 3, 2007.

19. Robert Nye and Floyd Allport respectively, quoted in Christian Borch, *The Politics of Crowds*, Cambridge University Press, 2012, p. 34.

20. Le Bon, *The Crowd*, p. 14.

21. Barrows, *Distorting Mirrors*, p. 19.

22. Le Bon, *The Crowd*, p. 14.

23. J. S. McClelland, *The Crowd and the Mob*, Unwin Hyman, 1989, p. 6.

24. Le Bon, *The Crowd*, pp. 15, 189.

25. Ibid., p. 15.

2 The Nuremberg Spectacle

1. Eric Westervelt, 'Off-Duty Police Officers Investigated, Charged with Participating in Capitol Riot', npr.org, 15 January 2021.

2. Mikael Thalen, 'Charlie Kirk Deletes Tweet Saying He Sent "80+ Buses Full of Patriots" to D.C.', dailydot.com, 9 January 2021.

3. Meg Kelly and Imogen Piper, 'Brazil's Military Police Initially Stood By as Bolsonaro Supporters Rioted', washingtonpost.com, 28 January 2023.

4. J. S. McClelland, *The Crowd and the Mob*, Unwin Hyman, 1989, p. 288.

5. Gustav Le Bon, *The Crowd: A Study of the Popular Mind*, T. Fisher Unwin, 1903, p. 135.

6. Le Bon's racism and sexism were extreme even for the period. Inferior races and women should not even be educated, he argued in academic journals, because rebellion, insanity, anarchist terrorism and the collapse of civilisation would surely follow. The quality of Le Bon's scientific method is nicely illustrated by his response to a report of Black girls translating Thucydides: he insisted that 'their skills would disappear once their skulls thickened.' See Susanna Barrows, *Distorting Mirrors: Visions of the Crowd in Late Nineteenth-Century France*, Yale University Press, 1981, p. 165.

7. Robert A. Nye, *The Origins of Crowd Psychology: Gustave Le Bon and the Crisis of Mass Democracy in the Third Republic*, Sage Publications, 1975, p. 179.

8. Le Bon, *The Crowd*, p. 83.

9. Joachim Fest, *The Face of the Third Reich*, Penguin, 1972, p. 148.

10. Barrows, *Distorting Mirrors*, p. 188.

11. Joshua Hagen and Robert Ostergren, 'Spectacle, Architecture and Place at the Nuremberg Party Rallies: Projecting a Nazi Vision of Past, Present and Future', *Cultural Geographies* 13, no. 2, 2006.

12. It is eerie that the remnants are still there. Art historian Barbara Miller Lane said in 1989: 'It is still hard to revisit images of the Zeppelinfeld without remembering – almost re-experiencing – the roar of the crowd in response to Hitler's exhortations.'

13. For context: the largest stadium in the world at present is the Rungrado 1st of May Stadium in Pyongyang, North Korea, with a reported 150,000 seats, followed by the 132,000-seat Narendra Modi Stadium in Ahmedabad, India.

14. Hagen and Ostergren, 'Spectacle, Architecture and Place'.

15. Barbara Miller Lane, 'Interpreting Nazi Architecture: The Case of Albert Speer', in Börje Magnusson et al. (eds), *Ultra terminum vagari: Scritti in onore di Carl Nylander*, Quasar, 1997.

16. Fest, *The Face of the Third Reich*, p. 104.

17. Raymond Williams, *Culture and Society 1780–1950*, Chatto and Windus, 1958, p. 319.
18. Wilhelm Reich, *The Mass Psychology of Fascism*, Orgone Institute Press, 1946, p. 70.
19. Jeffrey Brooks, *Thank You, Comrade Stalin!: Soviet Public Culture from Revolution to Cold War*, Princeton, 2000.
20. Hannah Arendt, *The Origins of Totalitarianism*, Meridian Books, 1958, p. 323.
21. Reich, *The Mass Psychology of Fascism*, p. 78.
22. Sigmund Freud, *Group Psychology and the Analysis of the Ego*, Bantam Books, 1960, p. 6.
23. Ibid., p. 13.
24. McClelland, *The Crowd and the Mob*, p. 277.
25. Le Bon, *The Crowd*, pp. 34–5.
26. This sounds like a somewhat adolescent critique of marketing and consumer capitalism, but it is there in black and white in Bernays's work.

3 'Feral Thugs'

1. Adam Elliott-Cooper, *Britain Is Not Innocent: A Netpol Report on the Policing of Black Lives Matter Protests in Britain's Towns and Cities in 2020*, Network for Police Monitoring, 2020, p. 20.
2. Joe Lo, 'Report: Met Police Endangered Black Lives Matter Supporters but Were Soft on the Far-Right', leftfootforward.org, 12 November 2020.
3. Elliott-Cooper, *Britain Is Not Innocent*, p. 29.
4. Govand Khalid Azeez, 'The Oriental Rebel in Western History', *Arab Studies Quarterly* 37, no. 3, 2015.
5. Gustav Le Bon, *The Psychology of Revolution*, G. P. Putnam's Sons, 1913, p. 71.
6. Vikram Dodd and Mark Wilding, 'Met Only Authorised Baton Rounds for Black-Led Events, FOI Reveals', theguardian.com, 6 August 2023. The Met said it only had data going back to 2017.
7. Tanzil Chowdhury, 'From the Colony to the Metropole: Race, Policing and the Colonial Boomerang', in Koshka Duff (ed.), *Abolishing the Police*, Dog Section Press, 2021.

8. Martin Thomas, *Violence and Colonial Order*, Cambridge University Press, 2012, pp. 70–1.

9. Susanna Barrows, *Distorting Mirrors: Visions of the Crowd in Late Nineteenth-Century France*, Yale University Press, 1981, pp. 141–4.

10. P. A. J. Waddington, *Strong Arm of the Law*, Oxford University Press, 1991, p. 125.

11. Kenneth Sloan, *Public Order and the Police*, Police Review Publishing, 1979, p. 25.

12. Association of Chief Police Officers (ACPO), Public Order Manual of Tactical Options and Related Matters, 1983, available at whatdotheyknow.com.

13. Matt Foot and Morag Livingstone, *Charged: How the Police Try to Suppress Protest*, Verso, 2022, p. 8.

14. Ibid., p. 5.

15. Gareth Peirce, 'Archive, 12 August 1985: How They Rewrote the Law at Orgreave', theguardian.com, 17 June 2014.

16. Laura Barton, 'Barton's Britain: Orgreave', theguardian.com, 9 June 2009.

17. When the case came to trial, the secret ACPO manual was alluded to publicly for the first time, which is how we know about it: it was accessed – albeit in redacted form – under court 'disclosure' rules, and under duress.

18. Mark Townsend, 'Olympic Games 2012: Police Plan Pre-emptive Arrests to Stop Disruption', theguardian.com, 2 June 2012.

19. *Public Order and the Police: A Report on the Events in Trafalgar Square, Sunday 17th to Monday 18th September, 1961*, National Council for Civil Liberties, 1961.

20. 1st Witness Statement of Angus McIntosh, Undercover Policing Inquiry, 3 December 2020, ucpi.org.uk.

21. I had my evidence used by the Home Affairs Committee, and put to Theresa May by a Labour backbencher: 'Dan Hancox says he asked repeatedly to leave Parliament Square, and was refused; are you calling him a liar?' 'No, erm, I'm not,' she replied, flannelling furiously and changing the subject.

22. The *Daily Express* offered an exceptional example of Le Bonian, anti-crowd conspiracism in this case. The outside agitators in the extremely hyper-local conflict between the people of Tottenham and the Met Police were, of course . . . the Soviet Union. The front-page headline for 8 October 1985 ran: '"Kill! Kill! Kill!" Moscow-Trained Hit Squad Gave Orders as Mob Hacked PC Blakelock to Death'.

23. Adam Elliot-Cooper and Deniz Yonucu, 'Racism, Policing, and the Black Resistance in Britain: A Conversation with Adam Elliot-Cooper', *PoLAR: Political and Legal Anthropology Review*, 8 November 2023, polarjournal.org.

24. Steve Reicher and Cliff Stott, *Mad Mobs and Englishmen? Myths and Realities of the 2011 Riots*, Constable & Robinson, 2011.

25. 'London Rioters of 2011 "from Boroughs Where There Were Tensions with Police"', News, University of Oxford, 9 March 2015, ox.ac.uk.

26. Daniel Briggs, 'Frustrations, Urban Relations and Temptations: Contextualising the English Riots', in Daniel Briggs (ed.), *The English Riots of 2011: A Summer of Discontent*, Waterside Press, 2012, available at repository.uel.ac.uk.

27. Since the introduction of universal suffrage in the UK in 1928, every single UK general election turnout in the twentieth century was above 70 per cent. In the twenty-first century, every single UK general election turnout has been below 70 per cent. The nadir was in 2001: 59.4 per cent.

28. 'London Riots: Teen Dad Brags He Got "the Whole Johnson & Johnson Set" Looting for His Baby Son', mirror.co.uk, 12 August 2011.

29. E. P. Thompson, 'The Moral Economy of the English Crowd in the Eighteenth Century', *Past and Present* 50, no. 1, 1971.

30. 'Archive on 4: Riot Remembered', BBC Sounds, 4 April 2020.

31. 'Police Liaison Officers', Network for Police Monitoring, netpol.org.

32. 'The Life Scientific: Clifford Stott on Riot Prevention', BBC Radio 4, 16 June 2020.

33. Clifford Stott, Geoff Pearson and Owen West, 'Enabling an Evidence -Based Approach to Policing Football in the UK', *Policing: A Journal of Policy and Practice* 14, no. 4, 2020.

34. Olivier Fillieule and Fabien Jobard, 'A Splendid Isolation: Protest Policing in France', Books and Ideas, 10 October 2016, booksand ideas.net.

35. All four of these key principles: '1. An alternative conception of crowd dynamics to that promoted by Gustave Le Bon, which is still central to the French philosophy of policing; 2. The facilitation and escort of street protests; 3. The development of communication at every stage of a policing operation; 4. The differentiation and targeting of interventions to restore order.' Ibid.

36. Organisers, of course, will do the opposite. The general rule of thumb, on estimating the size of a protest crowd, is to interpolate a number somewhere between the police estimate and the organisers' estimate. It is generally assumed that technology is now nearly at the stage whereby it will be possible to glean much more accurate estimates of protest numbers from aerial footage.

4 Among the Slum People

1. 'Empty Stadiums Have Shrunk Football Teams' Home Advantage', economist.com, 25 July 2020.

2. Another study of 5,000 matches carried out by two universities in 2021 found that the usual home advantage was halved during the Covid period. Dane McCarrick et al., 'Home Advantage during the COVID-19 Pandemic: Analyses of European Football Leagues', *Psychology of Sport and Exercise* 56, 2021.

3. 'Meet Block Seven', *The East Stand* (blog), 14 January 2022, eaststand hibs.com.

4. Sean Ingle, 'Football Hooliganism, Once the English Disease, Is More Like a Cold Sore Now', theguardian.com, 4 November 2013.

5. Giovanni Carnibella et al., *Football Violence in Europe: A Report to the Amsterdam Group*, Social Issues Research Centre, 1996, p. 87.

6. David Conn, 'Hillsborough: Evidence "Does Not Support Claims That Fans Had No Tickets"', theguardian.com, 29 June 2014.

7. *The Report of the Hillsborough Independent Panel*, The Stationery Office, September 2012, p. 23.

8. Ibid., p. 362.

9. Owen Gibson, 'What the Sun Said 15 Years Ago', theguardian.com, 7 July 2004.

10. David Conn, 'Hillsborough Families Attack "Ludicrous" Acquittals of Police', theguardian.com, 26 May 2021.

11. Adrian Tempany, *And the Sun Shines Now*, Faber, 2016, p. 94.

12. 'Police Keep Peace at Bradford City Match with Just Eight Liaison Officers', yorkshirepost.co.uk, 16 August 2017.

13. Clifford Stott, Geoff Pearson and Owen West, 'Enabling an Evidence-Based Approach to Policing Football in the UK', *Policing: A Journal of Policy and Practice* 14, no. 4, December 2020.

14. Jamie Greer, '"The Policing Is Proportionate and Necessary": The Authorities' View on Football Fan Disorder', jamiemgreer.medium.com, 23 September 2022.

15. This was the first season the aggregate Premier League attendance surpassed 15 million. Even the second tier of English football, the Championship, had an aggregate attendance of over 9 million, and the third over 5 million. 'Overall Football Attendance in the United Kingdom (UK) in 2021/22, by League', statista.com, 8 December 2022.

16. Daniel Brown, 'Football Fans Staggered by Police Chief's Ignorance towards Safe Standing', joe.co.uk, 2 January 2022.

17. 'Licensed Standing in Football Stadia: Post Implementation Evaluation', CFE Research, July 2023.

18. The organisation was initially formed in 1990 as the Football Licensing Authority, which was established under the Football Spectators Act 1989. It became the SGSA in 2011.

19. Source: Ken Scott of the SGSA. That figure refers to 50 per cent of matches in the Premiership and the English Football League, meaning the top four tiers of league football, as well as all matches played at Wembley. And 'without a police presence' means matches without any police at the stadium – they still may have had a match-day police deployment outside nearby railway stations, or in the town centre.

5 The World Turned Upside Down

1. *Notting Hill Carnival Crowd Movement Data Book*, Movement Strategies, 22 February 2017.
2. Jerome R. Mintz, *Carnival Song and Society*, Routledge, 1997, p. 204.
3. Richard Conniff, '20,000-Year-Old Cave Art from Borneo Depicts Humans Dancing', *Strange Behaviors* (blog), 6 November 2018, strangebehaviors.wordpress.com.
4. Aka charivari, or rough music: a theatrical community ritual and parade mocking cuckolds, or unfaithful or violent wives. David Underdown, *Revel, Riot, and Rebellion: Popular Politics and Culture in England 1603–1660*, Oxford University Press, 1987, pp. 101–3.
5. Ibid., p. 96.
6. Barbara Ehrenreich, *Dancing in the Streets: A History of Collective Joy*, Granta, 2007, pp. 104–5.
7. Until this point, worshippers 'stood or milled around, creating a very different dynamic than we find in today's churches'. Ibid., p. 77.
8. Peter Stallybrass and Allon White, *The Politics and Poetics of Transgression*, Cornell University Press, 1986, p. 178.
9. Ibid., p. 177.
10. Huw Lemmey, 'Party and Protest: The Radical History of Gay Liberation, Stonewall and Pride', theguardian.com, 25 June 2020.
11. Claudia Jones, 'A People's Art Is the Genesis of Their Freedom', 1959, available at blackbritishreader.tumblr.com.
12. Ashley Roach-McFarlane, 'The Forgotten Legacy of Claudia Jones: A Black Communist Radical Feminist', versobooks.com, 21 March 2021.
13. Roger Fowler et al., *Language and Control*, Routledge, 1989, p. 120.
14. Peter Evans, 'Fear of Reprisal Stops Public Helping Police, Newman Says', *The Times*, 31 August 1983.
15. Lizzy Buchan, 'Tory London Mayor Hopeful Accused of "Crude Culture Wars" over Notting Hill Carnival', mirror.co.uk, 24 August 2023.
16. Emma Youle, 'Notting Hill Carnival: New Data Reveals Crime Should Not Be the Story of the Weekend', huffingtonpost.co.uk, 24 August 2019.

17. Kirsten Robinson, 'Met Police Shared "Misleading" Figures on Number of Officers Injured at Notting Hill Carnival', metro.co.uk, 13 October 2022.
18. This fell to 500 after the pandemic. See '1 in 6 Festivals Came to an End as a Result of Covid', Association of Independent Festivals, 19 January 2023, aiforg.com.
19. *Here, There and Everywhere: 2023*, UK Music, 2023, p. 8.
20. 'Pissed' as in angry, not drunk – it's American English.
21. Fergus Neville, 'The Experience of Participating in Crowds: Shared Identity, Relatedness and Emotionality', PhD thesis, University of St Andrews, 2012.
22. Frankie Mullin, 'How UK Ravers Raged against the Ban', vice.com, 15 July 2014.
23. Ed Gillett, *Party Lines: Dance Music and the Making of Modern Britain*, Picador, 2023, p. 67.
24. Matt Foot and Morag Livingstone, *Charged: How the Police Try to Suppress Protest*, Verso, 2022, p. 157.
25. Ibid., p. 166.
26. Ehrenreich, *Dancing in the Streets*, pp. 225–47.
27. Anthony Sampson, 'From the Observer Archive, 16 September 1956: Teddy Boys Run Riot When the Clock Strikes One', theguardian.com, 16 September 2012.
28. 'Hardcore Dancing', 4 February 2021, Freebird Radio, web.archive.org /web/20210204221445/https://www.freebirdradio.net/acr/modules .php?name=Music_Sound&page=Hardcore_dancing.html.
29. Lindsay Abrahams, 'Mosh Pits Teach Us about the Physics of Collective Behavior', theatlantic.com, 13 February 2013.
30. Jesse L. Silverberg et al., 'Collective Motion of Moshers at Heavy Metal Concerts', *Physical Review Letters* 10, no. 22, 31 May 2013.

6 The Invention of Modern Life

1. Tony Hiss, *The Experience of Place: A New Way of Looking At and Dealing with Our Radically Changing Cities and Countryside*, Alfred A. Knopf, 1990, p. 8.

2. Orvar Löfgren, 'Sharing an Atmosphere: Spaces in Urban Commons', in Christian Borch and Martin Kornberger (eds), *Urban Commons: Rethinking the City*, Routledge, 2015, p. 74.

3. Walter Benjamin explained this alienation with the observation that Engels 'came from a Germany that was still provincial', effectively saying 'the poor kid wasn't ready for that yet', in the manner of Marty McFly playing 'Johnny B. Goode' to a bunch of baffled 1955 teenagers in *Back to the Future*.

4. This is tackled head-on in Lauren Elkin, *Flâneuse: Women Walk the City in Paris, New York, Tokyo, Venice and London*, Chatto & Windus, 2016.

5. Garnette Cadogan, 'Walking while Black', lithub.com, 8 July 2016.

6. Bill Bryson, *At Home: A Short History of Private Life*, Black Swan, 2010, p. 32.

7. Ibid., p. 31.

8. *Expo: Magic of the White City*, directed by Mark Bussler, Inecom Entertainment, 2005.

9. Caption to a popular photographic souvenir of the expo, 1893, national galleries.org.

10. 'Crowds Seek the City', *Chicago Record*, 17 August 1893.

11. Andrew Carnegie, 'Value of the World's Fair to the American People', *Engineering Magazine*, January 1894, available at worldsfairchicago 1893.com.

12. Carmen Dexl, 'Live Human Exhibits: The World Columbian Exposition as a Space of Empire', US Studies Online, 30 November 2020, usso.uk.

13. Karl Marx and Friedrich Engels, 'Review: May–October 1850', *Neue Rheinische Zeitung Revue*, 1 November 1850, available at marxists.org.

14. 'Egypt: Rab'a Killings Likely Crimes against Humanity', Human Rights Watch, 12 August 2014, hrw.org.

15. 'Bahrain', in *Country Reports on Human Rights Practices for 2011*, United States Department of State, 2012, p. 19, 2009-2017.state.gov.

16. Audrey Wachs, 'The Politics of Lower Manhattan's Privately Owned Public Spaces', Curbed, 25 July 2019, ny.curbed.com.

17. Rowan Moore, 'The London River Park: Place for the People or a Private Playground?', theguardian.com, 13 November 2011.

18. Eyako Heh and Joel Wainwright, 'No Privacy, No Peace: Urban Surveillance and the Movement for Black Lives', *Journal of Race, Ethnicity and the City* 3, no. 2, 2022.

19. Surveillance Studies Network, 'A Report on the Surveillance Society', September 2006.

20. Paul Bischoff, 'Surveillance Camera Statistics: Which Cities Have the Most CCTV Cameras?', Comparitech, 23 May 2023, comparitech. com.

21. Myles Zhang, 'The Privatization of Public Space in Lower Manhattan', 20 April 2021, myleszhang.org.

22. A European Environment Agency report found that solo car travel was worse for the environment than plane travel, in terms of passenger -per-kilometre emissions. *Transport and Environment Report 2020: Train or Plane?*, European Environment Agency, 2021.

23. 'How Barcelona Is Designing Its Streets for Health and Happiness', *Ideas That Happen* podcast, 19 April 2023.

24. Marta Bausells, 'Superblocks to the Rescue: Barcelona's Plan to Give Streets Back to Residents', theguardian.com, 17 May 2016.

25. Some of these were ticketed and carried a fee at the outset, but, like Glastonbury for many years, organisers largely tolerated non-paying gatecrashers, or were overrun by them, such that they were free if you wanted them to be.

26. 'ACFM Trip 36: Festivals', *#ACFM* podcast, 3 September 2023.

27. Dan Hancox, 'Revealed: Creeping Privatisation of London Parks in Summer', theguardian.com, 5 July 2019.

28. *The Impact of Events Tourism on London's Economy*, London & Partners, 2016, p. 4.

29. Angus Harrison, 'Why There Was Anti-Boiler Room Graffiti at Carnival', vice.com, 29 August 2017; Mike Urban, 'Lambeth Country Show Boycott in Response to the Great Brockwell Wall, Booze Ban, Body and Bag Searches', brixtonbuzz.com, 18 July 2018.

7 Myths and Scapegoats

1. 'File on 4: Catastrophe at the Academy', BBC Radio 4, 22 January 2023.
2. Keith Still, 'Crowd Safety and Crowd Risk Analysis', Crowd Risk Analysis Ltd, gkstill.com.
3. Will Pritchard, 'After Astroworld, What Is Being Done to Stop Crowd Crushes from Happening Again?', djmag.com, 8 March 2022.
4. Alice Saville, 'Trouble in the Stalls: When Audience Drama Upstages the Show', theguardian.com, 5 March 2022.
5. Louise Casey, *The Baroness Casey Review: An Independent Review of Events Surrounding the UEFA Euro 2020 Final 'Euro Sunday' at Wembley*, Baroness Casey of Blackstock, December 2021.
6. Rachel Manning, Mark Levine and Alan Collins, 'The Kitty Genovese Murder and the Social Psychology of Helping: The Parable of the 38 Witnesses', *American Psychologist* 62, no. 6, September 2007.
7. Anne Templeton et al., *Effective Strategies in Emergencies: First Responders' Views on Communicating and Coordinating with the Public*, UK Research and Innovation, May 2023.

Conclusion

1. Rafael Behr, 'The Tories Have Become Too Pungent for a Country That Likes Its Politics Plain', theguardian.com, 23 August 2023.
2. Tom Chivers, 'How the Mob Can Silence You', unherd.com, 8 December 2020.
3. 'Beyond Contagion: Understanding the Spread of Riots', *Beyond Contagion* podcast, 16 November 2021.

Index

city population (*continued*)
  designing the crowd out 195–6
  dysfunctional 201–2
  events economy 204–8
  fear of the crowd 31
  freedom of movement 183
  hostile architecture 196, 198
  impersonal meanness 179
  leisure 204–8
  mass urban social life begins
    184–8
  paradox of 208–10
  pedestrianisation 202–4
  people-watching 181
  policing 200–1
  population density 177–81, 208
  population growth 211
  privately owned public spaces
    (POPS) 197–8
  pro-crowd policies 202–4
  rush hour 179
strangers 179
  submersion in 181–2
  surging sea of humanity 186
  surveillance 199–200, 205
  traffic 201–2
  urban danger zones 178, 179, 180
  walking while Black 183
  walking while female 183
  walking while Muslim 183
urbanisation 11, 18, 51–3, 211
US Constitution 41
US Department of Homeland Security
  199
USSR, parades 67

validation 165–6
Valley Parade stadium fire, 1985 121
vanguard crowds 48–9
violence 12, 32
  absence of 34
  carnival 150–1

contagious 123
crowds tendency towards 32
football crowds 120–4
police and policing 9, 79–84,
  109–10, 171
rational 123
Violence and Colonial Order
  (Thomas) 76
virtue signalling 74

Waddington, Peter 92–3
walking while Black 183
walking while female 183
walking while Muslim 183
Walzer, Michael 113
wanderkessel 87
Washington Post (newspaper) 193
Weber, Max 17
Weimar Republic, collapse of 49
Weizman, Eyal, *The Roundabout
  Revolutions* 190–1, 192–3
Wembley, Euro 2020 final 221
West, Owen 132–3
White, Allon 17
White Plains, Tea Party rally 18
Whitelaw, Willie 77, 79, 80
Williams, John 127
Williams, Raymond 59–60, 69, 98
Williams, Timothy 93–4
Wimbledon FC 117, 136–7
woke mob 15, 225
Woodstock 9
Woodstock '99 163–5, 208
Wooldridge, Adrian 15
World Bank 180
world's fairs 184–8
Worswick, Melita 106, 106–7

Yorke, Thom 173
YouTube 119, 120

Zhang, Myles 201